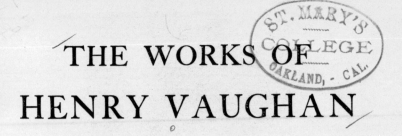

THE WORKS OF HENRY VAUGHAN

EDITED BY

LEONARD CYRIL MARTIN

M.A., B.Litt. (Oxon.)

LECTURER IN ENGLISH IN THE UNIVERSITY OF LUND, SWEDEN

VOLUME II

OXFORD

AT THE CLARENDON PRESS

1914

OXFORD UNIVERSITY PRESS

LONDON   EDINBURGH   GLASGOW   NEW YORK

TORONTO   MELBOURNE   BOMBAY

HUMPHREY MILFORD M.A.

PUBLISHER TO THE UNIVERSITY

CONTENTS.

VOL. II.

SILEX SCINTILLANS

	PAGE
Authoris (de se) Emblema	386
⟨Emblem⟩	to face 386
⟨Title-page⟩	387
The Authors Preface To the following Hymns	388
⟨Texts⟩	393
To . . . Jesvs Christ	394
⟨Vain Wits and eyes⟩	396
Regeneration	397
Death. *A Dialogue*	399
Resurrection and Immortality	400
Day of Judgement	402
Religion	404
The Search	405
Isaacs Marriage	408
The Brittish Church	410
The Lampe	410
Mans fall, and Recovery	411
The Showre	412
Distraction	413
The Pursuite	414
Mount of Olives	414
The Incarnation, and Passion	415
The Call	416
⟨Thou that know'st for whom I mourne⟩	416
Vanity of Spirit	418
The Retreate	419
⟨Come, come, what doe I here?⟩	420
Midnight	421
Content	422
⟨Joy of my life! while left me here⟩	422
The Storm	423
The Morning-watch	424
The Evening-watch. *A Dialogue*	425
⟨Silence, and stealth of dayes!⟩	425
Church-Service	426
Buriall	427

iv *Contents.*

	PAGE
Chearfulness	428
⟨Sure, there's a tye of Bodyes!⟩	429
Peace	430
The Passion	430
⟨And do they so? have they a Sense⟩	432
The Relapse	433
The Resolve	434
The Match	434
Rules *and* Lessons	436
Corruption	440
H. Scriptures	441
Unprofitableness	441
Christs Nativity	442
The Check	443
Disorder *and* frailty	444
Idle Verse	446
Son-dayes	447
Repentance	448
The Burial of an Infant	450
Faith	450
The Dawning	451
Admission	453
Praise	454
Dressing	455
Easter-day	456
Easter Hymn	457
The Holy Communion	457
Psalm 121	458
Affliction	459
The Tempest	460
Retirement	462
Love, and Discipline	463
The Pilgrimage	464
The Law, and the Gospel	465
The World	466
The Mutinie	468
The Constellation	469
The Shepheards	470
Misery	472
The Sap	475
Mount of Olives	476
Man	477
⟨I walkt the other day (to spend my hour,)⟩ . . .	478
Begging	480

Contents.

PART II

	PAGE
Ascension-day	481
Ascension-Hymn	482
⟨They are all gone into the world of light !⟩	483
White Sunday	485
The Proffer	486
Cock-crowing	488
The Starre	489
The Palm-tree	490
Joy . . . . ,	491
The Favour	492
The Garland	492
Love-sick	493
Trinity-Sunday	493
Psalme 104	494
The Bird	496
The Timber	497
The Jews	499
Begging	500
Palm-Sunday	501
Jesus weeping	502
The Daughter of *Herodias*	503
Jesus weeping	503
Providence	505
The Knot	506
The Ornament	507
St. Mary Magdalen	507
The Rain-bow	509
The Seed growing secretly	510
⟨As time one day by me did pass⟩	512
⟨Fair and yong light !⟩	513
The Stone	514
The dwelling-place	516
The Men of War	516
The Ass	518
The hidden Treasure	519
Childe-hood	520
The Night	522
Abels blood	523
Righteousness	524
Anguish	526
Tears	526
Jacobs Pillow, and Pillar	527

	PAGE
The Agreement.	528
The day of Judgement	530
Psalm 65	531
The Throne	533
Death	533
The Feast	534
The Obsequies	536
The Water-fall	537
Quickness	538
The Wreath	539
The Queer	539
The Book	540
To the Holy Bible	540
L'Envoy	541
An Alphabetical Table, Containing the several Titles of all the Hymns or Sacred Poems in these two Books	544

HERMETICAL PHYSICK

⟨Title-page⟩	547
The Translator To the ingenious Reader	548

THALIA REDIVIVA

⟨Title-page⟩	593
To the Most Honourable and truly Noble Henry Lord Marquis and Earl of *Worcester*, &c.	594
To the Reader	596
To *Mr.* Henry Vaughan *the Silurist: upon these and his former* Poems	597
Upon the Ingenious Poems *of his Learned Friend, Mr.* Henry Vaughan *the Silurist*	598
To the ingenious Author of Thalia Rediviva	599
To my worthy Friend, Mr. Henry Vaughan *the Silurist*	600
To his Learned Friend and Loyal Fellow-Prisoner, Thomas Powel *of* Cant. *Doctor of Divinity*	603
The King Disguis'd	605
The Eagle	606
To Mr. M. L. *upon his reduction of the* Psalms *into Method*	608
To the pious memorie of C. W. Esquire *who finished his Course here, and made his entrance into Immortality upon the* 13 *of* September, *in the year of* Redemption 1653	609
In Zodiacum Marcelli Palingenii	611
To Lysimachus, *the Author being with him in* London	612
On Sir Thomas Bodley's *Library ; the Author being then in* Oxford	613

Contents. vii

PAGE

The importunate Fortune, written to Doctor Powel of Cantre 614

To I. Morgan of White-Hall Esq; upon his sudden Journey
and succeeding Marriage 617

Fida: Or The Country-beauty: to Lysimachus . . . 618

Fida forsaken 620

To the Editor of the matchless Orinda 621

Upon sudden news of the much lamented death of Judge Trevers 622

To Etesia (for Timander,) the first Sight 623

The Character, to Etesia 624

To Etesia looking from her Casement at the full Moon . . 625

To Etesia parted from him, and looking back 626

In Etesiam lachrymantem 626

To Etesia going beyond Sea 626

Etesia absent 627

TRANSLATIONS

⟨Boethius, De Consolatione Philosophiæ⟩ Metrum 12. Lib. 3 . 628

Metrum 2. Lib. 3 . 630

Metrum 6. Lib. 4 . 631

Metrum 3. Lib. 4 . 633

Metrum 6. Lib. 3 . 634

The old man of Verona out of Claudian 635

The Sphere of Archimedes out of Claudian 635

The Phœnix out of Claudian 636

PIOUS THOUGHTS AND EJACULATIONS

To his Books 639

Looking Back 640

The Shower 641

Discipline 641

The Ecclipse 641

Affliction 642

Retirement 642

The Revival 643

The Day-spring 643

The Recovery 644

The Nativity 645

The true Christmas 646

The Request 647

Jordanis 648

Servilii Fatum, sive Vindicta divina 648

De Salmone 649

The World 649

Contents.

	PAGE
The Bee	652
To Christian Religion	654
Daphnis. An Elegiac *Eclogue*	656
TRANSLATIONS IN DR. THOMAS POWELL'S *HUMANE INDUSTRY*	661
APPENDIX I. Poems of uncertain authorship	665
APPENDIX II. Vaughan's Letters to John Aubrey and Anthony Wood	667
NOTES	677
INDEX OF FIRST LINES	709

SILEX SCINTILLANS

Authoris (de se) Emblema.

Tentâsti, fateor, sine vulnere sœpius, & me
    Consultum voluit Vox, sine voce, frequens ;
Ambivit placido divinior aura meatu,
    Et frustrà sancto murmure prœmonuit.
Surdus eram, mutusq; Silex: Tu, (quanta tuorum
    Cura tibi est!) aliâ das renovare viâ,
Permutas Curam ; Jamq; irritatus Amorem
    Posse negas, & vim, Vi, superare paras,
Accedis propior, molemq̦, & Saxea rumpis
    Pectora, sitq; Caro, quod fuit ante Lapis.   10
En lacerum ! Cœlosq; tuos ardentia tandem
    Fragmenta, & liquidas ex Adamante genas.
Sic olim undantes Petras, Scopulosq; vomentes
    Curâsti, O populi providus usq; tui!
Quam miranda tibi manus est ! Moriendo, revixi ;
    Et fractas jam sum ditior inter opes.

Emblem and Poem only in 1650. 4 prœmonuit.] prœmonuit 1650. 10 Lapis.]
Lapis 1650.

Silex Scintillans:

SACRED

POEMS

And private

EJACULATIONS.

The second Edition, In two Books;
By *Henry Vaughan*, Silurist.

Job chap. 35. ver. 10, 11.

Where is God my Maker, who giveth Songs in
the night ?
Who teacheth us more then the beasts of the
earth, and maketh us wiser then the fowls
of heaven ?

London, Printed for *Henry Crips*, and *Lodo-*
wick Lloyd, next to the Castle in *Cornhil*,
and in *Popes-head Alley*. 1655.

The Authors
PREFACE
To the following
HYMNS.

That this Kingdom hath abounded with those ingenious persons, which in the late notion are termed *Wits*, is too well known. Many of them having cast away all their fair portion of time, in no better imployments, then a deliberate search, or ex-cogitation of *idle words*, and a most vain, insatiable desire to be reputed *Poets*; leaving behinde them no other Monuments of those excellent abilities conferred upon them, but such as they may (with a *Predecessor* of theirs) term *Parricides*, and a soul-killing Issue; for that is the Βραβεῖον, and Laureate *Crown*, which idle
10 *Poems* will certainly bring to their unrelenting Authors.

And well it were for them, if those willingly-studied and wilfully-published vanities could defile no *spirits*, but their own; but the *case* is far worse. These *Vipers* survive their *Parents*, and for many ages after (like *Epidemic* diseases) infect whole Generations, corrupting always and unhallowing the best-gifted *Souls*, and the most capable *Vessels*: for whose sanctification and well-fare, the glorious *Son* of God laid down his *life*, and suffered the pretious *blood* of his blessed and innocent *heart* to be poured out. In the mean time it cannot be denyed, but these men are
20 had in remembrance, though we cannot say with any comfort, *Their memorial is blessed;* for, that I may speak no more then the truth (let their passionate *worshippers* say what they please) all the commendations that can be justly given them, will amount to no more, then what *Prudentius* the Christian-sacred *Poet* bestowed upon *Symmachus*;

Os dignum æterno tinctum quod fulgeat auro
Si mallet laudare deum : cui sordida monstra
Prætulit, & liquidam temeravit crimine vocem ;
Haud aliter, quàm cum rastris qui tentat eburnis
30 *Cænosum versare solum, &c. ——*

Preface and texts (page 393) only in 1655.

In English thus,

A wit most worthy in tryed Gold to shine,
Immortal Gold ! had he sung the divine
Praise of his Maker : to whom he preferr'd
Obscene, vile fancies, and prophanely marr'd
A rich, rare stile with sinful, lewd contents ;
No otherwise, then if with Instruments
Of polish'd Ivory, some drudge should stir
A dirty sink, *&c.* ——

This *comparison* is nothing odious, and it is as *true*, as it is 10 *apposite* ; for a *good* wit in a *bad* subject, is (as *Solomon* said of the *fair* and *foolish woman*) *Like a jewel of gold in a swines snowt*, Prov. 11. 22. Nay, the more acute the *Author is*, there is so much the more danger and death in the *work*. Where the *Sun* is busie upon a *dung-hill*, the *issue* is always some unclean *vermine*. Divers persons of eminent piety and learning (I meddle not with the seditious and *Schismatical*) have, long before my time, taken notice of this *malady* ; for the complaint against *vitious verse*, even by peaceful and obedient *spirits*, is of some antiquity in this Kingdom. And yet, as if the evil consequence 20 attending this inveterate *error*, were but a small thing, there is sprung very lately another prosperous *device* to assist it in the subversion of *souls*. Those that want the *Genius* of *verse*, fall to *translating* ; and the people are (every *term*) plentifully furnished with various *Foraign vanities* ; so that the most lascivious compositions of *France* and *Italy* are here *naturalized* and made *English* : And this (as it is sadly observed) with so much favor and success, that nothing *takes* (as they rightly phrase it) like a *Romance*. And very frequently (if that *Character* be not an *Ivy-bush*) the *buyer* receives this lewd ware from *persons of honor* : 30 who want not reason to forbear, much private misfortune having sprung from no other *seed* at first, then some infectious and dissolving *Legend*.

To continue (after years of discretion) in this *vanity*, is an inexcusable desertion of *pious sobriety* : and to persist so to the end, is a wilful despising of Gods *sacred exhortations*, by a constant, sensual volutation or wallowing in *impure thoughts* and *scurrilous conceits*, which both defile their Authors, and as many more, as they are communicated to. If *every idle word shall be accounted for*, and if *no corrupt communication should proceed out of our* 40 *mouths*, how desperate (I beseech you) is their condition, who all their life time, and out of meer design, study *lascivious fictions* :

then carefully record and publish them, that instead of *grace* and *life*, they *may minister sin and death* unto their readers? It was wisely considered, and piously said by one, *That he would read no idle books ; both in regard of love to his own soul, and pity unto his that made them, for* (said he) *if I be corrupted by them, their Composer is immediatly a cause of my ill: and at the day of reckoning (though now dead) must give an account for it, because I am corrupted by his bad example, which he left behinde him: I will write none, lest I hurt them that come after me ; I will read*
10 *none, lest I augment his punishment that is gone before me. I will neither write, nor read, lest I prove a foe to my own soul: while I live, I sin too much ; let me not continue longer in wickedness, then I do in life.* It is a sentence of sacred authority, that *he that is dead, is freed from sin* ; because he cannot in that *state*, which is without the *body*, sin any more ; but he that writes *idle books*, makes for himself another *body*, in which he always *lives*, and *sins* (after *death*) as *fast* and as *foul*, as ever he did in his *life* ; which very consideration, deserves to be a sufficient *Antidote* against this evil disease.

20 And here, because I would prevent a just *censure* by my free *confession*, I must remember, that I my self have for many years together, languished of this very *sickness* ; and it is no long time since I have recovered. But (blessed be God for it!) I have by his saving assistance supprest my *greatest follies*, and those which escaped from me, are (I think) as innoxious, as most of that *vein* use to be ; besides, they are interlined with many virtuous, and some pious mixtures. What I speak of them, is truth ; but let no man mistake it for an *extenuation* of faults, as if I intended an *Apology* for *them*, or my *self*, who am conscious
30 of so much *guilt* in *both*, as can never be expiated without *special sorrows*, and that cleansing and pretious *effusion* of my Almighty Redeemer : and if the world will be so charitable, as to grant my request, I do here most humbly and earnestly beg that none would read them.

But an idle or sensual *subject* is not all the *poyson* in these Pamphlets. Certain Authors have been so irreverendly bold, as to dash *Scriptures*, and the *sacred Relatives* of *God* with their impious conceits ; And (which I cannot speak without grief of heart) some of those desperate *adventurers* may (I think) be reckoned amongst
40 the principal or most learned Writers of *English verse.*

Others of a later *date*, being corrupted (it may be) by that evil *Genius*, which came in with the publique distractions, have stuffed

11 *neither*] *ne ther 1655*   25 *e caped 1655* (?)

their books with *Oathes, horrid Execrations,* and a most gross and studied *filthiness.* But the *hurt* that ensues by the publication of *pieces* so notoriously ill, lies heavily upon the *Stationers* account, who ought in conscience to refuse them, when they are put into his hands. No *loss* is so doleful as that *gain,* that will endamage the soul ; he that *prints* lewdness and impieties, is that mad man in the *Proverbs,* who *casteth firebrands, arrows and death.*

The suppression of this pleasing and prevailing *evil,* lies not altogether in the power of the *Magistrate* ; for it will flie abroad 10 in *Manuscripts,* when it fails of entertainment at the *press.* The true remedy lies wholly in their bosoms, who are the gifted persons, by a wise exchange of *vain* and *vitious subjects,* for *divine Themes* and *Celestial praise.* The *performance* is easie, and were it the most difficult in the world, the *reward* is so glorious, that it infinitely transcends it : for *they that turn many to righteousness, shall shine like the stars for ever and ever* : whence follows this undenyable *inference,* That the *corrupting of many,* being a contrary *work,* the *recompense* must be so too ; and then I know nothing reserved for them, but *the blackness of darkness for ever* ; 20 from which (O God !) deliver all penitent and reformed *Spirits* !

The first, that with any effectual success attempted a *diversion* of this foul and overflowing *stream,* was the blessed man, Mr. *George Herbert,* whose holy *life* and *verse* gained many pious *Converts,* (of whom I am the least) and gave the first check to a most flourishing and admired *wit* of his time. After him followed diverse,—*Sed non passibus æquis ;* they had more of *fashion,* then *force* : And the *reason* of their so vast *distance* from him, besides differing *spirits* and *qualifications* (for his *measure* was eminent) I suspect to be, because they aimed more at *verse,* 30 then *perfection* ; as may be easily gathered by their frequent *impressions,* and numerous *pages* : Hence sprang those wide, those weak, and lean *conceptions,* which in the most inclinable *Reader* will scarce give any nourishment or help to *devotion* ; for not flowing from a true, practick piety, it was impossible they should effect those things abroad, which they never had acquaintance with at home ; being onely the productions of a common spirit, and the obvious ebullitions of that light humor, which takes the pen in hand, out of no other consideration, then to be seen in print. It is true indeed, that to give up our thoughts to pious 40 *Themes* and *Contemplations* (if it be done for pieties sake) is a great *step* towards *perfection* ; because it will *refine,* and *dispose*

17 *like*] *l ke 1655* (?)

to devotion and sanctity. And further, it will *procure* for us (so easily communicable is that *loving spirit*) some small *prelibation* of those heavenly *refreshments*, which descend but seldom, and then very sparingly, upon *men* of an ordinary or indifferent *holyness*; but he that desires to excel in this kinde of *Hagiography*, or holy writing, must strive (by all means) for *perfection* and true *holyness*, that a *door may be opened to him in heaven*, Rev. 4. 1. and then he will be able to write (with *Hierotheus* and holy *Herbert*) A *true Hymn.*

10 To effect this in some measure, I have begged leave to communicate this my poor *Talent* to the *Church*, under the *protection* and *conduct* of her *glorious Head*: who (if he will vouchsafe to *own* it, and *go along* with it) can make it as useful now in the *publick*, as it hath been to me in *private.* In the *perusal* of it, you will (peradventure) observe some *passages*, whose *history* or *reason* may seem something *remote*; but were they brought *nearer*, and plainly exposed to your view, (though that (perhaps) might quiet your *curiosity*) yet would it not conduce much to your greater *advantage.* And therefore I must desire you to 20 accept of them in that *latitude*, which is already alowed them. By the last *Poems* in the book (were not that *mistake* here prevented) you would judge all to be *fatherless*, and the *Edition* posthume; for (indeed) *I was nigh unto death*, and am still at no great distance from it; which was the necessary reason for that solemn and accomplished *dress*, you will now finde this *impression* in.

But *the God of the spirits of all flesh*, hath granted me a further use of *mine*, then I did look for in the *body*; and when I expected, and had (by his assistance) prepared for a *message* of *death*, then 30 did he *answer* me with *life*; I hope to his *glory*, and my great *advantage*: that I may flourish not with *leafe* onely, but with some *fruit* also; which *hope* and earnest *desire* of his poor *Creature*, I humbly beseech him to perfect and fulfil for his dear *Sons* sake, unto *whom*, with *him* and the most holy and loving *Spirit*, be ascribed by *Angels*, by *Men*, and by all his *Works*, All Glory, and Wisdom, and Dominion, in this the *temporal* and in the *Eternal* Being. *Amen.*

Newton by *Usk*, near
Sketh-rock, Septem. 30.
40 1 6 5 4.

O Lord, the hope of Israel, all they that forsake thee shall be ashamed ; and they that depart from thee, shall be written in the earth, because they have forsaken the Lord, the fountain of living waters.

Heal me, O Lord, and I shall be healed ; save me, and I shall be saved, for thou art my health, and my great deliverer.

I said in the cutting off of my days, I shall go to the gates of the grave ; I have deprived my self of the residue of my years.

I said, I shall not see the Lord, even the Lord in the Land of the living : I shall behold man no more with the Inhabitants of the 10 *world.*

O Lord ! by thee doth man live, and from thee is the life of my spirit : therefore wilt thou recover me, and make me to live.

Thou hast in love to my soul delivered it from the pit of corruption ; for thou hast cast all my sins behinde thy back.

For thy names sake hast thou put off thine anger ; for thy praise hast thou refrained from me, that I should not be cut off.

For the grave cannot praise thee, death cannot celebrate thee : they that go down into the pit, cannot hope for thy truth.

The living, the living, he shall praise thee, as I do this day : the 20 *Father to the children shall make known thy truth.*

O Lord ! thou hast been merciful, thou hast brought back my life from corruption : thou hast redeemed me from my sin.

They that follow after lying vanities, forsake their own mercy.

Therefore shall thy songs be with me, and my prayer unto the God of my life.

I will go unto the altar of my God, unto God, the joy of my youth ; and in thy fear will I worship towards thy holy temple.

I will sacrifice unto thee with the voice of thanksgiving ; I will pay that which I have vowed : salvation is of the Lord. 30

To my most merciful, my most
loving, and dearly loved Redeemer, the ever blessed,
the onely Holy and

J U S T O N E ,

JESVS CHRIST,

The Son of the living

G O D,

And the sacred

Virgin Mary.

I.

My God! thou that didst dye for me,
These thy deaths fruits I offer thee;
Death that to me was life and light,
But dark and deep pangs to thy sight.
Some drops of thy all-quickning blood
Fell on my heart; those made it bud
And put forth thus, though Lord, before
The ground was curst, and void of store.
Indeed I had some here to hire
Which long resisted thy desire,   10
That ston'd thy servants, and did move
To have the murthred for thy love;
But Lord, I have expell'd them, and so bent,
Beg, thou wouldst take thy Tenants Rent.

II.

Dear Lord, 'tis finished! and now he
That copyed it, presents it thee.
'Twas thine first, and to thee returns,
From thee it shin'd, though here it burns;

The first verse alone appears in 1650 and is headed simply The Dedication.
1 God!] God, *1650*   2 thee;] thee. *1650*   3 life] life, *1650*   6 heart;]
heart, *1650*   those] these *1650*   9 Indeed] Indeed, (*set in*) *1650*   12 love;]
Love, *1650*   13 But] But, *1650*   bent,] bent *1650*   14 Beg,] Begge *1650*

If the Sun rise on rocks, is't right,
To call it their inherent light?   20
No, nor can I say, this is mine,
For, dearest Jesus, 'tis all thine.
As thy cloaths, (when thou with cloaths wert clad)
Both light from thee, and virtue had,
And now (as then within this place)
Thou to poor rags dost still give grace.
This is the earnest thy love sheds,
The *Candle* shining on some heads,
Till at thy charges they shall be,
Cloath'd all with immortality.   30

My dear Redeemer, the worlds light,
And life too, and my hearts delight!
For all thy mercies and thy truth
Shew'd to me in my sinful youth,
For my sad failings and my wilde
Murmurings at thee, when most milde:
For all my secret faults, and each
Frequent relapse and wilful breach,
For all designs meant against thee,
And ev'ry publish'd vanity   40
Which thou divinely hast forgiven,
While thy blood wash'd me white as heaven:
I nothing have to give to thee,
But this thy own gift, given to me;
Refuse it not! for now thy *Token*
Can tell thee where a heart is broken.

Revel. cap. 1. *ver.* 5, 6, 7.
*Unto him that loved us, and washed us from our sins in his own
blood.*
*And hath made us Kings and Priests unto God and his Father;
to him be glory and dominion, for ever and ever.   Amen.*
*Behold, he cometh with clouds, and every eye shall see him, and
they also which pierced him; and all kinreds of the earth shall wail
because of him: even so.   Amen.*

6 (*prose*) *of*] *af 1655*

¶

Vain Wits and eyes
Leave, and be wise :
Abuse not, shun not holy fire,
But with true tears wash off your mire.
Tears and these flames will soon grow kinde,
And mix an eye-salve for the blinde.
Tears cleanse and supple without fail,
And fire will purge your callous veyl.
Then comes the light! which when you spy,
And see your nakedness thereby,   10
Praise him, who dealt his gifts so free
In tears to you, in fire to me.

These verses in 1655 only

Silex Scintillans, &c.

Regeneration.

A Ward, and still in bonds, one day
      I stole abroad,
It was high-spring, and all the way
      Primros'd, and hung with shade;
    Yet, was it frost within,
      And surly winds
Blasted my infant buds, and sinne
      Like Clouds ecclips'd my mind.

2.

Storm'd thus; I straight perceiv'd my spring
      Meere stage, and show,   10
My walke a monstrous, mountain'd thing
      Rough-cast with Rocks, and snow;
    And as a Pilgrims Eye
      Far from reliefe,
Measures the melancholy skye
      Then drops, and rains for griefe,

3.

So sigh'd I upwards still, at last
      'Twixt steps, and falls
I reach'd the pinacle, where plac'd
      I found a paire of scales,   20
    I tooke them up and layd
      In th'one late paines,
The other smoake, and pleasures weigh'd
      But prov'd the heavier graines;

4.

With that, some cryed, *Away*; straight I
      Obey'd, and led
Full East, a faire, fresh field could spy
      Some call'd it, *Jacobs Bed*;
    A Virgin-soile, which no
      Rude feet ere trod,   30
Where (since he stept there,) only go
      Prophets, and friends of God.

6 And surly winds] The surly wind *L 1847*: And surly wind *L 1858-1883*
31 stept] slept *anonymous conjecture in G*

5.

Here, I repos'd ; but scarse well set,
                A grove descryed
Of stately height, whose branches met
                And mixt on every side ;
                I entred, and once in
                        (Amaz'd to see't,)
Found all was chang'd, and a new spring
                Did all my senses greet ;   40

6.

The unthrift Sunne shot vitall gold
                A thousand peeces,
And heaven its azure did unfold
                Checqur'd with snowie fleeces,
                The aire was all in spice
                        And every bush
A garland wore ; Thus fed my Eyes
                But all the Eare lay hush.

7.

Only a little Fountain lent
                Some use for Eares,   50
And on the dumbe shades language spent
                The Musick of her teares ;
                I drew her neere, and found
                        The Cisterne full
Of divers stones, some bright, and round
                Others ill-shap'd, and dull.

8.

The first (pray marke,) as quick as light
                Danc'd through the floud,
But, th'last more heavy then the night
                Nail'd to the Center stood ;   60
                I wonder'd much, but tyr'd
                        At last with thought,
My restless Eye that still desir'd
                As strange an object brought ;

48 Eare] Earth *G* : ear[th] *C*   63 desir'd] desir'd, *LGCB*

9.

It was a banke of flowers, where I descried
(Though 'twas mid-day,)
Some fast asleepe, others broad-eyed
And taking in the Ray,
Here musing long, I heard
A rushing wind   70
Which still increas'd, but whence it stirr'd
No where I could not find ;

10.

I turn'd me round, and to each shade
Dispatch'd an Eye,
To see, if any leafe had made
Least motion, or Reply,
But while I listning sought
My mind to ease
By knowing, where 'twas, or where not,
It whisper'd ; *Where I please.*   80

Lord, then said I, *On me one breath,*
And let me dye before my death!

Cant. Cap. 5. ver. 17.
Arise O North, and come thou South-wind, and blow upon my
garden, that the spices thereof may flow out.

Death.

A Dialogue.

Soule. 'Tis a sad Land, that in one day
Hath dull'd thee thus, when death shall freeze
Thy bloud to Ice, and thou must stay
Tenant for Yeares, and Centuries,
How wilt thou brook't ? ——

Body. I cannot tell, ——
But if all sence wings not with thee,
And something still be left the dead,
I'le wish my Curtaines off to free
Me from so darke, and sad a bed ;   10

A neast of nights, a gloomie sphere,
Where shadowes thicken, and the Cloud
Sits on the Suns brow all the yeare,
And nothing moves without a shrowd ;

Soule. 'Tis so : But as thou sawest that night
    Wee travell'd in, our first attempts
    Were dull, and blind, but Custome straight
    Our feares, and falls brought to contempt,

    Then, when the gastly *twelve* was past
    We breath'd still for a blushing *East*,   20
    And bad the lazie Sunne make hast,
    And on sure hopes, though long, did feast ;

    But when we saw the Clouds to crack
    And in those Cranies light appear'd,
    We thought the day then was not slack,
    And pleas'd our selves with what wee feard ;

    Just so it is in death.   But thou
    Shalt in thy mothers bosome sleepe
    Whilst I each minute grone to know
    How neere Redemption creepes.   30

Then shall wee meet to mix again, and met,
'Tis last good-night, our Sunne shall never set.

Job. Cap: 10. *ver.* 21. 22.

*Before I goe whence I shall not returne, even to the land of dark-
nesse, and the shadow of death ;*

*A Land of darknesse, as darkenesse it selfe, and of the shadow of
death, without any order, and where the light is as darknesse.*

Resurrection and Immortality :

Heb. cap. 10. *ve:* 20.

*By that new, and living way, which he hath prepared for us,
through the veile, which is his flesh.*

Body.

I.

Oft have I seen, when that renewing breath
    That binds, and loosens death
Inspir'd a quickning power through the dead
        Creatures a bed,
      Some drowsie silk-worme creepe
        From that long sleepe

And in weake, infant hummings chime, and knell
About her silent Cell
Untill at last full with the vitall Ray
She wing'd away,   10
And proud with life, and sence,
Heav'ns rich Expence,
Esteem'd (vaine things!) of two whole Elements
As meane, and span-extents.
Shall I then thinke such providence will be
Lesse friend to me?
Or that he can endure to be unjust
Who keeps his Covenant even with our dust.

Soule.

2.

Poore, querulous handfull! was't for this
I taught thee all that is?   20
Unbowel'd nature, shew'd thee her recruits,
And Change of suits
And how of death we make
A meere mistake,
For no thing can to *Nothing* fall, but still
Incorporates by skill,
And then returns, and from the wombe of things
Such treasure brings
As *Phenix*-like renew'th
Both life, and youth;   30
For a preserving spirit doth still passe
Untainted through this Masse,
Which doth resolve, produce, and ripen all
That to it fall;
Nor are those births which we
Thus suffering see
Destroy'd at all; But when times restles wave
Their substance doth deprave
And the more noble *Essence* finds his house
Sickly, and loose,   40
He, ever young, doth wing
Unto that spring,
And *source* of spirits, where he takes his lot
Till time no more shall rot

D d

His passive Cottage; which (though laid aside,)
Like some spruce Bride,
Shall one day rise, and cloath'd with shining light
All pure, and bright
Re-marry to the soule, for 'tis most plaine
Thou only fal'st to be refin'd againe. 50

3.

Then I that here saw darkly in a glasse
But mists, and shadows passe,
And, by their owne weake *Shine*, did search the springs
And Course of things
Shall with Inlightned Rayes
Peirce all their wayes;
And as thou saw'st, I in a thought could goe
To heav'n, or Earth below
To reade some *Starre*, or *Min'rall*, and in State
There often sate, 60
So shalt thou then with me
(Both wing'd, and free,)
Rove in that mighty, and eternall light
Where no rude shade, or night
Shall dare approach us; we shall there no more
Watch stars, or pore
Through melancholly clouds, and say
Would it were Day!
One everlasting *Saboth* there shall runne
Without *Succession*, and without a *Sunne*. 70

Dan: Cap: 12. ver: 13.
But goe thou thy way untill the end be, for thou shalt rest, and
stand up in thy lot, at the end of the dayes.

Day of Judgement.

When through the North a fire shall rush
And rowle into the East,
And like a firie torrent brush
And sweepe up *South*, and *West*,

When all shall streame, and lighten round
And with surprizing flames
Both stars, and Elements confound
And quite blot out their names,

When thou shalt spend thy sacred store
       Of thunders in that heate   10
And low as ere they lay before
       Thy six-dayes-buildings beate,
When like a scrowle the heavens shal passe
       And vanish cleane away,
And nought must stand of that vast space
       Which held up night, and day,
When one lowd blast shall rend the deepe,
       And from the wombe of earth
Summon up all that are asleepe
       Unto a second birth,   20
When thou shalt make the Clouds thy seate,
       And in the open aire
The Quick, and dead, both small and great
       Must to thy barre repaire;
O then it wilbe all too late
       To say, *What shall I doe?*
Repentance there is out of date
       And so is *mercy* too;
Prepare, prepare me then, O God!
       And let me now begin   30
To feele my loving fathers *Rod*
       Killing the man of sinne!
Give me, O give me Crosses here,
       Still more afflictions lend,
That pill, though bitter, is most deare
       That brings health in the end;
Lord, God! I beg nor friends, nor wealth
       But pray against them both;
Three things I'de have, my soules chief health!
       And one of these seme loath,   40
A living *FAITH*, a *HEART* of flesh,
       The *WORLD* an Enemie.
This last will keepe the first two fresh,
       And bring me, where I'de be.

1 Pet. 4. 7.
Now the end of all things is at hand, be you therefore sober, and watching in prayer.

37 Lord, God] Lord God *C*   40 seme] semes *L* : same *G*

D d 2

Religion.

My God, when I walke in those groves,
And leaves thy spirit doth still fan,
I see in each shade that there growes
An Angell talking with a man.

Under a *Juniper*, some house,
Or the coole *Mirtles* canopie,
Others beneath an *Oakes* greene boughs,
Or at some *fountaines* bubling Eye;

Here *Jacob* dreames, and wrestles; there
Elias by a Raven is fed,   10
Another time by th' Angell, where
He brings him water with his bread;

In *Abr'hams* Tent the winged guests
(O how familiar then was heaven!)
Eate, drinke, discourse, sit downe, and rest
Untill the Coole, and shady *Even*;

Nay thou thy selfe, my God, in *fire*,
Whirle-winds, and *Clouds*, and the *soft voice*
Speak'st there so much, that I admire
We have no Conf'rence in these daies;   20

Is the truce broke? or 'cause we have
A mediatour now with thee,
Doest thou therefore old Treaties wave
And by appeales from him decree?

Or is't so, as some green heads say
That now all miracles must cease?
Though thou hast promis'd they should stay
The tokens of the Church, and peace;

No, no; Religion is a Spring
That from some secret, golden Mine   30
Derives her birth, and thence doth bring
Cordials in every drop, and Wine;

But in her long, and hidden Course
Passing through the Earths darke veines,
Growes still from better unto worse,
And both her taste, and colour staines,

Then drilling on, learnes to encrease
False *Ecchoes,* and Confused sounds,
And unawares doth often seize
On veines of *Sulphur* under ground ;　　　40

So poison'd, breaks forth in some Clime,
And at first sight doth many please,
But drunk, is puddle, or meere slime
And 'stead of Phisick, a disease ;

Just such a tainted sink we have
Like that *Samaritans* dead *Well,*
Nor must we for the Kernell crave
Because most voices like the *shell.*

Heale then these waters, Lord ; or bring thy flock,
Since these are troubled, to the springing rock,　　　50
Looke downe great Master of the feast ; O shine,
And turn once more our *Water* into *Wine* !

Cant. cap. 4. ver. 12.
My sister, my spouse is as a garden Inclosed, as a Spring shut up, and a fountain sealed up.

The Search.

'Tis now cleare day : I see a Rose
Bud in the bright East, and disclose
The Pilgrim-Sunne ; all night have I
Spent in a roving Extasie
To find my Saviour ; I have been
As far as *Bethlem,* and have seen
His Inne, and Cradle ; Being there
I met the *Wise-men,* askt them where
He might be found, or what starre can
Now point him out, grown up a Man ?　　　10
To *Egypt* hence I fled, ran o're
All her parcht bosome to *Nile's* shore
Her yearly nurse ; came back, enquir'd
Amongst the *Doctors,* and desir'd
To see the *Temple,* but was shown
A little dust, and for the Town
A heap of ashes, where some sed
A small bright sparkle was a bed,
Which would one day (beneath the pole,)
Awake, and then refine the whole.　　　20

Tyr'd here, I come to *Sychar*; thence
To *Jacobs wel,* bequeathed since
Unto his sonnes, (where often they
In those calme, golden Evenings lay
Watring their flocks, and having spent
Those white dayes, drove home to the Tent
Their *well-fleec'd* traine ;) And here (O fate !)
I sit, where once my Saviour sate ;
The angry Spring in bubbles swell'd
Which broke in sighes still, as they fill'd,   30
And whisper'd, *Jesus had been there*
But *Jacobs children would not heare.*
Loath hence to part, at last I rise
But with the fountain in my Eyes,
And here a fresh search is decreed
He must be found, where he did bleed ;
I walke the garden, and there see
Idæa's of his Agonie,
And moving anguishments that set
His blest face in a bloudy sweat ;   40
I climb'd the Hill, perus'd the Crosse
Hung with my gaine, and his great losse,
Never did tree beare fruit like this,
Balsam of Soules, the bodyes blisse ;
But, O his grave ! where I saw lent
(For he had none,) a Monument,
An undefil'd, and new-heaw'd one,
But there was not the *Corner-stone* ;
Sure (then said I,) my Quest is vaine,
Hee'le not be found, where he was slaine,   50
So mild a Lamb can never be
'Midst so much bloud, and Crueltie ;
I'le to the Wilderness, and can
Find beasts more mercifull then man,
He liv'd there safe, 'twas his retreat
From the fierce *Jew,* and *Herods* heat,
And forty dayes withstood the fell,
And high temptations of hell ;
With Seraphins there talked he
His fathers flaming ministrie,   60
He heav'nd their *walks,* and with his eyes
Made those wild shades a Paradise,

Thus was the desert sanctified
To be the refuge of his bride ;
I'le thither then ; see, It is day,
The Sun's broke through to guide my way.
    But as I urg'd thus, and writ down
What pleasures should my Journey crown,
What silent paths, what shades, and Cells,
Faire, virgin-flowers, and hallow'd *Wells*   70
I should rove in, and rest my head
Where my deare Lord did often tread,
Sugring all dangers with successe,
Me thought I heard one singing thus ;

1.
Leave, leave, thy gadding thoughts ;
Who Pores
and spies
Still out of Doores
descries
Within them nought.   80

2.
The skinne, and shell of things
Though faire,
are not
Thy wish, nor pray'r
but got
By meer Despair
of wings.

3.
To rack old Elements,
or Dust
and say   90
Sure here he must
needs stay
Is not the way,
nor just.

Search well another world ; who studies this,
Travels in Clouds, seeks *Manna*, where none is.

Acts Cap. 17. ver. 27, 28.
That they should seek the Lord, if happily they might feel after him,
and finde him, though he be not far off from every one of us, for in
him we live, and move, and have our being.

84 pray'r] Pray'r, *1650*   89 Dust] Dust; *1650*

Isaacs Marriage.

Gen. cap. 24. ver. 63.

And Isaac *went out to pray in the field at the Even-tide, and he lift up his eyes, and saw, and behold, the Camels were coming.*

Praying ! and to be married ? It was rare,
But now 'tis monstrous ; and that pious care
Though of our selves, is so much out of date,
That to renew't were to degenerate.
But thou a Chosen sacrifice wert given,
And offer'd up so early unto heaven
Thy flames could not be out ; Religion was
Ray'd into thee, like beams into a glasse,
Where, as thou grewst, it multipli'd and shin'd
The sacred Constellation of thy mind.   10
But being for a bride, prayer was such
A decryed course, sure it prevail'd not much.
Had'st ne'r an oath, nor Complement ? thou wert
An odde dull sutor ; Hadst thou but the art
Of these our dayes, thou couldst have coyn'd thee twenty
New sev'ral oathes, and Complements (too) plenty ;
O sad, and wilde excesse ! and happy those
White dayes, that durst no impious mirth expose !
When Conscience by lew'd use had not lost sense,
Nor bold-fac'd custome banish'd Innocence ;   20
Thou hadst no pompous train, nor *Antick* crowd
Of young, gay swearers, with their needlesse, lowd
Retinue ; All was here smooth as thy bride
And calm like her, or that mild Evening-tide ;
Yet, hadst thou nobler guests : Angels did wind
And rove about thee, guardians of thy minde,
These fetch'd thee home thy bride, and all the way
Advis'd thy servant what to do, and say ;
These taught him at the *well*, and thither brought
The Chast, and lovely object of thy thought ;   30

Title Isaacs] *Isaac's catchword 1655*   Marriage. *1650* : Marriage *1655*
3 date, *1650* : date. *1655*   4 renew't] renew't, *1650*   9 multipli'd]
multiply'd, *1650*
    11, 12   But being for a bride, sure, prayer was
              Very strange stuffe wherewith to court thy lasse, *1650*
   14 odde dull] odde, corse *1650*   18 dayes *1650* : daye *1655*
   19   When sinne, by sinning oft, had not lost sence, *1650*
   23 Retinue ; *1650* : Retinue *1655*   25 wind] wind, *1650*

But here was ne'r a Complement, not one
Spruce, supple cringe, or study'd look put on,
All was plain, modest truth : Nor did she come
In *rowles* and *Curles*, mincing and stately dumb,
But in a Virgins native blush and fears
Fresh as those roses, which the day-spring wears.
O sweet, divine simplicity ! O grace
Beyond a Curled lock, or painted face !
A *Pitcher* too she had, nor thought it much
To carry that, which some would scorn to touch ;   40
With which in mild, chast language she did wooe
To draw him drink, and for his Camels too.

    And now thou knewest her coming, It was time
To get thee wings on, and devoutly climbe
Unto thy God, for Marriage of all states
Makes most unhappy, or most fortunates ;
This brought thee forth, where now thou didst undress
Thy soul, and with new pinions refresh
Her wearied wings, which so restor'd did flye
Above the stars, a track unknown, and high,   50
And in her piercing flight perfum'd the ayer
Scatt'ring the *Myrrhe*, and incense of thy pray'r.
So from * *Lahai-roi's* Well some spicie cloud
Woo'd by the Sun swels up to be his shrowd,
And from his moist wombe weeps a fragrant showre,
Which, scatter'd in a thousand pearls, each flowre
And herb partakes, where having stood awhile
And something coold the parch'd, and thirstie Isle,
The thankful Earth unlocks her self, and blends,
A thousand odours, which (all mixt,) she sends
Up in one cloud, and so returns the skies
That dew they lent, a breathing sacrifice.   62

* A wel in the South Country where Ja-cob dwelt, between Cadesh, & Bered ; Heb. the well of him that liveth, and seeth me.

    Thus soar'd thy soul, who (though young,) didst inherit
Together with his bloud, thy fathers spirit,
Whose active zeal, and tried faith were to thee
Familiar ever since thy Infancie.

35-6   But in a frighted, virgin-blush approach'd
            Fresh as the morning, when 'tis newly Coach'd ; *1650*
  38 lock, *1650* : lock. *1655*   43 knewest] knewst *1650*   48 refresh
1650 : refrsh *1655*   49 restor'd *1650* : resto'd *1655*   flye *1650* : flee *1655*
51 ayer] ayre *1650* : ayer. *1655*   52 pray'r. *1650*: pray'r *1655*   53 Well]
Well, *1650*   55 his] her *LGCB*   58 thirstie *1650* : thirst *1655*
62 sacrifice. *1650* : sacrifice *1655*   66 Infancie.] Infancie, *1650*

Others were tym'd, and train'd up to't but thou
Diddst thy swift yeers in piety out-grow,
Age made them rev'rend, and a snowie head,
But thou wert so, e're time his snow could shed; 70
Then, who would truly limne thee out, must paint
First, a *young Patriarch*, then a *marri'd Saint.*

The Brittish Church.

Ah ! he is fled !
And while these here their *mists*, and *shadows* hatch,
My glorious head
Doth on those hills of Mirrhe, and Incense watch.
Haste, hast my dear,
The Souldiers here
Cast in their lots again,
That seamlesse coat
The Jews touch'd not,
These dare divide, and stain. 10

2.

O get thee wings !
Or if as yet (until these clouds depart,
And the day springs,)
Thou think'st it good to tarry where thou art,
Write in thy bookes
My ravish'd looks
Slain flock, and pillag'd fleeces,
And hast thee so
As a young Roe
Upon the mounts of spices. 20

*O Rosa Campi ! O lilium Convallium ! quomodò nunc
facta es pabulum Aprorum !*

The Lampe.

'Tis dead night round about: Horrour doth creepe
And move on with the shades; stars nod, and sleepe,
And through the dark aire spin a firie thread
Such as doth gild the lazie glow-worms bed.

67 to't] to't, *1650*   3 head *1650*: head. *1655*

Yet, burn'st thou here, a full day; while I spend
My rest in Cares, and to the dark world lend
These flames, as thou dost thine to me; I watch
That houre, which must thy life, and mine dispatch;
But still thou doest out-goe me, I can see
Met in thy flames, all acts of piety;   10
Thy light, is *Charity*; Thy heat, is *Zeale*;
And thy aspiring, active fires reveale
Devotion still on wing; Then, thou dost weepe
Still as thou burn'st, and the warme droppings creepe
To measure out thy length, as if thou'dst know
What stock, and how much time were left thee now;
Nor dost thou spend one teare in vain, for still
As thou dissolv'st to them, and they distill,
They're stor'd up in the socket, where they lye,
When all is spent, thy last, and sure supply,   20
And such is true repentance, ev'ry breath
Wee spend in sighes, is treasure after death;
Only, one point escapes thee; That thy Oile
Is still out with thy flame, and so both faile;
But whensoe're I'm out, both shalbe in,
And where thou mad'st an end, there I'le begin.

Mark Cap. 13. ver. 35.
*Watch you therefore, for you know not when the master of the
house commeth, at Even, or at mid-night, or at the Cock-crowing, or
in the morning.*

Mans fall, and Recovery.

Farewell you Everlasting hills! I'm Cast
Here under Clouds, where stormes, and tempests blast
   This sully'd flowre
Rob'd of your Calme, nor can I ever make
Transplanted thus, one leafe of his t'awake,
   But ev'ry houre
He sleepes, and droops, and in this drowsie state
Leaves me a slave to passions, and my fate;
   Besides I've lost
A traine of lights, which in those Sun-shine dayes   10
Were my sure guides, and only with me stayes
   (Unto my cost,)

One sullen beame, whose charge is to dispense
More punishment, than knowledge to my sense;
    Two thousand yeares
I sojourn'd thus; at last *Jeshuruns* king
Those famous tables did from *Sinai* bring;
    These swell'd my feares,
Guilts, trespasses, and all this Inward Awe,
For sinne tooke strength, and vigour from the Law.   20
    Yet have I found
A plenteous way, (thanks to that holy one!)
To cancell all that e're was writ in stone,
    His saving wound
Wept bloud, that broke this Adamant, and gave
To sinners Confidence, life to the grave;
    This makes me span
My fathers journeys, and in one faire step
O're all their pilgrimage, and labours leap,
    For God (made man,)   30
Reduc'd th'Extent of works of faith; so made
Of their *Red Sea*, a *Spring*; I wash, they wade.

Rom. Cap. 18. ver. 19.
As by the offence of one, the fault came on all men to condem-
nation; So by the Righteousness of one, the benefit abounded
towards all men to the Justification of life.

The Showre.

'Twas so, I saw thy birth: That drowsie Lake
From her faint bosome breath'd thee, the disease
Of her sick waters, and Infectious Ease.
    But, now at Even
    Too grosse for heaven,
Thou fall'st in teares, and weep'st for thy mistake.

2.

Ah! it is so with me; oft have I prest
Heaven with a lazie breath, but fruitles this
Peirc'd not; Love only can with quick accesse
    Unlock the way,   10
    When all else stray
The smoke, and Exhalations of the brest.

3.
Yet, if as thou doest melt, and with thy traine
Of drops make soft the Earth, my eyes could weep
O're my hard heart, that's bound up, and asleep,
      Perhaps at last
    (Some such showres past,)
My God would give a Sun-shine after raine.

Distraction.

O knit me, that am crumbled dust! the heape
    Is all dispers'd, and cheape;
  Give for a handfull, but a thought
    And it is bought;
      Hadst thou
Made me a starre, a pearle, or a rain-bow,
    The beames I then had shot
    My light had lessend not,
      But now
I find my selfe the lesse, the more I grow;   10
    The world
Is full of voices; Man is call'd, and hurl'd
    By each, he answers all,
    Knows ev'ry note, and call,
      Hence, still
Fresh dotage tempts, or old usurps his will.
Yet, hadst thou clipt my wings, when Coffin'd in
    This quicken'd masse of sinne,
  And saved that light, which freely thou
    Didst then bestow,   20
      I feare
I should have spurn'd, and said thou didst forbeare;
    Or that thy store was lesse,
    But now since thou didst blesse
      So much,
I grieve, my God! that thou hast made me such.
      I grieve?
O, yes! thou know'st I doe; Come, and releive
    And tame, and keepe downe with thy light
    Dust that would rise, and dimme my sight,   30
    Lest left alone too long
    Amidst the noise, and throng,
      Oppressed I
Striving to save the whole, by parcells dye.

The Pursuite.

Lord! what a busie, restles thing
    Hast thou made man?
Each day, and houre he is on wing,
    Rests not a span;
Then having lost the Sunne, and light
    By clouds surpriz'd
He keepes a Commerce in the night
    With aire disguis'd;
Hadst thou given to this active dust
    A state untir'd,   10
The lost Sonne had not left the huske
    Nor home desir'd;
That was thy secret, and it is
    Thy mercy too,
For when all failes to bring to blisse,
    Then, this must doe.
Ah! Lord! and what a Purchase will that be
To take us sick, that sound would not take thee?

Mount of Olives.

Sweete, sacred hill! on whose fair brow
My Saviour sate, shall I allow
    Language to love
And Idolize some shade, or grove,
Neglecting thee? such ill-plac'd wit,
Conceit, or call it what you please
    Is the braines fit,
    And meere disease;

2.

Cotswold, and *Coopers* both have met
With learned swaines, and Eccho yet   10
    Their pipes, and wit;
But thou sleep'st in a deepe neglect
Untouch'd by any; And what need
The sheep bleat thee a silly Lay
    That heard'st both reed
    And sheepward play?

9 *Cotswold,*] *Cottswold, catchword 1655*

3.

Yet, if Poets mind thee well
They shall find thou art their hill,
   And fountaine too,
Their Lord with thee had most to doe ;   20
He wept once, walkt whole nights on thee,
And from thence (his suff'rings ended,)
     Unto glorie
     Was attended ;

4.

Being there, this spacious ball
Is but his narrow footstoole all,
   And what we thinke
Unsearchable, now with one winke
He doth comprise ; But in this aire
When he did stay to beare our Ill   30
     And sinne, this Hill
     Was then his Chaire.

The Incarnation, and Passion.

Lord ! when thou didst thy selfe undresse
Laying by thy robes of glory,
To make us more, thou wouldst be lesse,
And becam'st a wofull story.

To put on Clouds instead of light,
And cloath the morning-starre with dust,
Was a translation of such height
As, but in thee, was ne'r exprest ;

Brave wormes, and Earth ! that thus could have
A God Enclos'd within your Cell,   10
Your maker pent up in a grave,
Life lockt in death, heav'n in a shell ;

Ah, my deare Lord ! what couldst thou spye
In this impure, rebellious clay,
That made thee thus resolve to dye
For those that kill thee every day ?

O what strange wonders could thee move
To slight thy precious bloud, and breath !
Sure it was *Love*, my Lord ; for *Love*
Is only stronger far than death.   20

The Call.

Come my heart ! come my head
In sighes, and teares !
'Tis now, since you have laine thus dead
Some twenty years ;
Awake, awake,
Some pitty take
Upon your selves——
Who never wake to grone, nor weepe,
Shall be sentenc'd for their sleepe.

2.

Doe but see your sad estate,
How many sands
Have left us, while we careles sate
With folded hands ;
What stock of nights,
Of dayes, and yeares
In silent flights
Stole by our eares,
How ill have we our selves bestow'd
Whose suns are all set in a Cloud ?

3.

Yet, come, and let's peruse them all ;
And as we passe,
What sins on every minute fall
Score on the glasse ;
Then weigh, and rate
Their heavy State
Untill
The glasse with teares you fill ;
That done, we shalbe safe, and good,
Those beasts were cleane, that chew'd the Cud.

¶

Thou that know'st for whom I mourne,
And why these teares appeare,
That keep'st account, till he returne
Of all his dust left here ;

As easily thou mightst prevent
    As now produce these teares,
And adde unto that day he went
    A faire supply of yeares.
But 'twas my sinne that forc'd thy hand
    To cull this *Prim-rose* out,   10
That by thy early choice forewarn'd
    My soule might looke about.
O what a vanity is man !
    How like the Eyes quick winke
His Cottage failes; whose narrow span
    Begins even at the brink !
Nine months thy hands are fashioning us,
    And many yeares (alas !)
E're we can lisp, or ought discusse
    Concerning thee, must passe;   20
Yet have I knowne thy slightest things
    A *feather*, or a *shell*,
A *stick*, or *Rod* which some Chance brings
    The best of us excell,
Yea, I have knowne these shreds out last
    A faire-compacted frame
And for one *Twenty* we have past
    Almost outlive our name.
Thus hast thou plac'd in mans outside
    Death to the Common Eye,   30
That heaven within him might abide,
    And close eternitie ;
Hence, youth, and folly (mans first shame,)
    Are put unto the slaughter,
And serious thoughts begin to tame
    The wise-mans-madnes *Laughter* ;
Dull, wretched wormes ! that would not keepe
    Within our first faire bed,
But out of *Paradise* must creepe
    For ev'ry foote to tread ;   40
Yet, had our Pilgrimage bin free,
    And smooth without a thorne,
Pleasures had foil'd Eternitie,
    And *tares* had choakt the *Corne*.
Thus by the Crosse Salvation runnes,
    Affliction is a mother,

Whose painfull throws yield many sons,
    Each fairer than the other;
A silent teare can peirce thy throne,
    When lowd Joyes want a wing,   50
And sweeter aires streame from a grone,
    Than any arted string;
Thus, Lord, I see my gaine is great,
    My losse but little to it,
Yet something more I must intreate
    And only thou canst doe it.
O let me (like him,) know my End!
    And be as glad to find it,
And whatsoe'r thou shalt Commend,
    Still let thy Servant mind it!   60
Then make my soule white as his owne,
    My faith as pure, and steddy,
And deck me, Lord, with the same Crowne
    Thou hast crownd him already!

Vanity of Spirit.

Quite spent with thoughts I left my Cell, and lay
Where a shrill spring tun'd to the early day.
    I beg'd here long, and gron'd to know
    Who gave the Clouds so brave a bow,
    Who bent the spheres, and circled in
    Corruption with this glorious Ring,
    What is his name, and how I might
    Descry some part of his great light.
I summon'd nature: peirc'd through all her store,
Broke up some seales, which none had touch'd before,   10
    Her wombe, her bosome, and her head
    Where all her secrets lay a bed
    I rifled quite, and having past
    Through all the Creatures, came at last
    To search my selfe, where I did find
    Traces, and sounds of a strange kind.
Here of this mighty spring, I found some drills,
With Ecchoes beaten from th' eternall hills;
    Weake beames, and fires flash'd to my sight,
    Like a young East, or Moone-shine night,   20
    Which shew'd me in a nook cast by

21 Which] Wich *1655* (*from* With *l.* 23?)

A peece of much antiquity,
With Hyerogliphicks quite dismembred,
And broken letters scarce remembred.
I tooke them up, and (much Joy'd,) went about
T' unite those peeces, hoping to find out
 The mystery; but this neer done,
 That little light I had was gone:
 It griev'd me much.   At last, said I,
 Since in these veyls my Ecclips'd Eye   30
 May not approach thee, (for at night
 Who can have commerce with the light?)
 I'le disapparell, and to buy
 But one half glaunce, most gladly dye.

The Retreate.

Happy those early dayes! when I
Shin'd in my Angell-infancy.
Before I understood this place
Appointed for my second race,
Or taught my soul to fancy ought
But a white, Celestiall thought,
When yet I had not walkt above
A mile, or two, from my first love,
And looking back (at that short space,)
Could see a glimpse of his bright-face;   10
When on some *gilded Cloud*, or *flowre*
My gazing soul would dwell an houre,
And in those weaker glories spy
Some shadows of eternity;
Before I taught my tongue to wound
My Conscience with a sinfull sound,
Or had the black art to dispence
A sev'rall sinne to ev'ry sence,
But felt through all this fleshly dresse
Bright *shootes* of everlastingnesse.   20
 O how I long to travell back
And tread again that ancient track!
That I might once more reach that plaine,
Where first I left my glorious traine,
From whence th' Inlightned spirit sees
That shady City of Palme trees;

 10 see *1650*: fee *B. M. copy of 1655* (?)

E e 2

But (ah !) my soul with too much stay
Is drunk, and staggers in the way.
Some men a forward motion love,
But I by backward steps would move,   30
And when this dust falls to the urn
In that state I came return.

¶

Come, come, what doe I here?
    Since he is gone
Each day is grown a dozen year,
    And each houre, one ;
    Come, come !
    Cut off the sum,
By these soil'd teares !
    (Which only thou
    Know'st to be true,)
Dayes are my feares.   10

2.

Ther's not a wind can stir,
    Or beam passe by,
But strait I think (though far,)
    Thy hand is nigh ;
    Come, come !
Strike these lips dumb :
This restles breath
That soiles thy name,
Will ne'r be tame
Untill in death.   20

3.

Perhaps some think a tombe
    No house of store,
But a dark, and seal'd up wombe,
    Which ne'r breeds more.
    Come, come !
Such thoughts benum ;
But I would be
With him I weep
A bed, and sleep
To wake in thee.   30

¶ Midnight.

When to my Eyes
(Whilst deep sleep others catches,)
Thine hoast of spyes
The starres shine in their watches,
I doe survey
Each busie Ray,
And how they work, and wind,
And wish each beame
My soul doth streame,
With the like ardour shin'd ;   10
What Emanations,
Quick vibrations
And bright stirs are there ?
What thin Ejections,
Cold Affections,
And slow motions here ?

2.

Thy heav'ns (some say,)
Are a firie-liquid light,
Which mingling aye
Streames, and flames thus to the sight.   20
Come then, my god !
Shine on this bloud,
And water in one beame,
And thou shalt see
Kindled by thee
Both liquors burne, and streame.
O what bright quicknes,
Active brightnes,
And celestiall flowes
Will follow after   30
On that water,
Which thy spirit blowes !

Math. Cap. 3. ver. xi.
*I indeed baptize you with water unto repentance, but he that com-
meth after me, is mightier than I, whose shooes I am not worthy to
beare, he shall baptize you with the holy Ghost, and with fire.*

Title Midnight] Mid-night *catchword 1655*

¶ Content.

Peace, peace ! I know 'twas brave,
 But this corse fleece
I shelter in, is slave
 To no such peece.
 When I am gone,
I shall no ward-robes leave
 To friend, or sonne
But what their own homes weave,

2.

Such, though not proud, nor full,
 May make them weep,   10
And mourn to see the wooll
 Outlast the sheep ;
 Poore, Pious weare !
Hadst thou bin rich, or fine
 Perhaps that teare
Had mourn'd thy losse, not mine.

3.

Why then these curl'd, puff'd points,
 Or a laced story ?
Death sets all out of Joint
 And scornes their glory ; 20
 Some Love a *Rose*
In hand, some in the skin ;
 But crosse to those,
I would have mine *within*.

¶

Joy of my life ! while left me here,
 And still my Love !
How in thy absence thou dost steere
 Me from above !
 A life well lead
This truth commends,
 With quick, or dead
It never ends.

2.

Stars are of mighty use : The night
    Is dark, and long ;   10
The Rode foul, and where one goes right,
    Six may go wrong.
    One twinkling ray
    Shot o'r some cloud,
    May clear much way
    And guide a croud.

3.

Gods Saints are shining lights : who stays
    Here long must passe
O're dark hills, swift streames, and steep ways
    As smooth as glasse ;   20
    But these all night
    Like Candles, shed
    Their beams, and light
    Us into Bed.

4.

They are (indeed,) our Pillar-fires
    Seen as we go,
They are that Cities shining spires
    We travell too ;
    A swordlike gleame
    Kept man for sin   30
    First *Out* ; This beame
    Will guide him *In*.

The Storm.

I see the use : and know my bloud
    Is not a Sea,
But a shallow, bounded floud
    Though red as he ;
Yet have I flows, as strong as his,
    And boyling stremes that rave
With the same curling force, and hisse,
    As doth the mountain'd wave.

2.

But when his waters billow thus,
    Dark storms, and wind   10
Incite them to that fierce discusse,
    Else not Inclin'd,
Thus the Enlarg'd, inraged air
    Uncalmes these to a floud,
But still the weather that's most fair
    Breeds tempests in my bloud ;

3.

Lord, then round me with weeping Clouds,
    And let my mind
In quick blasts sigh beneath those shrouds
    A spirit-wind,   20
So shall that storme purge this *Recluse*
    Which sinfull ease made foul,
And *wind*, and *water* to thy use
    Both *wash*, and *wing* my soul.

The Morning-watch.

O Joyes! Infinite sweetnes ! with what flowres,
And shoots of glory, my sòul breakes, and buds !
    All the long houres
    Of night, and Rest
    Through the still shrouds
    Of sleep, and Clouds,
    This Dew fell on my Breast ;
    O how it *Blouds*,
And *Spirits* all my Earth ! heark ! In what Rings,
And *Hymning Circulations* the quick world   10
    Awakes, and sings ;
    The rising winds,
    And falling springs,
    Birds, beasts, all things
    Adore him in their kinds.
    Thus all is hurl'd
In sacred *Hymnes*, and *Order*, The great *Chime*
And *Symphony* of nature.   Prayer is
    The world in tune,
    A spirit-voyce,   20
    And vocall joyes

Whose *Eccho is* heav'ns blisse.
O let me climbe
When I lye down !   The Pious soul by night
Is like a clouded starre, whose beames though sed
To shed their light
Under some Cloud
Yet are above,
And shine, and move   30
Beyond that mistie shrowd.
So in my Bed
That Curtain'd grave, though sleep, like ashes, hide
My lamp, and life, both shall in thee abide.

The Evening-watch.

A Dialogue.

Farewell ! I goe to sleep ; but when   *Body.*
The day-star springs, I'le wake agen.

Goe, sleep in peace ; and when thou lyest   *Soul.*
Unnumber'd in thy dust, when all this frame
Is but one dramme, and what thou now descriest
In sev'rall parts shall want a name,
Then may his peace be with thee, and each dust
Writ in his book, who ne'r betray'd mans trust !

Amen ! but hark, e'r we two stray,   *Body.*
How many hours do'st think 'till day ?   10

Ah ! go ; th'art weak, and sleepie.   Heav'n   *Soul.*
Is a plain watch, and without figures winds
All ages up ; who drew this Circle even
He fils it ; Dayes, and hours are *Blinds.*
Yet, this take with thee ; The last gasp of time
Is thy first breath, and mans *eternall Prime.*

¶

Silence, and stealth of dayes ! 'tis now
Since thou art gone,
Twelve hundred houres, and not a brow
But Clouds hang on.
As he that in some Caves thick damp
Lockt from the light,
Fixeth a solitary lamp,
To brave the night

And walking from his Sun, when past
  That glim'ring Ray   10
Cuts through the heavy mists in haste
  Back to his day,
So o'r fled minutes I retreat
  Unto that hour
Which shew'd thee last, but did defeat
  Thy light, and pow'r,
I search, and rack my soul to see
  Those beams again,
But nothing but the snuff to me
  Appeareth plain ;   20
That dark, and dead sleeps in its known,
  And common urn,
But those fled to their Makers throne,
  There shine, and burn ;
O could I track them ! but souls must
  Track one the other,
And now the spirit, not the dust
  Must be thy brother.
Yet I have one *Pearle* by whose light
  All things I see,   30
And in the heart of Earth, and night
  Find Heaven, and thee.

Church-Service.

Blest be the God of Harmony, and Love !
   The God above !
   And holy dove !
Whose Interceding, spirituall grones
   Make restless mones
   For dust, and stones,
  For dust in every part,
  But a hard, stonie heart.

    2.

O how in this thy Quire of Souls I stand
   (Propt by thy hand)   10
   A heap of sand !
Which busie thoughts (like winds) would scatter quite

And put to flight,
But for thy might;
Thy hand alone doth tame
Those blasts, and knit my frame,

3.

So that both stones, and dust, and all of me
Joyntly agree
To cry to thee,
And in this Musick by thy Martyrs bloud   20
Seal'd, and made good
Present, O God!
The Eccho of these stones
—— My sighes, and grones.

Buriall.

O thou! the first fruits of the dead
And their dark bed,
When I am cast into that deep
And senseless sleep
The wages of my sinne,
O then,
Thou great Preserver of all men!
Watch o're that loose
And empty house,
Which I sometimes liv'd in.   10

2.

It is (in truth!) a ruin'd peece
Not worth thy Eyes,
And scarce a room but wind, and rain
Beat through, and stain
The seats, and Cells within;
Yet thou
Led by thy Love wouldst stoop thus low,
And in this Cott
All filth, and spott,
Didst with thy servant Inne.   20

3.

And nothing can, I hourely see,
       Drive thee from me,
Thou art the same, faithfull, and just
          In life, or Dust;
       Though then (thus crumm'd) I stray
             In blasts,
Or Exhalations, and wasts
          Beyond all Eyes
          Yet thy love spies
    That Change, and knows thy Clay.   30

4.

The world's thy boxe: how then (there tost;)
          Can I be lost?
But the delay is all; Tyme now
          Is old, and slow,
       His wings are dull, and sickly;
             Yet he
Thy servant is, and waits on thee,
          Cutt then the summe,
          Lord haste, Lord come,
    O come Lord *Jesus* quickly!   40

Rom. Cap. 8. ver. 23.
*And not only they, but our selves also, which have the first fruits
of the spirit, even wee our selves grone within our selves, waiting for
the adoption, to wit, the redemption of our body.*

Chearfulness.

Lord, with what courage, and delight
          I doe each thing
When thy least breath sustaines my wing!
          I shine, and move
          Like those above,
       And (with much gladnesse
          Quitting sadnesse,)
Make me faire dayes of every night.

2.

Affliction thus, meere pleasure is,
          And hap what will,
If thou be in't, 'tis welcome still;   10

But since thy rayes
In Sunnie dayes
Thou dost thus lend
And freely spend,
Ah! what shall I return for this?

3.

O that I were all Soul! that thou
Wouldst make each part
Of this poor, sinfull frame pure heart!
Then would I drown
My single one,
And to thy praise
A Consort raise
Of *Hallelujahs* here below.

¶

Sure, there's a tye of Bodyes! and as they
Dissolve (with it,) to Clay,
Love languisheth, and memory doth rust
O'r-cast with that cold dust;
For things thus *Center'd*, without *Beames*, or *Action*
Nor give, nor take *Contaction*,
And man is such a Marygold, these fled,
That shuts, and hangs the head.

2.

Absents within the Line Conspire, and *Sense*
Things distant doth unite,
Herbs sleep unto the *East*, and some fowles thence
Watch the Returns of light;
But hearts are not so kind: false, short delights
Tell us the world is brave,
And wrap us in Imaginary flights
Wide of a faithfull grave;
Thus *Lazarus* was carried out of town;
For 'tis our foes chief art
By distance all good objects first to drown,
And then besiege the heart.
But I will be my own *Deaths-head*; and though
The flatt'rer say, *I live,*
Because Incertainties we cannot know
Be sure, not to believe.

Peace.

My Soul, there is a Countrie
    Far beyond the stars,
Where stands a winged Centrie
    All skilfull in the wars,
There above noise, and danger
    Sweet peace sits crown'd with smiles,
And one born in a Manger
    Commands the Beauteous files,
He is thy gracious friend,
    And (O my Soul awake !)   10
Did in pure love descend
    To die here for thy sake,
If thou canst get but thither,
    There growes the flowre of peace,
The Rose that cannot wither,
    Thy fortresse, and thy ease ;
Leave then thy foolish ranges ;
    For none can thee secure,
But one, who never changes,
    Thy God, thy life, thy Cure.   20

The Passion.

    O my chief good !
    My dear, dear God !
    When thy blest bloud
Did Issue forth forc'd by the Rod,
    What pain didst thou
    Feel in each blow !
    How didst thou weep,
    And thy self steep
In thy own precious, saving teares !
    What cruell smart   10
    Did teare thy heart !
    How didst thou grone it
    In the spirit,
O thou, whom my soul Loves, and feares !

Peace 2 Far] Afar *LB*

2.

Most blessed Vine !
Whose juice so good
I feel as Wine,
But thy faire branches felt as bloud,
How wert thou prest
To be my feast !　　　　　20
In what deep anguish
Didst thou languish,
What springs of Sweat, and bloud did drown thee !
How in one path
Did the full wrath
Of thy great Father
Crowd, and gather,
Doubling thy griefs, when none would own thee !

3.

How did the weight
Of all our sinnes,　　　　　30
And death unite
To wrench, and Rack thy blessed limbes !
How pale, and bloudie
Lookt thy Body !
How bruis'd, and broke
With every stroke !
How meek, and patient was thy spirit !
How didst thou cry,
And grone on high
Father forgive,　　　　　40
And let them live,
I dye to make my foes inherit !

4.

O blessed Lamb !
That took'st my sinne,
That took'st my shame
How shall thy dust thy praises sing !
I would I were
One hearty tear !
One constant spring !
Then would I bring　　　　　50
Thee two small mites, and be at strife

Which should most vie,
My heart, or eye,
Teaching my years
In smiles, and tears
To weep, to sing, thy *Death*, my *Life*.

Rom. Cap. 8. ver. 19.

Etenim res Creatæ exerto Capite observantes expectant revelationem Filiorum Dei.

And do they so? have they a Sense
    Of ought but Influence?
Can they their heads lift, and expect,
    And grone too? why th'Elect
Can do no more: my volumes sed
    They were all dull, and dead,
They judg'd them senslesse, and their state
    Wholly Inanimate.
    Go, go; Seal up thy looks,
    And burn thy books.   10

                    2.
I would I were a stone, or tree,
    Or flowre by pedigree,
Or some poor high-way herb, or Spring
    To flow, or bird to sing!
Then should I (tyed to one sure state,)
    All day expect my date;
But I am sadly loose, and stray
    A giddy blast each way;
    O let me not thus range!
    Thou canst not change.   20

                    3.
Sometimes I sit with thee, and tarry
    An hour, or so, then vary.
Thy other Creatures in this Scene
    Thee only aym, and mean;
Some rise to seek thee, and with heads
    Erect peep from their beds;
Others, whose birth is in the tomb,
    And cannot quit the womb,
    Sigh there, and grone for thee,
        Their liberty.   30

4.

O let not me do lesse ! shall they
    Watch, while I sleep, or play ?
Shall I thy mercies still abuse
    With fancies, friends, or newes ?
O brook it not ! thy bloud is mine,
    And my soul should be thine ;
O brook it not ! why wilt thou stop
    After whole showres one drop ?
      Sure, thou wilt joy to see
        Thy sheep with thee.   40

The Relapse.

My God, how gracious art thou ! I had slipt
    Almost to hell,
And on the verge of that dark, dreadful pit
    Did hear them yell,
But O thy love ! thy rich, almighty love
    That sav'd my soul,
And checkt their furie, when I saw them move,
    And heard them howl ;
O my sole Comfort, take no more these wayes,
    This hideous path,   10
And I wil mend my own without delayes,
    Cease thou thy wrath !
I have deserv'd a thick, Egyptian damp,
    Dark as my deeds,
Should *mist* within me, and put out that lamp
    Thy spirit feeds ;
A darting Conscience full of stabs, and fears ;
    No shade but *Yewgh,*
Sullen, and sad Ecclipses, Cloudie spheres,
    These are my due.   20
But he that with his bloud, (a price too deere,)
    My scores did pay,
Bid me, by vertue from him, chalenge here
    The brightest day ;
Sweet, downie thoughts ; soft *Lilly*-shades ; Calm streams ;
    Joyes full, and true ;
Fresh, spicie mornings ; and eternal beams
    These are his due.

The Resolve.

I have consider'd it; and find
  A longer stay
Is but excus'd neglect. To mind
  One path, and stray
Into another, or to none,
  Cannot be love;
When shal that traveller come home,
  That will not move?
If thou wouldst thither, linger not,
  Catch at the place,   10
Tell youth, and beauty they must rot,
  They'r but a *Case*;
Loose, parcell'd hearts wil freeze: The Sun
  With scatter'd locks
Scarce warms, but by contraction
  Can heat rocks;
Call in thy *Powers*; run, and reach
  Home with the light,
Be there, before the shadows stretch,
  And *Span* up night;   20
Follow the *Cry* no more: there is
  An ancient way
All strewed with flowres, and happiness
  And fresh as *May*;
There turn, and turn no more; Let wits,
  Smile at fair eies,
Or lips; But who there weeping sits,
  Hath got the *Prize*.

The Match.

Dear friend! whose holy, ever-living lines
  Have done much good
To many, and have checkt my blood,
My fierce, wild blood that still heaves, and inclines,
  But is still tam'd
  By those bright fires which thee inflam'd;

11 beauty] beautie, *WR* (*1650*)   16 heat rocks] heat the rocks *LG*
17 run] run on, *L* 18 light,] light; *WR* (*all editions*) 20 night;]
night: *WR* (*1667*) 25 wits,] wits *WR* (*1663, 1667*) 27 lips;] lips
WR (*1667*)

Here I joyn hands, and thrust my stubborn heart
    Into thy *Deed*,
  There from no *Duties* to be freed,
And if hereafter *youth*, or *folly* thwart   10
    And claim their share,
  Here I renounce the pois'nous ware.

ii

Accept, dread Lord, the poor Oblation,
    It is but poore,
  Yet through thy Mercies may be more.
O thou ! that canst not wish my souls damnation,
    Afford me life,
  And save me from all inward strife !
Two *Lifes* I hold from thee, my gracious Lord,
    Both cost thee deer,
  For one, I am thy Tenant here ;
The other, the true life, in the next world   10
    And endless is,
  O let me still mind *that* in *this* !
To thee therefore my *Thoughts, Words, Actions*
    I do resign,
  Thy will in all be done, not mine.
Settle my *house*, and shut out all distractions
    That may unknit
  My heart, and thee planted in it ;
Lord *Jesu* ! thou didst bow thy blessed head
    Upon a tree,   20
  O do as much, now unto me !
O hear, and heal thy servant ! Lord, strike dead
    All lusts in me,
  Who onely wish life to serve thee ?
Suffer no more this dust to overflow
    And drown my eies,
  But seal, or pin them to thy skies.
And let this *grain* which here in tears I sow
    Though *dead*, and *sick*,
  Through thy *Increase* grow *new*, and *quick*.   30

Rules *and* Lessons.

When first thy Eies unveil, give thy Soul leave
To do the like ; our Bodies but forerun
The spirits duty ; True hearts spread, and heave
Unto their God, as flow'rs do to the Sun.
  Give him thy first thoughts then ; so shalt thou keep
  Him company all day, and in him sleep.

Yet, never sleep the Sun up ; Prayer shou'd
Dawn with the day ; There are set, awful hours
'Twixt heaven, and us ; The *Manna* was not good
After Sun-rising, far-day sullies flowres.   10
  Rise to prevent the Sun ; sleep doth sins glut,
  And heav'ns gate opens, when this world's is shut.

Walk with thy fellow-creatures : note the *hush*
And *whispers* amongst them. There's not a *Spring,*
Or *Leafe* but hath his *Morning-hymn* ; Each *Bus*
And *Oak* doth know *I AM* ; canst thou not sing ?
  O leave thy Cares, and follies ! go this way
  And thou art sure to prosper all the day.

Serve God before the world ; let him not go
Until thou hast a blessing, then resigne   20
The whole unto him ; and remember who
Prevail'd by *wrestling* ere the *Sun* did *shine.*
  Poure *Oyle* upon the *stones,* weep for thy sin,
  Then journey on, and have an eie to heav'n.

Mornings are *Mysteries* ; the first worlds *Youth,*
Mans *Resurrection,* and the futures *Bud*
Shrowd in their births : The Crown of life, light, truth
Is stil'd their *starre,* the *stone,* and *hidden food.*
  Three *blessings* wait upon them, two of which
  Should move ; They make us *holy, happy,* rich.   30

When the world's up, and ev'ry swarm abroad,
Keep thou thy temper, mix not with each Clay ;
Dispatch necessities, life hath a load
Which must be carri'd on, and safely may.
  Yet keep those cares without thee, let the heart
  Be Gods alone, and choose the better part.

Through all thy *Actions, Counsels,* and *Discourse,*
Let *Mildness,* and *Religion* guide thee out,
If truth be thine, what needs a brutish force?
But what's not *good,* and *just* ne'r go about.   40
    Wrong not thy Conscience for a rotten stick,
    That gain is dreadful, which makes spirits sick.

To God, thy Countrie, and thy friend be true,
If *Priest,* and *People* change, keep thou thy ground.
Who sels Religion, is a *Judas Jew,*
And, oathes once broke, the soul cannot be sound.
    The perjurer's a devil let loose: what can
    Tie up his hands, that dares mock God, and man?

Seek not the same steps with the *Crowd*; stick thou
To thy sure trot; a Constant, humble mind   50
Is both his own Joy, and his Makers too;
Let folly dust it on, or lag behind.
    A sweet *self-privacy* in a right soul
    Out-runs the Earth, and lines the utmost pole.

To all that seek thee, bear an open heart;
Make not thy breast a *Labyrinth,* or *Trap*;
If tryals come, this wil make good thy part,
For honesty is safe, come what can hap;
    It is the good mans *feast*; The prince of flowres
    Which thrives in *storms,* and smels best after *showres.*   60

Seal not thy Eyes up from the poor, but give
Proportion to their *Merits,* and thy *Purse*;
Thou mai'st in Rags a mighty Prince relieve
Who, when thy sins call for't, can fence a Curse.
    Thou shalt not lose one *mite.* Though waters stray,
    The Bread we cast returns in fraughts one day.

Spend not an hour so, as to weep another,
For tears are not thine own; If thou giv'st words
Dash not thy *friend,* nor *Heav'n*; O smother
A vip'rous thought; some *Syllables* are *Swords.*   70
    Unbitted tongues are in their penance double,
    They shame their *owners,* and the *hearers* trouble.

63 Prince] Prlnce *1655*   69 not thy *friend*] not with them thy
friend L: not thyself, thy friend *G*

Injure not modest bloud, whose *spirits* rise
In judgement against *Lewdness*; that's base wit
That voyds but *filth*, and *stench*.   Hast thou no prize
But *sickness*, or *Infection*? stifle it.
  Who makes his jests of sins, must be at least
  If not a very *devill*, worse than a *Beast*.

Yet, fly no friend, if he be such indeed,
But meet to quench his *Longings*, and thy *Thirst*; 80
Allow your Joyes *Religion*; That done, speed
And bring the same man back, thou wert at first.
  Who so returns not, cannot pray aright,
  But shuts his door, and leaves God out all night.

To highten thy *Devotions*, and keep low
All mutinous thoughts, what busines e'r thou hast
Observe God in his works; here *fountains* flow,
Birds sing, *Beasts* feed, *Fish* leap, and th'*Earth* stands fast;
  Above are restles *motions*, running *Lights*,
  Vast Circling *Azure*, giddy *Clouds*, days, nights. 90

When *Seasons* change, then lay before thine Eys
His wondrous *Method*; mark the various *Scenes*
In heav'n; *Hail, Thunder, Rain-bows, Snow*, and *Ice,
Calmes, Tempests, Light*, and *darknes* by his means;
  Thou canst not misse his Praise; Each *tree, herb, flowre*
  Are shadows of his *wisedome*, and his Pow'r.

To *meales* when thou doest come, give him the praise
Whose *Arm* supply'd thee; Take what may suffice,
And then be thankful; O admire his ways
Who fils the worlds unempty'd granaries ! 100
  A thankles feeder is a *Theif*, his feast
  A very *Robbery*, and himself no *guest*.

High-noon thus past, thy time decays; provide
Thee other thoughts; Away with friends, and mirth;
The Sun now stoops, and hasts his beams to hide
Under the dark, and melancholy Earth.
  All but preludes thy End.   Thou art the man
  Whose *Rise, hight*, and *Descent* is but a span.

76 stifle] stiflle *1655*   82 at] all *1655* (*from* 84?)

Yet, set as he doth, and 'tis well.   Have all
Thy Beams home with thee : trim thy *Lamp*, buy *Oyl*,   110
And then set forth ; who is thus drest, The *Fall*
Furthers his glory, and gives death the foyl.
   Man is a *Summers day* ; whose *youth*, and *fire*
   Cool to a glorious *Evening*, and Expire.

When night comes, list thy deeds ; make plain the way
'Twixt Heaven, and thee ; block it not with delays,
But perfect all before thou sleep'st ; Then say
Ther's one Sun more strung on my Bead of days.
   What's good score up for Joy ; The bad wel scann'd
   Wash off with tears, and get thy *Masters* hand.   120

Thy Accounts thus made, spend in the grave one houre
Before thy time ; Be not a stranger there
Where thou may'st sleep whole ages ; Lifes poor flowr
Lasts not a night sometimes.   Bad spirits fear
   This Conversation ; But the good man lyes
   Intombed many days before he dyes.

Being laid, and drest for sleep, Close not thy Eys
Up with thy Curtains ; Give thy soul the wing
In some good thoughts ; So when the day shall rise
And thou *unrak'st* thy *fire*, those *sparks* will bring   130
   New *flames* ; Besides where these lodge vain *heats* mourn
   And die ; That *Bush* where God is, shall not burn.

When thy *Nap's* over, stir thy fire, unrake
In that *dead age* ; one beam i'th' dark outvies
Two in the day ; Then from the *Damps*, and *Ake*
Of night shut up thy *leaves*, be Chast ; God prys
   Through thickest nights ; Though then the Sun be far
   Do thou the works of *Day*, and rise a *Star*.

Briefly, *Doe as thou would'st be done unto,*
Love God, and Love thy Neighbour ; Watch, and Pray.   140
These are the *Words*, and *Works* of life ; This do,
And live ; who doth not thus, hath lost *Heav'ns way.*
   O lose it not ! look up, wilt Change those *Lights*
   For *Chains* of *Darknes*, and *Eternal Nights* ?

125 Conversation] Coversation *1655*

Corruption.

Sure, It was so.   Man in those early days
    Was not all stone, and Earth,
He shin'd a little, and by those weak Rays
    Had some glimpse of his birth.
He saw Heaven o'r his head, and knew from whence
    He came (condemned,) hither,
And, as first Love draws strongest, so from hence
    His mind sure progress'd thither.
Things here were strange unto him : Swet, and till
    All was a thorn, or weed,   10
Nor did those last, but (like himself,) dyed still
    As soon as they did *Seed*,
They seem'd to quarrel with him ; for that Act
    That fel him, foyl'd them all,
He drew the Curse upon the world, and Crackt
    The whole frame with his fall.
This made him long for *home*, as loath to stay
    With murmurers, and foes ;
He sigh'd for *Eden*, and would often say
    Ah ! what bright days were those ?   20
Nor was Heav'n cold unto him ; for each day
    The vally, or the Mountain
Afforded visits, and still *Paradise* lay
    In some green shade, or fountain.
Angels lay *Leiger* here ; Each Bush, and Cel,
    Each Oke, and high-way knew them,
Walk but the fields, or sit down at some *wel*,
    And he was sure to view them.
Almighty *Love* ! where art thou now ? mad man
    Sits down, and freezeth on,   30
He raves, and swears to stir nor fire, nor fan,
    But bids the thread be spun.
I see, thy Curtains are Close-drawn ; Thy bow
    Looks dim too in the Cloud,
Sin triumphs still, and man is sunk below
    The Center, and his shrowd ;
All's in deep sleep, and night ; Thick darknes lyes
    And hatcheth o'r thy people ;
But hark ! what trumpets that ? what Angel cries
    Arise ! Thrust in thy sickle.   40

H. Scriptures.

Welcome dear book, souls Joy, and food! The feast
  Of Spirits, Heav'n extracted lyes in thee;
  Thou art lifes Charter, The Doves spotless neast
Where souls are hatch'd unto Eternitie.

In thee the hidden stone, the *Manna* lies,
  Thou art the great *Elixir*, rare, and Choice;
  The Key that opens to all Mysteries,
The *Word* in Characters, God in the *Voice*.

O that I had deep Cut in my hard heart
  Each line in thee! Then would I plead in groans   10
  Of my Lords penning, and by sweetest Art
Return upon himself the *Law*, and *Stones*.
  Read here, my faults are thine. This Book, and I
  Will tell thee so; *Sweet Saviour thou didst dye!*

Unprofitablenes.

How rich, O Lord! how fresh thy visits are!
'Twas but Just now my bleak leaves hopeles hung
  Sullyed with dust and mud;
Each snarling blast shot through me, and did share
Their Youth, and beauty, Cold showres nipt, and wrung
  Their spiciness, and bloud;
But since thou didst in one sweet glance survey
Their sad decays, I flourish, and once more
  Breath all perfumes, and spice;
I smell a dew like *Myrrh*, and all the day   10
Wear in my bosome a full Sun; such store
  Hath one beame from thy Eys.
But, ah, my God! what fruit hast thou of this?
What one poor leaf did ever I yet fall
  To wait upon thy wreath?
Thus thou all day a thankless weed doest dress,
And when th' hast done, a stench, or fog is all
  The odour I bequeath.

14 yet] let *GB*

Christs Nativity.

Awake, glad heart! get up, and Sing,
It is the Birth-day of thy King,
 Awake! awake!
 The Sun doth shake
Light from his locks, and all the way
Breathing Perfumes, doth spice the day.

2.

Awak, awak! heark, how th' *wood* rings,
Winds whisper, and the busie *springs*
 A Consort make;
 Awake, awake!   10
Man is their high-priest, and should rise
To offer up the sacrifice.

3.

I would I were some *Bird*, or Star,
Flutt'ring in woods, or lifted far
 Above this *Inne*
 And Rode of sin!
Then either Star, or *Bird*, should be
Shining, or singing still to thee.

4.

I would I had in my best part
Fit Roomes for thee! or that my heart 20
 Were so clean as
 Thy manger was!
But I am all filth, and obscene,
Yet, if thou wilt, thou canst make clean.

5.

Sweet *Jesu*! will then; Let no more
This Leper haunt, and soyl thy door,
 Cure him, Ease him
 O release him!
And let once more by mystick birth
The Lord of life be borne in Earth. 30

7 Awak] Awake *catchword 1655*

I I.

How kind is heav'n to man! If here
    One sinner doth amend
Strait there is Joy, and ev'ry sphere
    In musick doth Contend;
And shall we then no voices lift?
    Are mercy, and salvation
Not worth our thanks? Is life a gift
    Of no more acceptation?
Shal he that did come down from thence,
    And here for us was slain,   10
Shal he be now cast off? no sense
    Of all his woes remain?
Can neither Love, nor suff'rings bind?
    Are we all stone, and Earth?
Neither his bloudy passions mind,
    Nor one day blesse his birth?
    Alas, my God! Thy birth now here
    Must not be numbred in the year.

The Check.

Peace, peace! I blush to hear thee; when thou art
    A dusty story
A speechlesse heap, and in the midst my heart
    In the same livery drest
    Lyes tame as all the rest;
When six years thence digg'd up, some youthfull Eie
    Seeks there for Symmetry
But finding none, shal leave thee to the wind,
    Or the next foot to Crush,
    Scatt'ring thy kind   10
And humble dust, tell then dear flesh
    Where is thy glory?

2.

As he that in the midst of day Expects
    The hideous night,
Sleeps not, but shaking off sloth, and neglects,
    Works with the Sun, and sets
    Paying the day its debts;

That (for Repose, and darknes bound,) he might
    Rest from the fears i'th' night;
So should we too.   All things teach us to die   20
    And point us out the way
      While we passe by
    And mind it not; play not away
      Thy glimpse of light.

3.

View thy fore-runners: Creatures giv'n to be
    Thy youths Companions,
Take their leave, and die; Birds, beasts, each tree
    All that have growth, or breath
    Have one large language, *Death.*
O then play not! but strive to him, who Can   30
    Make these sad shades pure Sun,
Turning their mists to beams, their damps to day,
    Whose pow'r doth so excell
      As to make Clay
    A spirit, and true glory dwell
      In dust, and stones.

4.

Heark, how he doth Invite thee! with what voice
    Of Love, and sorrow
He begs, and Calls; *O that in these thy days*
    Thou knew'st but thy own good!   40
    Shall not the Crys of bloud,
Of Gods own bloud awake thee?   He bids beware
    Of drunknes, surfeits, Care,
But thou sleep'st on; wher's now thy protestation,
    Thy Lines, thy Love?   Away,
      Redeem the day,
The day that gives no observation,
      Perhaps to morrow.

Disorder *and* frailty.

When first thou didst even from the grave
And womb of darknes becken out
My brutish soul, and to thy slave
Becam'st thy self, both guide, and Scout;

    42 thee] thet *1655*

Even from that hour
Thou gotst my heart; And though here tost
By winds, and bit with frost
I pine, and shrink
Breaking the link
'Twixt thee, and me; And oftimes creep   10
Into th' old silence, and dead sleep,
Quitting thy way
All the long day,
Yet, sure, my God! I love thee most.
Alas, thy love!

2.

I threaten heaven, and from my Cell
Of Clay, and frailty break, and bud
Touch'd by thy fire, and breath; Thy bloud
Too, is my Dew, and springing wel.
But while I grow   20
And stretch to thee, ayming at all
Thy stars, and spangled hall,
Each fly doth tast,
Poyson, and blast
My yielding leaves; sometimes a showr
Beats them quite off, and in an hour
Not one poor shoot
But the bare root
Hid under ground survives the fall.
Alas, frail weed!   30

3.

Thus like some sleeping Exhalation
(Which wak'd by heat, and beams, makes up
Unto that Comforter, the Sun,
And soars, and shines; But e'r we sup
And walk two steps
Cool'd by the damps of night, descends,
And, whence it sprung, there ends,)
Doth my weak fire
Pine, and retire,
And (after all my hight of flames,)   40
In sickly Expirations tames

23 tast,] tast *1655*

Leaving me dead
On my first bed
Untill thy Sun again ascends.
Poor, falling Star !

4.

O, is ! but give wings to my fire,
And hatch my soul, untill it fly
Up where thou art, amongst thy tire
Of Stars, above Infirmity ;
Let not perverse,   50
And foolish thoughts adde to my Bil
Of forward sins, and Kil
That seed, which thou
In me didst sow,
But dresse, and water with thy grace
Together with the seed, the place ;
And for his sake
Who died to stake
His life for mine, tune to thy will
My heart, my verse.   60

Hosea Cap. 6. ver. 4.

*O Ephraim what shall I do unto thee ? O Judah how shall I
intreat thee ? for thy goodness is as a morning Cloud, and as the
early Dew it goeth away.*

Idle Verse.

Go, go, queint folies, sugred sin,
    Shadow no more my door ;
I will no longer Cobwebs spin,
    I'm too much on the score.

For since amidst my youth, and night,
    My great preserver smiles,
Wee'l make a Match, my only light,
    And Joyn against their wiles ;

Blind, desp'rate *fits*, that study how
    To dresse, and trim our shame,   10
That gild rank poyson, and allow
    Vice in a fairer name ;

46 is] yes *LGCB*

The *Purles* of youthfull bloud, and bowles,
    Lust in the Robes of Love,
The idle talk of feav'rish souls
    Sick with a scarf, or glove ;

Let it suffice my warmer days
    Simper'd, and shin'd on you,
Twist not my Cypresse with your Bays,
    Or Roses with my Yewgh ;   20

Go, go, seek out some greener thing,
    It snows, and freezeth here ;
Let Nightingales attend the spring,
    Winter is all my year.

Son-dayes.

Bright shadows of true Rest ! some shoots of blisse,
          Heaven once a week ;
The next worlds gladnes prepossest in this ;
          A day to seek
Eternity in time ; the steps by which
We Climb above all ages ; Lamps that light
Man through his heap of dark days ; and the rich,
And full redemption of the whole weeks flight.

2.

The Pulleys unto headlong man ; times bower ;
          The narrow way ;   10
Transplanted Paradise ; Gods walking houre ;
          The Cool o'th' day ;
The Creatures *Jubile*; Gods parle with dust ;
Heaven here ; Man on those hills of Myrrh, and flowres ;
Angels descending ; the Returns of Trust ;
A Gleam of glory, after six-days-showres.

3.

The Churches love-feasts ; Times Prerogative,
          And Interest
Deducted from the whole ; The Combs, and hive,
          And home of rest.   20

4 seek *L 1858, 1883 GCB* : seek ; *1655*   *Title* Son-dayes] Sondays
catchword 1655

The milky way Chalkt out with Suns ; a Clue
That guides through erring hours ; and in full story
A taste of Heav'n on earth ; the pledge, and Cue
Of a full feast ; And the Out Courts of glory.

Repentance.

Lord, since thou didst in this vile Clay
    That sacred Ray
Thy spirit plant, quickning the whole
With that one grains Infused wealth,
My forward flesh creept on, and subtly stole
Both growth, and power ; Checking the health
And heat of thine : That little gate
And narrow way, by which to thee
The Passage is, He term'd a grate
And Entrance to Captivitie ;   10
Thy laws but nets, where some small birds
(And those but seldome too) were caught,
Thy Promises but empty words
Which none but Children heard, or taught.
This I believed : And though a friend
Came oft from far, and whisper'd, *No* ;
Yet that not sorting to my end
I wholy listen'd to my foe.
Wherefore, pierc'd through with grief, my sad
Seduced soul sighs up to thee,   20
To thee who with true light art Clad
And seest all things just as they be.
Look from thy throne upon this Rowl
Of heavy sins, my high transgressions,
Which I Confesse withall my soul,
My God, Accept of my Confession.
    It was last day
(Touch'd with the guilt of my own way)
I sate alone, and taking up
    The bitter Cup,   30
Through all thy fair, and various store
Sought out what might outvie my score.
    The blades of grasse, thy Creatures feeding,
    The trees, their leafs ; the flowres, their seeding ;

4 Infused *1650* : Infufed *B. M. copy of 1655* (?)   5 flesh] flest *1655*

The Dust, of which I am a part,
The Stones much softer than my heart,
The drops of rain, the sighs of wind,
The Stars to which I am stark blind,
The Dew thy herbs drink up by night,
The beams they warm them at i'th' light,   40
All that have signature or life,
I summon'd to decide this strife,
And lest I should lack for Arrears,
A spring ran by, I told her tears,
But when these came unto the scale,
My sins alone outweigh'd them all.
O my dear God! my life, my love!
Most blessed lamb! and mildest dove!
Forgive your penitent Offender,
And no more his sins remember,   50
Scatter these shades of death, and give
Light to my soul, that it may live;
Cut me not off for my transgressions,
Wilful rebellions, and suppressions,
But give them in those streams a part
Whose spring is in my Saviours heart.
Lord, I confesse the heynous score,
And pray, I may do so no more,
Though then all sinners I exceed
O think on this; *Thy Son did bleed;*   60
O call to mind his wounds, his woes,
His Agony, and bloudy throws;
Then look on all that thou hast made,
And mark how they do fail, and fade,
The heavens themselves, though fair and bright
Are dark, and unclean in thy sight,
How then, with thee, Can man be holy
Who doest thine Angels charge with folly?
O what am I, that I should breed
Figs on a thorne, flowres on a weed!   70
I am the gourd of sin, and sorrow
Growing o'r night, and gone to morrow,
In all this *Round* of life and death
Nothing's more vile than is my breath,
Profanenes on my tongue doth rest,
Defects, and darknes in my brest,

Pollutions all my body wed,
And even my soul to thee is dead,
Only in him, on whom I feast,
Both soul, and body are well drest,   80
    His pure perfection quits all score,
    And fills the Boxes of his poor ;
He is the Center of long life, and light,
I am but finite, He is Infinite.
O let thy *Justice* then in him Confine,
And through his merits, make thy mercy mine !

The Burial

Of an Infant.

Blest Infant Bud, whose Blossome-life
Did only look about, and fal,
Wearyed out in a harmles strife
Of tears, and milk, the food of all ;

Sweetly didst thou expire : Thy soul
Flew home unstain'd by his new kin,
For ere thou knew'st how to be foul,
Death *wean'd* thee from the world, and sin.

Softly rest all thy Virgin-Crums !
Lapt in the sweets of thy young breath,   10
Expecting till thy Saviour Comes
To *dresse* them, and *unswadle* death.

Faith.

Bright, and blest beame ! whose strong projection
    Equall to all,
Reacheth as well things of dejection
    As th' high, and tall ;
How hath my God by raying thee
    Inlarg'd his spouse,
And of a private familie
    Made open house ?
All may be now Co-heirs ; no noise
    Of *Bond*, or *Free*   10
Can Interdict us from those Joys
    That wait on thee,

The Law, and Ceremonies made
    A glorious night,
Where Stars, and Clouds, both light, and shade
    Had equal right;
But, as in nature, when the day
    Breaks, night adjourns,
Stars shut up shop, mists pack away,
    And the Moon mourns;   20
So when the Sun of righteousness
    Did once appear,
That Scene was chang'd, and a new dresse
    Left for us here;
Veiles became useles, Altars fel,
    Fires smoking die;
And all that sacred pomp, and shel
    Of things did flie;
Then did he shine forth, whose sad fall,
    And bitter fights   30
Were figur'd in those mystical,
    And Cloudie Rites;
And as i'th' natural Sun, these three,
    Light, motion, heat,
So are now *Faith, Hope, Charity*
    Through him Compleat;
Faith spans up blisse; what sin, and death
    Put us quite from,
Lest we should run for't out of breath,
    Faith brings us home;   40
So that I need no more, but say
    I do believe,
And my most loving Lord straitway
    Doth answer, *Live.*

The Dawning.

Ah! what time wilt thou come? when shall that crie
    The *Bridegroome's Comming*! fil the sky?
    Shall it in the Evening run
    When our words and works are done?
    Or wil thy all-surprizing light
      Break at midnight?

When either sleep, or some dark pleasure
Possesseth mad man without measure ;
Or shal these early, fragrant hours
    Unlock thy bowres ?   10
And with their blush of light descry
Thy locks crown'd with eternitie ;
Indeed, it is the only time
That with thy glory doth best chime,
All now are stirring, ev'ry field
    Ful hymns doth yield,
The whole Creation shakes off night,
And for thy shadow looks the light,
Stars now vanish without number,
Sleepie Planets set, and slumber,   20
The pursie Clouds disband, and scatter,
All expect some sudden matter,
Not one beam triumphs, but from far
    That morning-star ;

O at what time soever thou
(Unknown to us,) the heavens wilt bow,
And, with thy Angels in the *Van*,
Descend to Judge poor careless man,
Grant, I may not like puddle lie
In a Corrupt securitie,   30
Where, if a traveller water crave,
He finds it dead, and in a grave ;
But as this restless, vocall *Spring*
All day, and night doth run, and sing,
And though here born, yet is acquainted
Elsewhere, and flowing keeps untainted ;
So let me all my busie age
In thy free services ingage,
And though (while here) of force I must
Have Commerce somtimes with poor dust,   40
And in my flesh, though vile, and low,
As this doth in her Channel, flow,
Yet let my Course, my aym, my Love,
And chief acquaintance be above ;
So when that day, and hour shal come
In which thy self wil be the Sun,
Thou'lt find me drest and on my way,
Watching the Break of thy great day.

Admission.

How shril are silent tears? when sin got head
    And all my Bowels turn'd
To brasse, and iron; when my stock lay dead,
    And all my powers mourn'd;
    Then did these drops (for Marble sweats,
        And Rocks have tears,)
    As rain here at our windows beats,
        Chide in thine Ears;

2.

No quiet couldst thou have: nor didst thou wink,
    And let thy Begger lie,   10
But e'r my eies could overflow their brink
    Didst to each drop reply;
    Bowels of Love! at what low rate,
        And slight a price
    Dost thou relieve us at thy gate,
        And stil our Cries?

3.

Wee are thy Infants, and suck thee; If thou
    But hide, or turn thy face,
Because where thou art, yet, we cannot go,
    We send tears to the place,   20
    These find thee out, and though our sins
        Drove thee away,
    Yet with thy love that absence wins
        Us double pay.

4.

O give me then a thankful heart! a heart
    After thy own, not mine;
So after thine, that all, and ev'ry part
    Of mine, may wait on thine;
    O hear! yet not my tears alone,
        Hear now a floud,   30
    A floud that drowns both tears, and grones,
        My Saviours bloud.

Praise.

King of Comforts ! King of life !
    Thou hast cheer'd me,
And when fears, and doubts were rife,
    Thou hast cleer'd me !

Not a nook in all my Breast
    But thou fill'st it,
Not a thought, that breaks my rest,
    But thou kill'st it ;

Wherefore with my utmost strength
    I wil praise thee,   10
And as thou giv'st line, and length,
    I wil raise thee ;

Day, and night, not once a day
    I will blesse thee,
And my soul in new array
    I will dresse thee ;

Not one minute in the year
    But I'l mind thee,
As my seal, and bracelet here
    I wil bind thee ;   20

In thy word, as if in heaven
    I wil rest me,
And thy promise 'til made even
    There shall feast me.

Then, thy sayings all my life
    They shal please me,
And thy bloudy wounds, and strife
    They wil ease me ;

With thy grones my daily breath
    I will measure,   30
And my life hid in thy death
    I will treasure.

Though then thou art
    Past thought of heart
All perfect fulness,
    And canst no whit
    Accesse admit
From dust and dulness ;

Yet to thy name
(As not the same   40
With thy bright Essence,)
Our foul, Clay hands
At thy Commands
Bring praise, and Incense;

If then, dread Lord,
When to thy board
Thy wretch comes begging,
He hath a flowre
Or (to his pow'r,)
Some such poor Off'ring;   50

When thou hast made
Thy begger glad,
And fill'd his bosome,
Let him (though poor,)
Strow at thy door
That one poor Blossome.

Dressing.

O thou that lovest a pure, and whitend soul!
That feedst among the Lillies, 'till the day
Break, and the shadows flee; touch with one Coal
My frozen heart; and with thy secret key

Open my desolate rooms; my gloomie Brest
With thy cleer fire refine, burning to dust
These dark Confusions, that within me nest,
And soyl thy Temple with a sinful rust.

Thou holy, harmless, undefil'd high-priest!
The perfect, ful oblation for all sin,   10
Whose glorious conquest nothing can resist,
But even in babes doest triumph still and win;

Give to thy wretched one
Thy mysticall *Communion*,
That, absent, he may see,
Live, die, and rise with thee;
Let him so follow here, that in the end
He may take thee, as thou doest him intend.

3 flee] ssee *1655*

Give him thy private seal,
Earnest, and sign ; Thy gifts so deal   20
That these forerunners here
May make the future cleer ;
Whatever thou dost bid, let faith make good,
Bread for thy body, and Wine for thy blood.
Give him (with pitty) love,
Two flowres that grew with thee above ;
Love that shal not admit
Anger for one short fit,
And pitty of such a divine extent
That may thy members, more than mine, resent.   30

Give me, my God ! thy grace,
The beams, and brightnes of thy face,
That never like a beast
I take thy sacred feast,
Or the dread mysteries of thy blest bloud
Use, with like Custome, as my Kitchin food.
Some sit to thee, and eat
Thy body as their Common meat,
O let not me do so !
Poor dust should ly still low,   40
Then kneel my soul, and body ; kneel, and bow ;
If *Saints*, and *Angels* fal down, much more thou.

Easter-day.

Thou, whose sad heart, and weeping head lyes low,
Whose Cloudy brest cold damps invade,
Who never feel'st the Sun, nor smooth'st thy brow,
But sitt'st oppressed in the shade,
Awake, awake,
And in his Resurrection partake,
Who on this day (that thou might'st rise as he,)
Rose up, and cancell'd two deaths due to thee.

Awake, awake ; and, like the Sun, disperse
All mists that would usurp this day ;   10
Where are thy Palmes, thy branches, and thy verse ?
Hosanna! heark ; why doest thou stay ?
Arise, arise,
And with his healing bloud anoint thine Eys,
Thy inward Eys ; his bloud will cure thy mind,
Whose spittle only could restore the blind.

Easter Hymn.

Death, and darkness get you packing,
Nothing now to man is lacking,
All your triumphs now are ended,
And what *Adam* marr'd, is mended;
Graves are beds now for the weary,
Death a nap, to wake more merry;
Youth now, full of pious duty,
Seeks in thee for perfect beauty,
The weak, and aged tir'd, with length
Of daies, from thee look for new strength,   10
And Infants with thy pangs Contest
As pleasant, as if with the brest;
 Then, unto him, who thus hath thrown
Even to Contempt thy kingdome down,
And by his blood did us advance
Unto his own Inheritance,
To him be glory, power, praise,
From this, unto the last of daies.

The Holy Communion.

Welcome sweet, and sacred feast; welcome life!
 Dead I was, and deep in trouble;
But grace, and blessings came with thee so rife,
That they have quicken'd even drie stubble;
 Thus soules their bodies animate,
 And thus, at first, when things were rude,
  Dark, void, and Crude
They, by thy Word, their beauty had, and date;
  All were by thee,
  And stil must be,   10
 Nothing that is, or lives,
But hath his Quicknings, and reprieves
 As thy hand opes, or shuts;
  Healings, and Cuts,
Darkness, and day-light, life, and death
Are but meer leaves turn'd by thy breath.
 Spirits without thee die,
  And blackness sits
 On the divinest wits,
As on the Sun Ecclipses lie.   20

 Title (1) Easter] Easter- *catchword 1655*

But that great darkness at thy death
When the veyl broke with thy last breath,
 Did make us see
 The way to thee;
And now by these sure, sacred ties,
 After thy blood
 (Our sov'rain good,)
 Had clear'd our eies,
 And given us sight;
Thou dost unto thy self betroth   30
 Our souls, and bodies both
 In everlasting light.

Was't not enough that thou hadst payd the price
 And given us eies
When we had none, but thou must also take
 Us by the hand
 And keep us still awake,
 When we would sleep,
 Or from thee creep,
Who without thee cannot stand?   40

Was't not enough to lose thy breath
And blood by an accursed death,
 But thou must also leave
 To us that did bereave
Thee of them both, these seals the means
 That should both cleanse
  And keep us so,
  Who wrought thy wo?
O rose of *Sharon*! O the Lilly
 Of the valley!   50
How art thou now, thy flock to keep,
Become both *food*, and *Shepheard* to thy sheep

Psalm 121.

Up to those bright, and gladsome hils
 Whence flowes my weal, and mirth,
I look, and sigh for him, who fils
 (Unseen,) both heaven, and earth.

He is alone my help, and hope,
    That I shall not be moved,
His watchful Eye is ever ope,
    And guardeth his beloved;

The glorious God is my sole stay,
    He is my Sun, and shade,   10
The cold by night, the heat by day,
    Neither shall me invade.

He keeps me from the spite of foes,
    Doth all their plots controul,
And is a shield (not reckoning those,)
    Unto my very soul.

Whether abroad, amidst the Crowd,
    Or els within my door,
He is my Pillar, and my Cloud,
    Now, and for evermore.   20

Affliction.

Peace, peace; It is not so. Thou doest miscall
    Thy Physick; Pils that change
Thy sick Accessions into setled health,
This is the great *Elixir* that turns gall
To wine, and sweetness; Poverty to wealth,
    And brings man home, when he doth range.
    Did not he, who ordain'd the day,
        Ordain night too?
    And in the greater world display
    What in the lesser he would do?   10
All flesh is Clay, thou know'st; and but that God
    Doth use his rod,
And by a fruitfull Change of frosts, and showres
    Cherish, and bind thy *pow'rs*,
Thou wouldst to weeds, and thistles quite disperse,
    And be more wild than is thy verse;
Sickness is wholsome, and Crosses are but curbs
    To check the mule, unruly man,
They are heavens husbandry, the famous fan
    Purging the floor which Chaff disturbs.   20

Were all the year one constant Sun-shine, wee
     Should have no flowres,
All would be drought, and leanness ; not a tree
     Would make us bowres ;
Beauty consists in colours ; and that's best
     Which is not fixt, but flies, and flowes ;
The settled *Red* is dull, and *whites* that rest
     Something of sickness would disclose.
          Vicissitude plaies all the game,
               Nothing that stirrs,   30
               Or hath a name,
          But waits upon this wheel,
Kingdomes too have their Physick, and for steel,
     Exchange their peace, and furrs.
Thus doth God *Key* disorder'd man
          (Which none else can,)
Tuning his brest to rise, or fall ;
And by a sacred, needfull art
Like strings, stretch ev'ry part
Making the whole most Musicall.   40

The Tempest.

How is man parcell'd out ? how ev'ry hour
     Shews him himself, or somthing he should see ?
     This late, long heat may his Instruction be,
And tempests have more in them than a showr.

          When nature on her bosome saw
               Her Infants die,
          And all her flowres wither'd to straw,
               Her brests grown dry ;
          She made the Earth their nurse, & tomb,
               Sigh to the sky,   10
          'Til to those sighes fetch'd from her womb
               Rain did reply,
          So in the midst of all her fears
               And faint requests
          Her Earnest sighes procur'd her tears
               And fill'd her brests.

O that man could do so! that he would hear
    The world read to him! all the vast expence
    In the Creation shed, and slav'd to sence
Makes up but lectures for his eie, and ear.   20

Sure, mighty love foreseeing the discent
    Of this poor Creature, by a gracious art
    Hid in these low things snares to gain his heart,
And layd surprizes in each Element.

All things here shew him heaven; *Waters* that fall
    Chide, and fly up; *Mists* of corruptest fome
    Quit their first beds & mount; trees, herbs, flowres, all
Strive upwards stil, and point him the way home.

How do they cast off grossness? only *Earth*,
    And *Man* (like *Issachar*) in lodes delight,   30
    Water's refin'd to *Motion*, Aire to *Light*,   ** Light,*
Fire to all * three, but man hath no such mirth.   *Motion,*
                                                        heat.

Plants in the *root* with Earth do most Comply,
    Their *Leafs* with water, and humiditie,
    The *Flowres* to air draw neer, and subtiltie,
And *seeds* a kinred fire have with the sky.

All have their *keyes*, and set *ascents*; but man
    Though he knows these, and hath more of his own,
    Sleeps at the ladders foot; alas! what can
These new discoveries do, except they drown?   40

Thus groveling in the shade, and darkness, he
    Sinks to a dead oblivion; and though all
    He sees, (like *Pyramids*,) shoot from this ball
And less'ning still grow up invisibly,

Yet hugs he stil his durt; The *stuffe* he wears
    And painted trimming takes down both his eies,
    Heaven hath less beauty than the dust he spies,
And money better musick than the *Spheres*.

Life's but a blast, he knows it; what? shal straw,
    And bul-rush-fetters temper his short hour?   50
    Must he nor sip, nor sing? grows ne'r a flowr
To crown his temples? shal dreams be his law?

O foolish man! how hast thou lost thy sight?
   How is it that the Sun to thee alone
   Is grown thick darkness, and thy bread, a stone?
Hath flesh no softness now? mid-day no light?

Lord! thou didst put a soul here; If I must
   Be broke again, for flints will give no fire
   Without a steel, O let thy power cleer
Thy gift once more, and grind this flint to dust!   60

Retirement.

Who on yon throne of Azure sits,
   Keeping close house
   Above the morning-starre,
   Whose meaner showes,
And outward utensils these glories are
   That shine and share
   Part of his mansion; He one day
   When I went quite astray
   Out of meer love
   By his mild Dove   10
Did shew me home, and put me in the way.

2.

Let it suffice at length thy fits
   And lusts (said he,)
   Have had their wish, and way;
   Presse not to be
Still thy own foe, and mine; for to this day
   I did delay,
   And would not see, but chose to wink,
   Nay, at the very brink
   And edge of all   20
   When thou wouldst fall
My *love-twist* held thee up, my *unseen link.*

3.

I know thee well; for I have fram'd
   And hate thee not,
   Thy spirit too is mine;
   I know thy lot,

Extent, and end, for my hands drew the line
    Assigned thine ;
If then thou would'st unto my seat,
     'Tis not th'applause, and feat   30
      Of dust, and clay
      Leads to that way,
But from those follies a resolv'd Retreat.

4.

Now here below where yet untam'd
    Thou doest thus rove
  I have a house as well
    As there above,
In it my *Name*, and *honour* both do dwell
    And shall untill
I make all new ; there nothing gay   40
    In perfumes, or Array,
      Dust lies with dust
      And hath but just
The same Respect, and room, with ev'ry clay.

5.

A faithful school where thou maist see
    In Heraldrie
  Of stones, and speechless Earth
    Thy true descent ;
Where dead men preach, who can turn feasts, and mirth
    To funerals, and *Lent*.   50
There dust that out of doors might fill
    Thy eies, and blind thee still,
      Is fast asleep ;
      Up then, and keep
Within those doors, (my doors) dost hear ? *I will.*

Love, and Discipline.

Since in a land not barren stil
(Because thou dost thy grace distil,)
My lott is faln, Blest be thy will !

And since these biting frosts but kil
Some tares in me which choke, or spil
That seed thou sow'st, Blest be thy skil !

Blest be thy Dew, and blest thy frost,
And happy I to be so crost,
And cur'd by Crosses at thy cost.

The Dew doth Cheer what is distrest,   10
The frosts ill weeds nip, and molest,
In both thou work'st unto the best.

Thus while thy sev'ral mercies plot,
And work on me now cold, now hot,
The work goes on, and slacketh not,

For as thy hand the weather steers,
So thrive I best, 'twixt joyes, and tears,
And all the year have some grean Ears.

The Pilgrimage.

As travellours when the twilight's come,
And in the sky the stars appear,
The past daies accidents do summe
With, *Thus wee saw there, and thus here.*

Then *Jacob*-like lodge in a place
(A place, and no more, is set down,)
Where till the day restore the race
They rest and dream homes of their own.

So for this night I linger here,
And full of tossings too and fro,   10
Expect stil when thou wilt appear
That I may get me up, and go.

I long, and grone, and grieve for thee,
For thee my words, my tears do gush,
O that I were but where I see!
Is all the note within my Bush.

As Birds rob'd of their native wood,
Although their Diet may be fine,
Yet neither sing, nor like their food,
But with the thought of home do pine;   20

So do I mourn, and hang my head,
And though thou dost me fullnes give,
Yet look I for far better bread
Because by this man cannot live.

O feed me then! and since I may
Have yet more days, more nights to Count,
So strengthen me, Lord, all the way,
That I may travel to thy Mount.

Heb. Cap. xi. ver. 13.

*And they Confessed, that they were strangers, and Pilgrims on the
earth.*

The Law, and the Gospel.

Lord, when thou didst on *Sinai* pitch
And shine from *Paran*, when a firie Law
Pronounc'd with thunder, and thy threats did thaw
Thy Peoples hearts, when all thy weeds were rich
  And Inaccessible for light,
    Terrour, and might,
How did poor flesh (which after thou didst weare,)
    Then faint, and fear!
Thy Chosen flock, like leafs in a high wind,
Whisper'd obedience, and their heads Inclin'd.   10

2.

  But now since we to *Sion* came,
And through thy bloud thy glory see,
With filial Confidence we touch ev'n thee;
And where the other mount all clad in flame,
  And threatning Clouds would not so much
    As 'bide the touch,
We Climb up this, and have too all the way
    Thy hand our stay,
Nay, thou tak'st ours, and (which ful Comfort brings)
Thy Dove too bears us on her sacred wings.   20

3.

  Yet since man is a very brute
And after all thy Acts of grace doth kick,
Slighting that health thou gav'st, when he was sick,
Be not displeas'd, If I, who have a sute
  To thee each houre, beg at thy door
    For this one more;
O plant in me thy *Gospel*, and thy *Law*,
    Both *Faith*, and *Awe*;
So twist them in my heart, that ever there
I may as wel as *Love*, find too thy *fear*!   30

4.

Let me not spil, but drink thy bloud,
Not break thy fence, and by a black Excess
Force down a Just Curse, when thy hands would bless;
Let me not scatter, and despise my food,
    Or nail those blessed limbs again
        Which bore my pain;
So Shall thy mercies flow: for while I fear,
        I know, thou'lt bear,
But should thy mild Injunction nothing move me,
I would both think, and Judge I did not love thee.   40

John Cap. 14. ver. 15.
If ye love me, keep my Commandements.

The World.

I saw Eternity the other night
Like a great *Ring* of pure and endless light,
    All calm, as it was bright,
And round beneath it, Time in hours, days, years
        Driv'n by the spheres
Like a vast shadow mov'd, In which the world
        And all her train were hurl'd;
The doting Lover in his queintest strain
        Did their Complain,
Neer him, his Lute, his fancy, and his flights,   10
        Wits sour delights,
With gloves, and knots the silly snares of pleasure
        Yet his dear Treasure
All scatter'd lay, while he his eys did pour
        Upon a flowr.

2.

The darksome States-man hung with weights and woe
Like a thick midnight-fog mov'd there so slow
    He did nor stay, nor go;
Condemning thoughts (like sad Ecclipses) scowl
        Upon his soul,   20
And Clouds of crying witnesses without
        Pursued him with one shout.
Yet dig'd the Mole, and lest his ways be found
        Workt under ground,

11 sour] so our *1655*

Where he did Clutch his prey, but one did see
    That policie,
Churches and altars fed him, Perjuries
    Were gnats and flies,
It rain'd about him bloud and tears, but he
    Drank them as free.   30

3.

The fearfull miser on a heap of rust
Sate pining all his life there, did scarce trust
    His own hands with the dust,
Yet would not place one peece above, but lives
    In feare of theeves.
Thousands there were as frantick as himself
    And hug'd each one his pelf,
The down-right Epicure plac'd heav'n in sense
    And scornd pretence
While others slipt into a wide Excesse   40
    Said little lesse ;
The weaker sort slight, triviall wares Inslave
    Who think them brave,
And poor, despised truth sate Counting by
    Their victory.

4.

Yet some, who all this while did weep and sing,
And sing, and weep, soar'd up into the *Ring*,
    But most would use no wing.
O fools (said I,) thus to prefer dark night
    Before true light,   50
To live in grots, and caves, and hate the day
    Because it shews the way,
The way which from this dead and dark abode
    Leads up to God,
A way where you might tread the Sun, and be
    More bright than he.
But as I did their madnes so discusse
    One whisper'd thus,
This Ring the Bride-groome did for none provide
    But for his bride.   60

John Cap. 2. ver. 16, 17.
All that is in the world, the lust of the flesh, the lust of the Eys,
and the pride of life, is not of the father, but is of the world.
  And the world passeth away, and the lusts thereof, but he that
doth the will of God abideth for ever.

The Mutinie.

Weary of this same Clay, and straw, I laid
Me down to breath, and casting in my heart
The after-burthens, and griefs yet to come,
    The heavy sum
So shook my brest, that (sick and sore dismai'd)
My thoughts, like water which some stone doth start
Did quit their troubled Channel, and retire
Unto the banks, where, storming at those bounds,
They murmur'd sore; But I, who felt them boyl
    And knew their Coyl,   10
Turning to him, who made poor sand to tire
And tame proud waves, If yet these barren grounds
    And thirstie brick must be (said I)
    My taske, and Destinie,

2.

Let me so strive and struggle with thy foes
(Not thine alone, but mine too,) that when all
Their Arts and force are built unto the height
    That Babel-weight
May prove thy glory, and their shame; so Close
And knit me to thee, That though in this vale   20
Of sin, and death I sojourn, yet one Eie
May look to thee, To thee the finisher
And Author of my faith; so shew me home
    That all this fome
And frothie noise which up and down doth flie
May find no lodging in mine Eie, or Eare,
    O seal them up! that these may flie
    Like other tempests by.

3.

Not but I know thou hast a shorter Cut
To bring me home, than through a wildernes,   30
A Sea, or Sands and Serpents; Yet since thou
    (As thy words show)
Though in this desart I were wholy shut,
Canst light and lead me there with such redress
That no decay shal touch me; O be pleas'd
To fix my steps, and whatsoever path
Thy sacred and eternal wil decreed
    For thy bruis'd reed

O give it ful obedience, that so seiz'd
Of all I have, I may nor move thy wrath   40
  Nor grieve thy *Dove*, but soft and mild
    Both live and die thy Child.

Revel. Cap. 2. ver. 17.

To him that overcometh wil I give to eate of the hidden Manna,
*and I wil give him a white stone, and in the stone a new name
written, which no man knoweth, saving he that receiveth it.*

The Constellation.

Fair, order'd lights (whose motion without noise
  Resembles those true Joys
Whose spring is on that hil where you do grow
  And we here tast sometimes below,)

With what exact obedience do you move
  Now beneath, and now above,
And in your vast progressions overlook
  The darkest night, and closest nook!

Some nights I see you in the gladsome East,
  Some others neer the West,   10
And when I cannot see, yet do you shine
  And beat about your endles line.

Silence, and light, and watchfulnes with you
  Attend and wind the Clue,
No sleep, nor sloth assailes you, but poor man
  Still either sleeps, or slips his span.

He grops beneath here, and with restless Care
  First makes, then hugs a snare,
Adores dead dust, sets heart on Corne and grass
  But seldom doth make heav'n his glass.   20

Musick and mirth (if there be musick here)
  . Take up, and tune his year,
These things are Kin to him, and must be had,
  Who kneels, or sighs a life is mad.

Perhaps some nights hee'l watch with you, and peep
  When it were best to sleep,
Dares know Effects, and Judge them long before,
  When th' herb he treads knows much, much more.

But seeks he your *Obedience, Order, Light,*
    Your calm and wel-train'd flight,   30
Where, though the glory differ in each star,
    Yet is there peace still, and no war?

Since plac'd by him who calls you by your names
    And fixt there all your flames,
Without Command you never acted ought
    And then you in your Courses fought.

But here Commission'd by a black self-wil
    The sons the father kil,
The Children Chase the mother, and would heal
    The wounds they give, by crying, zeale.   40

Then Cast her bloud, and tears upon thy book
    Where they for fashion look,
And like that Lamb which had the Dragons voice
    Seem mild, but are known by their noise.

Thus by our lusts disorder'd into wars
    Our guides prove wandring stars,
Which for these mists, and black days were reserv'd,
    What time we from our first love swerv'd.

Yet O for his sake who sits now by thee
    All crown'd with victory,   50
So guide us through this Darknes, that we may
    Be more and more in love with day;

Settle, and fix our hearts, that we may move
    In order, peace, and love,
And taught obedience by thy whole Creation,
    Become an humble, holy nation.

Give to thy spouse her perfect, and pure dress,
    Beauty and *holiness,*
And so repair these Rents, that men may see
    And say, *Where God is, all agree.*   60

The Shepheards.

Sweet, harmles livers! (on whose holy leisure
    Waits Innocence and pleasure,)
Whose leaders to those pastures, and cleer springs,
    Were *Patriarchs*, Saints, and Kings,

1 livers *L 1858 C*: lives *1655*

How happend it that in the dead of night
    You only saw true light,
While *Palestine* was fast a sleep, and lay
    Without one thought of Day?
Was it because those first and blessed swains
    Were pilgrims on those plains   10
When they receiv'd the promise, for which now
    'Twas there first shown to you?
'Tis true, he loves that Dust whereon they go
    That serve him here below,
And therefore might for memory of those
    His love there first disclose;
But wretched *Salem* once his love, must now
    No voice, nor vision know,
Her stately Piles with all their height and pride
    Now languished and died,   20
And *Bethlems* humble Cotts above them stept
    While all her Seers slept;
Her Cedar, firr, hew'd stones and gold were all
    Polluted through their fall,
And those once sacred mansions were now
    Meer emptiness and show,
This made the Angel call at reeds and thatch,
    Yet where the shepheards watch,
And Gods own lodging (though he could not lack,)
    To be a common *Rack*;   30
No costly pride, no soft-cloath'd luxurie
    In those thin Cels could lie,
Each stirring wind and storm blew through their Cots
    Which never harbour'd plots,
Only Content, and love, and humble joys
    Lived there without all noise,
Perhaps some harmless Cares for the next day
    Did in their bosomes play,
As where to lead their sheep, what silent nook,
    What springs or shades to look,   40
But that was all; And now with gladsome care
    They for the town prepare,
They leave their flock, and in a busie talk
    All towards *Bethlem* walk
To see their souls great shepheard, who was come
    To bring all straglers home,

12 'Twas] 'Iwas *1655*

Where now they find him out, and taught before
   That Lamb of God adore,
That Lamb whose daies great Kings and Prophets wish'd
   And long'd to see, but miss'd.   50
The first light they beheld was bright and gay
   And turn'd their night to day,
But to this later light they saw in him,
   Their day was dark, and dim.

Misery.

Lord, bind me up, and let me lye
A Pris'ner to my libertie,
If such a state at all can be
As an Impris'ment serving thee ;
The wind, though gather'd in thy fist,
Yet doth it blow stil where it list,
And yet shouldst thou let go thy hold
Those gusts might quarrel and grow bold.
  As waters here, headlong and loose
The lower grounds stil chase, and choose,   10
Where spreading all the way they seek
And search out ev'ry hole, and Creek ;
So my spilt thoughts winding from thee
Take the down-rode to vanitie,
Where they all stray and strive, which shal
Find out the first and steepest fal ;
I cheer their flow, giving supply
To what's already grown too high,
And having thus perform'd that part
Feed on those vomits of my heart.   20
I break the fence my own hands made
Then lay that trespasse in the shade,
Some fig-leafs stil I do devise
As if thou hadst nor ears, nor Eyes.
Excesse of friends, of words, and wine
Take up my day, while thou dost shine
All unregarded, and thy book
Hath not so much as one poor look.
If thou steal in amidst the mirth
And kindly tel me, *I am Earth*,   30
I shut thee out, and let that slip,
Such Musick spoils good fellowship.

Thus wretched I, and most unkind,
Exclude my dear God from my mind,
Exclude him thence, who of that Cel
Would make a Court, should he there dwel.
He goes, he yields ; And troubled sore
His holy spirit grieves therefore,
The mighty God, th' eternal King
Doth grieve for Dust, and Dust doth sing.   40
But I go on, haste to Devest
My self of reason, till opprest
And buried in my surfeits I
Prove my own shame and miserie.
Next day I call and cry for thee
Who shouldst not then come neer to me,
But now it is thy servants pleasure
Thou must (and dost) give him his measure.
Thou dost, thou com'st, and in a showr
Of healing sweets thy self dost powr   50
Into my wounds, and now thy grace
(I know it wel,) fils all the place ;
I sit with thee by this new light,
And for that hour th'art my delight,
No man can more the world despise
Or thy great mercies better prize.
I School my Eys, and strictly dwel
Within the Circle of my Cel,
That Calm and silence are my Joys
Which to thy peace are but meer noise.   60
At length I feel my head to ake,
My fingers Itch, and burn to take
Some new Imployment, I begin
To swel and fome and fret within.
" *The Age, the present times are not*
" *To snudge in, and embrace a Cot,*
" *Action and bloud now get the game,*
" *Disdein treads on the peaceful name,*
" *Who sits at home too bears a loade*
" *Greater than those that gad abroad.*   70
Thus do I make thy gifts giv'n me
The only quarrellers with thee,

58 Cel, *M*: Cel *1655*: Cel ; *LGCB*

I'd loose those knots thy hands did tie,
Then would go travel, fight or die.
Thousands of wild and waste Infusions
Like waves beat on my resolutions,
As flames about their fuel run
And work, and wind til all be done,
So my fierce soul bustles about
And never rests til all be out.   80
Thus wilded by a peevish heart
Which in thy musick bears no part
I storm at thee, calling my peace
A Lethargy, and meer disease,
Nay, those bright beams shot from thy eys
To calm me in these mutinies
I stile meer tempers, which take place
At some set times, but are thy grace.
    Such is mans life, and such is mine
The worst of men, and yet stil thine,   90
Stil thine thou know'st, and if not so
Then give me over to my foe.
Yet since as easie 'tis for thee
To make man good, as bid him be,
And with one glaunce (could he that gain,)
To look him out of all his pain,
O send me from thy holy hil
So much of strength, as may fulfil
All thy delight (what e'r they be)
And sacred Institutes in me;   100
Open my rockie heart, and fil
It with obedience to thy wil,
Then seal it up, that as none see,
So none may enter there but thee.
    O hear my God! hear him, whose bloud
Speaks more and better for my good!
O let my Crie come to thy throne!
My crie not pour'd with tears alone,
(For tears alone are often foul)
But with the bloud of all my soul,   110
With spirit-sighs, and earnest grones,
Faithful and most repenting mones,
With these I crie, and crying pine
Till thou both mend and make me thine.

99 delight] delights (?)

The Sap.

Come sapless Blossom, creep not stil on Earth
　　Forgetting thy first birth ;
'Tis not from dust, or if so, why dost thou
　　Thus cal and thirst for dew ?
It tends not thither, if it doth, why then
　　This growth and stretch for heav'n ?
Thy root sucks but diseases, worms there seat
　　And claim it for their meat.
Who plac'd thee here, did something then Infuse
　　Which now can tel thee news.　　　　　　　　10
There is beyond the Stars an hil of myrrh
　　From which some drops fal here,
On it the Prince of *Salem* sits, who deals
　　To thee thy secret meals,
There is thy Country, and he is the way
　　And hath withal the key.
Yet liv d he here sometimes, and bore for thee
　　A world of miserie,
For thee, who in the first mans loyns didst fal
　　From that hil to this vale,　　　　　　　　20
And had not he so done, it is most true
　　Two deaths had bin thy due ;
But going hence, and knowing wel what woes
　　Might his friends discompose,
To shew what strange love he had to our good
　　He gave his sacred bloud
By wil our sap, and Cordial ; now in this
　　Lies such a heav'n of bliss,
That, who but truly tasts it, no decay
　　Can touch him any way,　　　　　　　　30
Such secret life, and vertue in it lies
　　It wil exalt and rise
And actuate such spirits as are shed
　　Or ready to be dead,
And bring new too.　Get then this sap, and get
　　Good store of it, but let
The vessel where you put it be for sure
　　To all your pow'r most pure ;
There is at all times (though shut up) in you
　　A powerful, rare dew,　　　　　　　　40

Which only grief and love extract; with this
 Be sure, and never miss,
To wash your vessel wel: Then humbly take
 This balm for souls that ake,
And one who drank it thus, assures that you
 Shal find a Joy so true,
Such perfect Ease, and such a lively sense
 Of grace against all sins,
That you'l Confess the Comfort such, as even
 Brings to, and comes from Heaven.   50

Mount of Olives.

When first I saw true beauty, and thy Joys
Active as light, and calm without all noise
Shin'd on my soul, I felt through all my powr's
Such a rich air of sweets, as Evening showrs
Fand by a gentle gale Convey and breath
On some parch'd bank, crown'd with a flowrie wreath;
Odors, and Myrrh, and balm in one rich floud
O'r-ran my heart, and spirited my bloud,
My thoughts did swim in Comforts, and mine eie
Confest, *The world did only paint and lie.*   10
And where before I did no safe Course steer
But wander'd under tempests all the year,
Went bleak and bare in body as in mind,
And was blow'n through by ev'ry storm and wind,
I am so warm'd now by this glance on me,
That, midst all storms I feel a Ray of thee;
So have I known some beauteous *Paisage* rise
In suddain flowres and arbours to my Eies,
And in the depth and dead of winter bring
To my Cold thoughts a lively sense of spring.   20
 Thus fed by thee, who dost all beings nourish,
My wither'd leafs again look green and flourish,
I shine and shelter underneath thy wing
Where sick with love I strive thy name to sing,
Thy glorious name! which grant I may so do
That these may be thy *Praise*, and my *Joy* too.

Man.

Weighing the stedfastness and state
Of some mean things which here below reside,
Where birds like watchful Clocks the noiseless date
    And Intercourse of times divide,
Where Bees at night get home and hive, and flowrs
        Early, aswel as late,
Rise with the Sun, and set in the same bowrs ;

2.

I would (said I) my God would give
The staidness of these things to man ! for these
To his divine appointments ever cleave,   10
    And no new business breaks their peace ;
The birds nor sow, nor reap, yet sup and dine,
        The flowres without clothes live,
Yet *Solomon* was never drest so fine.

3.

Man hath stil either toyes, or Care,
He hath no root, nor to one place is ty'd,
But ever restless and Irregular
    About this Earth doth run and ride,
He knows he hath a home, but scarce knows where,
        He sayes it is so far   20
That he hath quite forgot how to go there.

4.

He knocks at all doors, strays and roams,
Nay hath not so much wit as some stones have
Which in the darkest nights point to their homes,
    By some hid sense their Maker gave ;
Man is the shuttle, to whose winding quest
        And passage through these looms
God order'd motion, but ordain'd no rest.

7 bowrs] howrs *G*

¶

I walkt the other day (to spend my hour,)
 Into a field
Where I sometimes had seen the soil to yield
 A gallant flowre,
But Winter now had ruffled all the bowre
 And curious store
I knew there heretofore.

2.

Yet I whose search lov'd not to peep and peer
 I'th' face of things
Thought with my self, there might be other springs 10
 Besides this here
Which, like cold friends, sees us but once a year,
 And so the flowre
Might have some other bowre.

3.

Then taking up what I could neerest spie
 I digg'd about
That place where I had seen him to grow out,
 And by and by
I saw the warm Recluse alone to lie
 Where fresh and green 20
He lived of us unseen.

4.

Many a question Intricate and rare
 Did I there strow,
But all I could extort was, that he now
 Did there repair
Such losses as befel him in this air
 And would e'r long
Come forth most fair and young.

5.

This past, I threw the Clothes quite o'r his head,
 And stung with fear 30
Of my own frailty dropt down many a tear
 Upon his bed,
Then sighing whisper'd, *Happy are the dead!*
 What peace doth now
 Rock him asleep below?

6.

And yet, how few believe such doctrine springs
  From a poor root
Which all the Winter sleeps here under foot
  And hath no wings
To raise it to the truth and light of things,   40
   But is stil trod
  By ev'ry wandring clod.

7.

O thou! whose spirit did at first inflame
  And warm the dead,
And by a sacred Incubation fed
  With life this frame
Which once had neither being, forme, nor name,
   Grant I may so
  Thy steps track here below,

8.

That in these Masques and shadows I may see 50
  Thy sacred way,
And by those hid ascents climb to that day
  Which breaks from thee
Who art in all things, though invisibly;
   Shew me thy peace,
  Thy mercy, love, and ease,

9.

And from this Care, where dreams and sorrows raign
  Lead me above
Where Light, Joy, Leisure, and true Comforts move
  Without all pain,   60
There, hid in thee, shew me his life again
   At whose dumbe urn
  Thus all the year I mourn.

57 Care] Cave *conj. G*

Begging.

King of Mercy, King of Love,
In whom I live, in whom I move,
Perfect what thou hast begun,
Let no night put out this Sun ;
Grant I may, my chief desire !
Long for thee, to thee aspire,
Let my youth, my bloom of dayes
Be my Comfort, and thy praise,
That hereafter, when I look
O'r the sullyed, sinful book,   10
I may find thy hand therein
Wiping out my shame, and sin.
O it is thy only Art
To reduce a stubborn heart,
And since thine is victorie,
Strong holds should belong to thee ;
Lord then take it, leave it not
Unto my dispose or lot,
But since I would not have it mine,
O my God, let it be thine !   20

Jude ver. 24, 25.

Now unto him that is able to keep us from falling, and to present us
faultless before the presence of his glory with exceeding joy,
To the only wise God, our Saviour, be glory, and majesty, Dominion
and power, now and ever, Amen.

FINIS.

Silex Scintillans, &c.

Ascension-day.

Lord Jesus ! with what sweetness and delights,
Sure, holy hopes, high joys and quickning flights
Dost thou feed thine ! O thou ! the hand that lifts
To him, who gives all good and perfect gifts.
Thy glorious, bright Ascension (though remov'd
So many Ages from me) is so prov'd
And by thy Spirit seal'd to me, that I
Feel me a sharer in thy victory.

      I soar and rise
      Up to the skies,   10
          Leaving the world their day,
      And in my flight,
      For the true light
          Go seeking all the way;
I greet thy Sepulchre, salute thy Grave,
That blest inclosure, where the Angels gave
The first glad tidings of thy early light,
And resurrection from the earth and night.
I see that morning in thy *Converts tears,
Fresh as the dew, which but this dawning wears?   20
I smell her spices, and her ointment yields,
As rich a scent as the now Primros'd-fields :
The Day-star smiles, and light with the deceast,
Now shines in all the Chambers of the East.
What stirs, what posting intercourse and mirth
Of Saints and Angels glorifie the earth ?
What sighs, what whispers, busie stops and stays ;
Private and holy talk fill all the ways ?
They pass as at the last great day, and run
In their white robes to seek the risen Sun ;   30
I see them, hear them, mark their haste, and move
Amongst them, with them, wing'd with faith and love.

      * *St. Mary Magdalene.*

---

23 light with the deceast] light, with Thee deceas'd, *C* : light with Thee
deceased *B*   30 risen] tisen *1655*

Thy forty days more secret commerce here,
After thy death and Funeral, so clear
And indisputable, shews to my sight
As the Sun doth, which to those days gave light.
I walk the fields of *Bethani* which shine
All now as fresh as *Eden*, and as fine.
Such was the bright world, on the first seventh day,
Before man brought forth sin, and sin decay ;   40
When like a Virgin clad in *Flowers* and *green*
The pure earth sat, and the fair woods had seen
No frost, but flourish'd in that youthful vest,
With which their great Creator had them drest :
When Heav'n above them shin'd like molten glass,
While all the Planets did unclouded pass ;
And Springs, like dissolv'd Pearls their Streams did pour
Ne'r marr'd with floods, nor anger'd with a showre.
With these fair thoughts I move in this fair place,
And the last steps of my milde Master trace ;   50
I see him leading out his chosen Train,
All sad with tears, which like warm Summer-rain
In silent drops steal from their holy eyes,
Fix'd lately on the Cross, now on the skies.
And now (eternal Jesus !) thou dost heave
Thy blessed hands to bless, these thou dost leave ;
The cloud doth now receive thee, and their sight
Having lost thee, behold two men in white !
Two and no more : *what two attest, is true,*
Was thine own answer to the stubborn Jew.   60
Come then thou faithful witness ! come dear Lord
Upon the Clouds again to judge this world !

Ascension-Hymn.

Dust and clay
Mans antient wear !
Here you must stay,
But I elsewhere ;
Souls sojourn here, but may not rest ;
Who will ascend, must be undrest.

And yet some
That know to die

Before death come,
  Walk to the skie   10
Even in this life ; but all such can
Leave behinde them the old Man.

  If a star
  Should leave the Sphære,
  She must first mar
  Her flaming wear,
And after fall, for in her dress
Of glory, she cannot transgress.

  Man of old
  Within the line   20
  Of *Eden* could
  Like the Sun shine
All naked, innocent and bright,
And intimate with Heav'n, as light ;

  But since he
  That brightness soil'd,
  His garments be
  All dark and spoil'd,
And here are left as nothing worth,
Till the Refiners fire breaks forth.   30

  Then comes he !
  Whose mighty light
  Made his cloathes be
  Like Heav'n, all bright ;
The Fuller, whose pure blood did flow
To make stain'd man more white then snow.

  Hee alone
  And none else can
  Bring bone to bone
  And rebuild man,   40
And by his all subduing might
Make clay ascend more quick then light.

¶

They are all gone into the world of light !
  And I alone sit lingring here ;
Their very memory is fair and bright,
  And my sad thoughts doth clear.

It glows and glitters in my cloudy brest
 Like stars upon some gloomy grove,
Or those faint beams in which this hill is drest,
 After the Sun's remove.

I see them walking in an Air of glory,
 Whose light doth trample on my days: 10
My days, which are at best but dull and hoary,
 Meer glimering and decays.

O holy hope! and high humility,
 High as the Heavens above!
These are your walks, and you have shew'd them me
 To kindle my cold love,

Dear, beauteous death! the Jewel of the Just,
 Shining no where, but in the dark;
What mysteries do lie beyond thy dust;
 Could man outlook that mark!   20

He that hath found some fledg'd birds nest, may know
 At first sight, if the bird be flown;
But what fair Well, or Grove he sings in now,
 That is to him unknown.

And yet, as Angels in some brighter dreams
 Call to the soul, when man doth sleep:
So some strange thoughts transcend our wonted theams,
 And into glory peep.

If a star were confin'd into a Tomb
 Her captive flames must needs burn there;   30
But when the hand that lockt her up, gives room,
 She'l shine through all the sphære.

O Father of eternal life, and all
 Created glories under thee!
Resume thy spirit from this world of thrall
 Into true liberty.

Either disperse these mists, which blot and fill
 My perspective (still) as they pass,
Or else remove me hence unto that hill,
 Where I shall need no glass.   40

White Sunday.

Wellcome white day! a thousand Suns,
Though seen at once, were black to thee;
For after their light, darkness comes,
But thine shines to eternity.

Those flames which on the Apostles rush'd
At this great feast, and in a tyre
Of cloven Tongues their heads all brush'd,
And crown'd them with Prophetic fire:

Can these new lights be like to those,
These lights of Serpents like the Dove? 10
Thou hadst no *gall*, ev'n for thy foes,
And thy two wings were *Grief* and *Love*.

Though then some boast that fire each day,
And on Christs coat pin all their shreds;
Not sparing openly to say,
His candle shines upon their heads:

Yet while some rays of that great light
Shine here below within thy Book,
They never shall so blinde my sight
But I will know which way to look. 20

For though thou doest that great light lock,
And by this lesser commerce keep:
Yet by these glances of the flock
I can discern Wolves from the Sheep.

Not, but that I have wishes too,
And pray, *These last may be as first*,
Or better; but thou long ago
Hast said, *These last should be the worst*.

Besides, thy method with thy own,
Thy own dear people pens our times, 30
Our stories are in theirs set down
And penalties spread to our Crimes.

Again, if worst and worst implies
A State, that no redress admits,
Then from thy Cross unto these days
The *rule* without *Exception* fits.

And yet, as in nights gloomy page
One silent star may interline :
So in this last and lewdest age,
Thy antient love on some may shine.   40

For, though we hourly breath decays,
And our best *note* and highest *ease*
Is but meer changing of the *keys*,
And a *Consumption* that doth please ;

Yet thou the great eternal Rock
Whose height above all ages shines,
Art still the same, and canst unlock
Thy waters to a soul that pines.

Since then thou art the same this day
And ever, as thou wert of old,   50
And nothing doth thy love allay
But our hearts dead and sinful cold :

As thou long since wert pleas'd to buy
Our drown'd estate, taking the Curse
Upon thy self, so to destroy
The knots we tyed upon thy purse,

So let thy grace now make the way
Even for thy love ; for by that means
We, who are nothing but foul clay,
Shal be fine gold, which thou didst cleanse.   60

O come ! refine us with thy fire !
Refine us ! we are at a loss.
Let not thy stars for *Balaams* hire
Dissolve into the common dross !

The Proffer.

Be still black Parasites,
Flutter no more ;
Were it still winter, as it was before,
You'd make no flights ;
But now the dew and Sun have warm'd my bowres,
You flie and flock to suck the flowers.

But you would honey make :
    These buds will wither,
And what you now extract, in harder weather
    Will serve to take ;   10
Wise husbands will (you say) there wants prevent,
  Who do not so, too late repent.

    O poys'nous, subtilc fowls !
      The flyes of hell
That buz in every ear, and blow on souls
    Until they smell
And rot, descend not here, nor think to stay,
  I've read, who 'twas, drove you away.

    Think you these longing eyes,
      Though sick and spent,   20
And almost famish'd, ever will consent
    To leave those skies,
That glass of souls and spirits, where well drest
  They shine in white (like stars) and rest.

    Shall my short hour, my inch,
      My one poor sand,
And crum of life, now ready to disband
    Revolt and flinch,
And having born the burthen all the day,
  Now cast at night my Crown away ?   30

    No, No ; I am not he,
      Go seek elsewhere.
I skill not your fine tinsel, and false hair,
    Your Sorcery
And smooth seducements : I'le not stuff my story
  With your Commonwealth and glory.

    There are, that will sow tares
      And scatter death
Amongst the quick, selling their souls and breath
    For any wares ;   40
But when thy Master comes, they'l finde and see
  There's a reward for them and thee.

11 husbands *LGCB* : husband *1655*

Then keep the antient way !
Spit out their phlegm
And fill thy brest with home ; think on thy dream :
A calm, bright day !
A Land of flowers and spices ! the word given,
If these be fair, O what is Heaven !

Cock-crowing.

Father of lights ! what Sunnie seed,
What glance of day hast thou confin'd
Into this bird ?   To all the breed
This busie Ray thou hast assign'd ;
    Their magnetisme works all night,
    And dreams of Paradise and light.

Their eyes watch for the morning hue,
Their little grain expelling night
So shines and sings, as if it knew
The path unto the house of light.   10
    It seems their candle, howe'r done,
    Was tinn'd and lighted at the sunne.

If such a tincture, such a touch,
So firm a longing can impowre
Shall thy own image think it much
To watch for thy appearing hour ?
    If a meer blast so fill the sail,
    Shall not the breath of God prevail ?

O thou immortall light and heat !
Whose hand so shines through all this frame,   20
That by the beauty of the seat,
We plainly see, who made the same.
    Seeing thy seed abides in me,
    Dwell thou in it, and I in thee.

To sleep without thee, is to die ;
Yea, 'tis a death partakes of hell :
For where thou dost not close the eye
It never opens, I can tell.
    In such a dark, Ægyptian border,
    The shades of death dwell and disorder.   30

Title Cock-growing] Cock crowing *catchword 1655* (?)

If joyes, and hopes, and earnest throws,
And hearts, whose Pulse beats still for light
Are given to birds ; who, but thee, knows
A love-sick souls exalted flight?
   Can souls be track'd by any eye
   But his, who gave them wings to flie?

Onely this Veyle which thou hast broke,
And must be broken yet in me,
This veyle, I say, is all the cloke
And cloud which shadows thee from me.   40
   This veyle thy full-ey'd love denies,
   And onely gleams and fractions spies.

O take it off ! make no delay,
But brush me with thy light, that I
May shine unto a perfect day,
And warme me at thy glorious Eye !
   O take it off ! or till it flee,
   Though with no Lilie, stay with me !

The Starre.

What ever 'tis, whose beauty here below
Attracts thee thus & makes thee stream & flow,
   And wind and curle, and wink and smile,
   Shifting thy gate and guile:

Though thy close commerce nought at all imbarrs
My present search, for Eagles eye not starrs,
   And still the lesser by the best
   And highest good is blest:

Yet, seeing all things that subsist and be,
Have their Commissions from Divinitie,   10
   And teach us duty, I will see
   What man may learn from thee.

First, I am sure, the Subject so respected
Is well disposed, for bodies once infected,
   Deprav'd or dead, can have with thee
   No hold, nor sympathie.

Next, there's in it a restless, pure desire
And longing for thy bright and vitall fire,
   Desire that never will be quench'd,
   Nor can be writh'd, nor wrench'd.   20

These are the Magnets which so strongly move
And work all night upon thy light and love,
  As beauteous shapes, we know not why,
   Command and guide the eye.

For where desire, celestiall, pure desire
Hath taken root, and grows, and doth not tire,
  There God a Commerce states, and sheds
   His Secret on their heads.

This is the Heart he craves; and who so will
But give it him, and grudge not; he shall feel   30
  That God is true, as herbs unseen
   Put on their youth and green.

The Palm-tree.

Deare friend sit down, and bear awhile this shade
As I have yours long since; This Plant, you see
So prest and bow'd, before sin did degrade
Both you and it, had equall liberty

With other trees: but now shut from the breath
And air of *Eden*, like a male-content
It thrives no where. This makes these weights (like death
And sin) hang at him; for the more he's bent

The more he grows. Celestial natures still
Aspire for home; This *Solomon* of old   10
By flowers and carvings and mysterious skill
Of Wings, and Cherubims, and Palms foretold.

This is the life which hid above with Christ
In God, doth always (hidden) multiply,
And spring, and grow, a tree ne'r to be pric'd,
A Tree, whose fruit is immortality.

Here Spirits that have run their race and fought
And won the fight, and have not fear'd the frowns
Nor lov'd the smiles of greatness, but have wrought
Their masters will, meet to receive their Crowns.   20

15 pric'd] prick'd *1655*

Here is the patience of the Saints: this Tree
Is water'd by their tears, as flowers are fed
With dew by night; but One you cannot see
Sits here and numbers all the tears they shed.

Here is their faith too, which if you will keep
When we two part, I will a journey make
To pluck a Garland hence, while you do sleep
And weave it for your head against you wake.

Joy.

Be dumb course measures, jar no more; to me
There is no discord, but your harmony.
False, jugling sounds; a grone well drest, where care
Moves in disguise, and sighs afflict the air:
Sorrows in white; griefs tun'd; a sugerd Dosis
Of Wormwood, and a Deaths-head crown'd with Roses.
He weighs not your forc'd accents, who can have
A lesson plaid him by a winde or wave.
Such numbers tell their days, whose spirits be
Lull'd by those Charmers to a Lethargy.   10
  But as for thee, whose faults long since require
More eyes then stars; whose breath could it aspire
To equal winds: would prove too short: Thou hast
Another mirth, a mirth though overcast
With clouds and rain, yet full as calm and fine
As those *clear heights* which above tempests shine.
          Therefore while the various showers
          Kill and cure the tender flowers,
          While the winds refresh the year
          Now with clouds, now making clear,   20
          Be sure under pains of death
          To ply both thine eyes and breath.
              As leafs in Bowers
              Whisper their hours,
              And Hermit-wells
              Drop in their Cells:
          So in sighs and unseen tears
          Pass thy solitary years,
And going hence, leave written on some Tree,
Sighs make joy sure, and shaking fastens thee.   30

The Favour.

O thy bright looks! thy glance of love
Shown, & but shown me from above!
Rare looks! that can dispense such joy
As without wooing wins the coy.
And makes him mourn, and pine and dye
Like a starv'd Eaglet, for thine eye.
Some kinde herbs here, though low & far,
Watch for, and know their loving star.
O let no star compare with thee!
Nor any herb out-duty me!   10
So shall my nights and mornings be
Thy time to shine, and mine to see.

The Garland.

Thou, who dost flow and flourish here below,
To whom a falling star and nine dayes glory,
Or some frail beauty makes the bravest shew,
Hark, and make use of this ensuing story.

When first my youthfull, sinfull age
 Grew master of my wayes,
Appointing errour for my Page,
 And darknesse for my dayes;
I flung away, and with full crie
 Of wild affections, rid   10
In post for pleasures, bent to trie
 All gamesters that would bid.
I played with fire, did counsell spurn,
 Made life my common stake;
But never thought that fire would burn,
 Or that a soul could ake.
Glorious deceptions, gilded mists,
 False joyes, phantastick flights,
Peeces of sackcloth with silk-lists,
 These were my prime delights. 20
I sought choice bowres, haunted the spring,
 Cull'd flowres and made me posies:
Gave my fond humours their full wing,
 And crown'd my head with Roses.

The Garland 1 below,] below. *1655* 21 bowres,] bowres *1655*
23 their] the r *1655* (?)

But at the height of this Careire
 I met with a dead man,
Who noting well my vain Abear,
 Thus unto me began :
Desist fond fool, be not undone,
 What thou hast cut to day   30
Will fade at night, and with this Sun
 Quite vanish and decay.

Flowres gather'd in this world, die here ; if thou
Wouldst have a wreath that fades not, let them grow,
And grow for thee ; who spares them here, shall find
A Garland, where comes neither rain, nor wind.

Love-sick.

Iesus, my life ! how shall I truly love thee ?
O that thy Spirit would so strongly move me,
That thou wert pleas'd to shed thy grace so farr
As to make man all pure love, flesh a star !
A star that would ne'r set, but ever rise,
So rise and run, as to out-run these skies,
These narrow skies (narrow to me) that barre,
So barre me in, that I am still at warre,
At constant warre with them. O come and rend,
Or bow the heavens ! Lord bow them and descend, 10
And at thy presence make these mountains flow,
These mountains of cold Ice in me ! Thou art
Refining fire, O then refine my heart,
My foul, foul heart ! Thou art immortall heat,
Heat motion gives ; Then warm it, till it beat,
So beat for thee, till thou in mercy hear,
So hear that thou must open : open to
A sinfull wretch, A wretch that caus'd thy woe,
Thy woe, who caus'd his weal ; so far his weal
That thou forgott'st thine own, for thou didst seal 20
Mine with thy blood, thy blood which makes thee mine,
Mine ever, ever ; And me ever thine.

Trinity-Sunday.

O holy, blessed, glorious three,
Eternall witnesses that be
In heaven, One God in trinitie !

   31 Will *catchword* : Whll *text 1655*

As here on earth (when men with-stood,)
The Spirit, Water, and the Blood,
Made my Lords Incarnation good :

So let the *Anty-types* in me
Elected, bought and seal'd for free,
Be own'd, sav'd, *Sainted* by you three !

Psalme 104.

Up, O my soul, and blesse the Lord.   O God,
  My God, how great, how very great art thou !
Honour and majesty have their abode
  With thee, and crown thy brow.

Thou cloath'st thy self with light, as with a robe,
  And the high, glorious heav'ns thy mighty hand
Doth spread like curtains round about this globe
  Of Air, and Sea, and Land.

The beams of thy bright Chambers thou dost lay
  In the deep waters, which no eye can find ;   10
The clouds thy chariots are, and thy path-way
  The wings of the swift wind.

In thy celestiall, gladsome messages
  Dispatch'd to holy souls, sick with desire
And love of thee, each willing Angel is
  Thy minister in fire.

Thy arm unmoveable for ever laid
  And founded the firm earth ; then with the deep
As with a vail thou hidst it, thy floods plaid
  Above the mountains steep.   20

At thy rebuke they fled, at the known voice
  Of their Lords thunder they retir'd apace :
Some up the mountains past by secret ways,
  Some downwards to their place.

For thou to them a bound hast set, a bound
  Which (though but sand) keeps in and curbs whole seas :
There all their fury, fome and hideous sound
  Must languish and decrease.

And as thy care bounds these, so thy rich love
  Doth broach the earth, and lesser brooks lets forth,   30
Which run from hills to valleys, and improve
  Their pleasure and their worth.

These to the beasts of every field give drink ;
  There the wilde asses swallow the cool spring :
And birds amongst the branches on their brink
   Their dwellings have and sing.

Thou from thy upper Springs above, from those
  Chambers of rain, where Heav'ns large bottles lie,
Doest water the parch'd hills, whose breaches close
   Heal'd by the showers from high.   40

Grass for the cattel, and herbs for mans use
  Thou mak'st to grow ; these (blest by thee) the earth
Brings forth, with wine, oyl, bread : All which infuse
   To mans heart strength and mirth.

Thou giv'st the trees their greenness, ev'n to those
  Cedars in *Lebanon*, in whose thick boughs
The birds their nests build ; though the Stork doth choose
   The fir-trees for her house.

To the wilde goats the high hills serve for folds,
  The rocks give Conies a retyring place :   50
Above them the cool Moon her known course holds,
   And the Sun runs his race.

Thou makest darkness, and then comes the night ;
  In whose thick shades and silence each wilde beast
Creeps forth, and pinch'd for food, with scent and sight
   Hunts in an eager quest.

The Lyons whelps impatient of delay
  Roar in the covert of the woods, and seek
Their meat from thee, who doest appoint the prey
   And feed'st them all the week.   60

This past, the Sun shines on the earth, and they
  Retire into their dens ; Man goes abroad
Unto his work, and at the close of day
   Returns home with his load.

O Lord my God, how many and how rare
  Are thy great works ! In wisdom hast thou made
Them all, and this the earth, and every blade
   Of grass, we tread, declare.

So doth the deep and wide sea, wherein are
  Innumerable, creeping things both small   70
And great : there ships go, and the shipmens fear
   The comely spacious Whale.

37 Thou] Thon 1655

These all upon thee wait, that thou maist feed
    Them in due season : what thou giv'st, they take ;
Thy bounteous open hand helps them at need,
    And plenteous meals they make.

When thou doest hide thy face (thy face which keeps
    All things in being) they consume and mourn :
When thou with-draw'st their breath, their vigour sleeps,
    And they to dust return.   80

Thou send'st thy spirit forth, and they revive,
    The frozen earths dead face thou dost renew.
Thus thou thy glory through the world dost drive,
    And to thy works art true.

Thine eyes behold the earth, and the whole stage
    Is mov'd and trembles, the hills melt & smoke
With thy least touch : lightnings and winds that rage
    At thy rebuke are broke.

Therefore as long as thou wilt give me breath
    I will in songs to thy great name imploy   90
That gift of thine, and to my day of death
    Thou shalt be all my joy.

Ile *spice* my thoughts with thee, and from thy word
    Gather true comforts ; but the wicked liver
Shall be consum'd.   O my soul, bless thy Lord !
    Yea, blesse thou him for ever !

The Bird.

Hither thou com'st : the busie wind all night
Blew through thy lodging, where thy own warm wing
Thy pillow was.   Many a sullen storm
(For which course man seems much the fitter born,)
    Rain'd on thy bed
    And harmless head.

And now as fresh and chearful as the light
Thy little heart in early hymns doth sing
Unto that *Providence*, whose unseen arm
Curb'd them, and cloath'd thee well and warm.   10
    All things that be, praise him ; and had
    Their lesson taught them, when first made.

75 Thy] They *catchword 1655*

So hills and valleys into singing break,
And though poor stones have neither speech nor tongue,
While active winds and streams both run and speak,
Yet stones are deep in admiration.
Thus Praise and Prayer here beneath the Sun
Make lesser mornings, when the great are done.

For each inclosed Spirit is a star
    Inlightning his own little sphære,   20
Whose light, though fetcht and borrowed from far,
    Both mornings makes, and evenings there.

But as these Birds of light make a land glad,
Chirping their solemn Matins on each tree :
So in the shades of night some dark fowls be,
Whose heavy notes make all that hear them, sad.

    The Turtle then in Palm-trees mourns,
        While Owls and Satyrs howl ;
    The pleasant Land to brimstone turns
        And all her streams grow foul.   30

Brightness and mirth, and love and faith, all flye,
Till the Day-spring breaks forth again from high.

The Timber.

Sure thou didst flourish once ! and many Springs,
Many bright mornings, much dew, many showers
Past ore thy head : many light *Hearts* and *Wings*
Which now are dead, lodg'd in thy living bowers.

And still a new succession sings and flies ;
Fresh Groves grow up, and their green branches shoot
Towards the old and still enduring skies,
While the low *Violet* thrives at their root.

But thou beneath the sad and heavy *Line*
Of death, dost waste all senseless, cold and dark ;   10
Where not so much as dreams of light may shine,
Nor any thought of greenness, leaf or bark.

And yet (as if some deep hate and dissent,
Bred in thy growth betwixt high winds and thee,
Were still alive) thou dost great storms resent
Before they come, and know'st how near they be.

       14 tongue] tongu *1655*   13 if] is *1655*

Else all at rest thou lyest, and the fierce breath
Of tempests can no more disturb thy ease ;
But this thy strange resentment after death
Means onely those, who broke (in life) thy peace.   20

So murthered man, when lovely life is done,
And his blood freez'd, keeps in the Center still
Some secret sense, which makes the dead blood run
At his approach, that did the body kill.

And is there any murth'rer worse then sin ?
Or any storms more foul then a lewd life ?
Or what *Resentient* can work more within,
Then true remorse, when with past sins at strife ?

He that hath left lifes vain joys and vain care,
And truly hates to be detain'd on earth,   30
Hath got an house where many mansions are,
And keeps his soul unto eternal mirth.

But though thus dead unto the world, and ceas'd
From sin, he walks a narrow, private way ;
Yet grief and old wounds make him sore displeas'd,
And all his life a rainy, weeping day.

For though he should forsake the world, and live
As meer a stranger, as men long since dead ;
Yet joy it self will make a right soul grieve
To think, he should be so long vainly lead.   40

But as shades set off light, so tears and grief
(Though of themselves but a sad blubber'd story)
By shewing the sin great, shew the relief
Far greater, and so speak my Saviors glory.

If my way lies through deserts and wilde woods ;
Where all the Land with scorching heat is curst ;
Better, the pools should flow with rain and floods
To fill my bottle, then I die with thirst.

Blest showers they are, and streams sent from above
Begetting *Virgins* where they use to flow ;   50
And trees of life no other waters love,
These upper springs and none else make them grow.

42 story)] story *1655*   50 *Virgins*] verdure *conj. Firth in C*

But these chaste fountains flow not till we dye;
Some drops may fall before, but a clear spring
And ever running, till we leave to fling
Dirt in her way, will keep above the skie.

Rom. Cap. 6. ver. 7.
He that is dead, is freed from sin.

The Jews.

When the fair year
Of your deliverer comes,
And that long frost which now benums
Your hearts shall thaw; when Angels here
Shall yet to man appear,
And familiarly confer
Beneath the Oke and Juniper:
When the bright *Dove*
Which now these many, many Springs
Hath kept above,   10
Shall with spread wings
Descend, and living waters flow
To make drie dust, and dead trees grow;

O then that I
Might live, and see the Olive bear
Her proper branches! which now lie
Scattered each where,
And without root and sap decay
Cast by the husband-man away.
And sure it is not far!   20
For as your fast and foul decays
Forerunning the bright morning-star,
Did sadly note his healing rayes
Would shine elsewhere, since you were blind,
And would be cross, when God was kinde:
So by all signs
Our fulness too is now come in,
And the same Sun which here declines
And sets, will few hours hence begin
To rise on you again, and look   30
Towards old *Mamre* and *Eshcols* brook.

For surely he
Who lov'd the world so, as to give
His onely Son to make it free,
Whose spirit too doth mourn and grieve
To see man lost, will for old love
From your dark hearts this veil remove.

Faith sojourn'd first on earth in you,
You were the dear and chosen stock :
The Arm of God, glorious and true,   40
Was first reveal'd to be your rock.

You were the *eldest* childe, and when
Your stony hearts despised love,
The *youngest,* ev'n the Gentiles then
Were chear'd, your jealousie to move.

Thus, Righteous Father ! doest thou deal
With Brutish men ; Thy gifts go round
By turns, and timely, and so heal
The lost Son by the newly found.

Begging.

I, do not go ! thou know'st, I'le dye !
My *Spring* and *Fall* are in thy book !
Or, if thou goest, do not deny
To lend me, though from far, one look !

My sins long since have made thee strange,
A very stranger unto me ;
No morning-meetings since this change,
Nor evening-walks have I with thee.

Why is my God thus slow and cold,
When I am most, most sick and sad ?   10
Well fare those blessed days of old
When thou didst hear the *weeping Lad* !

O do not thou do as I did,
Do not despise a Love-sick heart !
What though some clouds defiance bid
Thy Sun must shine in every part.

1 I,] I *1655* : O *1654*   go !] goe, *1654*   know'st,] know'st *1654*   dye !]
dye, *1654*   3 Or,] Or *1654*   7 since this change,] (since this change) *1654*
9 slow] hard *1654*   11 old] old, *1654*   15 bid] bid, *1654*

Though I have spoil'd, O spoil not thou !
Hate not thine own dear gift and token !
Poor birds sing best, and prettiest show,
When their nest is faln and broken.   20

Dear Lord ! restore thy ancient peace,
Thy quikning friendship, mans bright wealth !
And if thou wilt not give me ease
From sicknesse, give my spirit health !

Palm-Sunday.

Come, drop your branches, strow the way
   Plants of the day !
Whom sufferings make most green and gay.

The King of grief, the man of sorrow
Weeping still, like the wet morrow,
Your shades and freshness comes to borrow.

Put on, put on your best array ;
Let the joy'd rode make holy-day,
And flowers that into fields do stray,
Or secret groves, keep the high-way.   10

Trees, flowers & herbs ; birds, beasts & stones,
That since man fell, expect with groans
To see the lamb, which all at once,
Lift up your heads and leave your moans !
   For here comes he
   Whose death will be
Mans life, and your full liberty.

Hark ! how the children shril and high
   Hosanna cry,
Their joys provoke the distant skie,   20
Where thrones and Seraphins reply,
And their own Angels shine and sing
   In a bright ring :
   Such yong, sweet mirth
   Makes heaven and earth
Joyn in a joyful Symphony,

17 thou !] thou, *1654* 22 wealth !] wealth ; *1654*
13 which] come *LG* : whist *conj. M*

The harmless, yong and happy Ass,
Seen long before * this came to pass,
Is in these joys an high partaker
Ordain'd, and made to bear his Maker. 30

Dear feast of Palms, of Flowers and Dew !
Whose fruitful dawn sheds hopes and lights ;
Thy bright solemnities did shew,
The third glad day through two sad nights.

I'le get me up before the Sun,
I'le cut me boughs off many a tree,
And all alone full early run
To gather flowers to wellcome thee.

Then like the *Palm*, though wrong, I'le bear,
I will be still a childe, still meek 40
As the poor Ass, which the proud jear,
And onely my dear *Jesus* seek.

If I lose all, and must endure
The proverb'd griefs of holy *Job*,
I care not, so I may secure
But one *green Branch* and a *white robe*.

* *Zechariah, chap. 9. ver. 9.*

Jesus weeping.

S. Luke 19. *ver.* 41.

Blessed, unhappy City ? dearly lov'd
But still unkinde ! art this day nothing mov'd !
    Art senseless still ?   O can'st thou sleep
    When God himself for thee doth weep !
    Stiff-necked *Jews* ! your fathers breed
    That serv'd the calf, not *Abr'ams* seed,
    Had not the Babes *Hosanna* cryed,
    The stones had spoke, what you denyed.

Dear *Jesus* weep on ! pour this latter
Soul-quickning rain, this living water 10
    On their dead hearts ; but (O my fears !)
    They will drink blood, that despise tears.

39 though wrong] though wronged *L 1847 1858 C* : through wrong *G*
8 denyed.] denyed *1655*

My dear, bright Lord! my Morning-star!
Shed this live-dew on fields which far
From hence long for it! shed it there,
Where the starv'd earth groans for one tear!

This land, though with thy hearts blest extract fed,
Will nothing yield but thorns to wound thy head.

The Daughter of *Herodias.*

St. Matth. chap. 14. *ver.* 6. *&c.*

Vain, sinful Art! who first did fit
Thy lewd loath'd *Motions* unto *sounds,*
And made grave *Musique* like wilde *wit*
Erre in loose airs beyond her bounds?

What fires hath he heap'd on his head?
Since to his sins (as needs it must,)
His *Art* adds still (though he be dead,)
New fresh accounts of blood and lust.

Leave then * yong Sorceress ; the *Ice*
Will those coy spirits cast asleep,   10
Which teach thee now to please * his eyes
Who doth thy lothsome mother keep.

But thou hast pleas'd so well, he swears,
And gratifies thy sin with vows :
His shameless lust in publick wears,
And to thy soft arts strongly bows.

Skilful Inchantress and true bred !
Who out of evil can bring forth good?
Thy mothers nets in thee were spred,
She tempts to *Incest,* thou to *blood.*   20

* *Her name was* Salome; *in passing over a frozen river, the ice broke under
her, and chopt off her head.*
* Herod Antipas.

Jesus weeping.

St. John chap. 11. *ver.* 35.

My dear, Almighty Lord! why dost thou weep?
Why dost thou groan and groan again,
And with such deep,
Repeated sighs thy kinde heart pain,

Since the same sacred breath which thus
              Doth Mourn for us,
Can make mans dead and scatter'd bones
Unite, and raise up all that dyed, at once?

O holy groans ! Groans of the Dove !
O healing tears ! the tears of love !   10
Dew of the dead ! which makes dust move
And spring, how is't that you so sadly grieve,
              Who can relieve?

Should not thy sighs refrain thy store
Of tears, and not provoke to more?
Since two afflictions may not raign
In one at one time, as some feign.
Those blasts, which o'r our heads here stray,
If showers then fall, will showers allay,
As those poor Pilgrims oft have tryed,   20
Who in this windy world abide.

Dear Lord ! thou art all grief and love,
But which thou art most, none can prove.
Thou griev'st, man should himself undo,
And lov'st him, though he works thy wo.

'Twas not that vast, almighty measure
Which is requir'd to make up life,
(Though purchas'd with thy hearts dear treasure,)
              Did breed this strife
Of grief and pity in thy brest,   30
The throne where peace and power rest :
But 'twas thy love that (without leave,)
Made thine eyes melt, and thy heart heave ;
For though death cannot so undo
What thou hast done, (but though man too
Should help to spoil) thou canst restore
All better far then 'twas before ;
Yet, thou so full of pity art
(Pity which overflows thy heart !)
That, though the Cure of all mans harm   40
Is nothing to thy glorious arm,
Yet canst not thou that free Cure do,
But thou must sorrow for him too.

Then farewel joys ! for while I live,
My business here shall be to grieve :
A grief that shall outshine all joys
For mirth and life, yet without noise.
A grief, whose silent dew shall breed
Lilies and Myrrhe, where the curs'd seed
Did sometimes rule.   A grief so bright   50
'Twill make the Land of darkness light ;
And while too many sadly roam,
Shall send me (*Swan-like*) singing home.

Psal. **73**. ver. **25**.

*Whom have I in heaven but thee ? and there is none upon earth,
that I desire besides thee.*

Providence.

Sacred and secret hand !
By whose assisting, swift command
The Angel shewd that holy Well,
Which freed poor *Hagar* from her fears,
And turn'd to smiles the begging tears
Of yong, distressed *Ishmael.*

How in a mystick Cloud
(Which doth thy strange sure mercies shroud)
Doest thou convey man food and money
Unseen by him, till they arrive   10
Just at his mouth, that thankless hive
Which kills thy Bees, and eats thy honey !

If I thy servant be
(Whose service makes ev'n captives free,)
A fish shall all my tribute pay,
The swift-wing'd Raven shall bring me meat,
And I, like Flowers shall still go neat,
As if I knew no moneth but *May.*

I will not fear what man,
With all his plots and power can ;   20
Bags that wax old may plundered be,
But none can sequester or let
A state that with the Sun doth set
And comes next morning fresh as he.

Poor birds this doctrine sing,
And herbs which on dry hills do spring
Or in the howling wilderness
Do know thy dewy morning-hours,
And watch all night for mists or showers,
Then drink and praise thy bounteousness   30

May he for ever dye
Who trusts not thee ! but wretchedly
Hunts gold and wealth, and will not lend
Thy service, nor his soul one day :
May his Crown, like his hopes, be clay,
And what he saves, may his foes spend !

If all my portion here,
The measure given by thee each year
Were by my causeless enemies
Usurp'd ; it never should me grieve   40
Who know, how well thou canst relieve,
Whose hands are open as thine eyes.

Great King of love and truth !
Who would'st not hate my froward youth,
And wilt not leave me, when grown old ;
Gladly will I, like *Pontick* sheep,
Unto their wormwood-diet keep
Since thou hast made thy Arm my fold.

The Knot.

Bright Queen of Heaven ! Gods Virgin Spouse
        The glad worlds blessed maid !
Whose beauty tyed life to thy house,
        And brought us saving ayd.

Thou art the true Loves-knot ; by thee
        God is made our Allie,
And mans inferior Essence he
        With his did dignifie.

For Coalescent by that Band
        We are his body grown,   10
Nourished with favors from his hand
        Whom for our head we own.

And such a Knot, what arm dares loose,
    What life, what death can sever?
Which us in him, and him in us
    United keeps for ever.

The Ornament.

The lucky world shewd me one day
Her gorgeous Mart and glittering store,
Where with proud haste the rich made way
To buy, the poor came to adore.

Serious they seem'd and bought up all
The latest Modes of pride and lust,
Although the first must surely fall,
And the last is most loathsome dust.

But while each gay, alluring wear
With idle hearts and busie looks   10
They viewd, (for idleness hath there
Laid up all her Archives and books.)

Quite through their proud and pompous file
Blushing, and in meek weeds array'd
With native looks, which knew no guile,
Came the sheep-keeping *Syrian* Maid.

Whom strait the shining Row all fac'd
Forc'd by her artless looks and dress,
While one cryed out, We are disgrac'd
For she is bravest, you confess.   20

St. Mary Magdalen.

Dear, beauteous Saint! more white then day,
When in his naked, pure array;
Fresher then morning-flowers which shew
As thou in tears dost, best in dew.
How art thou chang'd! how lively-fair,
Pleasing and innocent an air,
Not tutor'd by thy glass, but free,
Native and pure shines now in thee!
But since thy beauty doth still keep
Bloomy and fresh, why dost thou weep?   10

19 one] once *1655*   6 an] and *1655*

This dusky state of sighs and tears
Durst not look on those smiling years,
When *Magdal-*castle was thy seat,
Where all was sumptuous, rare and neat.
Why lies this *Hair* despised now
Which once thy care and art did show?
Who then did dress the much lov'd toy,
In *Spires, Globes,* angry *Curls* and coy,
Which with skill'd negligence seem'd shed
About thy curious, wilde, yong head?   20
Why is this rich, this *Pistic* Nard
Spilt, and the box quite broke and marr'd?
What pretty sullenness did hast
Thy easie hands to do this waste?
Why art thou humbled thus, and low
As earth, thy lovely head dost bow?
Dear *Soul!* thou knew'st, flowers here on earth
At their Lords foot-stool have their birth;
Therefore thy wither'd self in haste
Beneath his blest feet thou didst cast,   30
That at the root of this green tree
Thy great decays restor'd might be.
Thy curious vanities and rare;
Odorous ointments kept with care,
And dearly bought, (when thou didst see
They could not cure, nor comfort thee,)
Like a wise, early Penitent
Thou sadly didst to him present,
Whose interceding, meek and calm
Blood, is the worlds all-healing *Balm.*   40
This, this Divine Restorative
Call'd forth thy tears, which ran in live
And hasty drops, as if they had
(Their Lord so near) sense to be glad.
Learn, *Ladies,* here the faithful cure
Makes beauty lasting, fresh and pure;
Learn *Marys* art of tears, and then
Say, *You have got the day from men.*
Cheap, mighty Art! her Art of love,
Who lov'd much and much more could move;   50

33 rare, *L 1847*: rare; *1655*: rare *LGCB*

Her Art! whose memory must last
Till truth through all the world be past,
Till his abus'd, despised flame
Return to Heaven, from whence it came,
And send a fire down, that shall bring
Destruction on his ruddy wing.

Her Art! whose pensive, weeping eyes,
Were once sins loose and tempting spies,
But now are fixed stars, whose light
Helps such dark straglers to their sight.   60

Self-boasting *Pharisee*! how blinde
A Judge wert thou, and how unkinde?
It was impossible, that thou
Who wert all false, should'st true grief know;
Is't just to judge her faithful tears
By that foul rheum thy false eye wears?

This Woman (say'st thou) *is a sinner:*
And sate there none such at thy dinner?
Go Leper, go; wash till thy flesh
Comes like a childes, spotless and fresh;   70
He is still leprous, that still paints:
Who Saint themselves, they are no *Saints*.

The Rain-bow.

Still yong and fine! but what is still in view
We slight as old and soil'd, though fresh and new.
How bright wert thou, when *Shems* admiring eye
Thy burnisht, flaming *Arch* did first descry!
When *Terah, Nahor, Haran, Abram, Lot,*
The youthful worlds gray fathers in one knot,
Did with intentive looks watch every hour
For thy new light, and trembled at each shower!
When thou dost shine darkness looks white and fair,
Storms turn to Musick, clouds to smiles and air:
Rain gently spends his honey-drops, and pours
Balm on the cleft earth, milk on grass and flowers.
Bright pledge of peace and Sun-shine! the sure tye
Of thy Lords hand, the * object of his eye.

* *Gen. chap.* 9. *ver.* 16.

10 Storms *conj. H. H. Vaughan in G*: Forms *1655 LCB*

When I behold thee, though my light be dim,
Distant and low, I can in thine see him,
Who looks upon thee from his glorious throne
And mindes the Covenant 'twixt *All* and *One.*
O foul, deceitful men ! my God doth keep
His promise still, but we break ours and sleep.   20
After the *Fall*, the first sin was in *Blood*,
And *Drunkenness* quickly did succeed the flood ;
But since *Christ* dyed, (as if we did devise
To lose him too, as well as *Paradise*,)
These two grand sins we joyn and act together,
Though blood & drunkeness make but foul, foul weather.
Water (though both Heavens windows and the deep,
Full forty days o'r the drown'd world did weep,)
Could not reform us, and blood (in despight)
Yea Gods own blood we tread upon and slight.   30
So those bad daughters, which God sav'd from fire,
While *Sodom* yet did smoke, lay with their sire.

Then peaceful, signal bow, but in a cloud
Still lodged, where all thy unseen arrows shrowd,
I will on thee, as on a Comet look,
A Comet, the sad worlds ill-boding book ;
Thy light as luctual and stain'd with woes
I'le judge, where penal flames sit mixt and close.
For though some think, thou shin'st but to restrain
Bold storms, and simply dost attend on rain,   40
Yet I know well, and so our sins require,
Thou dost but Court cold rain, till *Rain* turns *Fire.*

The Seed growing secretly.

S. Mark 4. 26.

If this worlds friends might see but once
What some poor man may often feel,
Glory, and gold, and Crowns and Thrones
They would soon quit and learn to kneel.

My dew, my dew ! my early love,
My souls bright food, thy absence kills !
Hover not long, eternal Dove !
Life without thee is loose and spills.

26 weather.] weather *1655.*

Somthing I had, which long ago
Did learn to suck, and sip, and taste,
But now grown sickly, sad and slow,
Doth fret and wrangle, pine and waste.

O spred thy sacred wings and shake
One living drop! one drop life keeps!
If pious griefs Heavens joys awake,
O fill his bottle! thy childe weeps!

Slowly and sadly doth he grow,
And soon as left, shrinks back to ill;
O feed that life, which makes him blow
And spred and open to thy will!

For thy eternal, living wells
None stain'd or wither'd shall come near:
A fresh, immortal *green* there dwells,
And spotless *white* is all the wear.

Dear, secret *Greenness!* nurst below
Tempests and windes, and winter-nights,
Vex not, that but one sees thee grow,
That *One* made all these lesser lights.

If those bright joys he singly sheds
On thee, were all met in one Crown,
Both Sun and Stars would hide their heads;
And Moons, though full, would get them down.

Let glory be their bait, whose mindes
Are all too high for a low Cell:
Though Hawks can prey through storms and winds,
The poor Bee in her hive must dwel.

Glory, the Crouds cheap tinsel still
To what most takes them, is a drudge;
And they too oft take good for ill,
And thriving vice for vertue judge.

What needs a Conscience calm and bright
Within it self an outward test?
Who breaks his glass to take more light,
Makes way for storms into his rest.

Then bless thy secret growth, nor catch
At noise, but thrive unseen and dumb;
Keep clean, bear fruit, earn life and watch
Till the white winged Reapers come!

¶

As time one day by me did pass
 Through a large dusky glasse
 He held, I chanc'd to look
 And spyed his curious book
Of past days, where sad Heav'n did shed
A mourning light upon the dead.

Many disordered lives I saw
 And foul records which thaw
 My kinde eyes still, but in
 A fair, white page of thin   10
And ev'n, smooth lines, like the Suns rays,
Thy name was writ, and all thy days.

O bright and happy Kalendar!
 Where youth shines like a star
 All pearl'd with tears, and may
 Teach age, *The Holy way*;
Where through thick pangs, high agonies
Faith into life breaks, and death dies.

As some meek *night-piece* which day quails,
 To candle-light unveils: 20
 So by one beamy line
 From thy bright lamp did shine,
In the same page thy humble grave
Set with green herbs, glad hopes and brave.

Here slept my thoughts dear mark! which dus
 Seem'd to devour, like rust;
 But dust (I did observe)
 By hiding doth preserve,
As we for long and sure recruits,
Candy with sugar our choice fruits.   30

O calm and sacred bed where lies
 In deaths dark mysteries
 A beauty far more bright
 Then the noons cloudless light
For whose dry dust green branches bud
And robes are bleach'd in the *Lambs* blood.

22 shine, *M*: shine; *1655*: shine *LGCB*   36 blood.] blood *1655*

Sleep happy ashes ! (blessed sleep !)
   While haplesse I still weep ;
   Weep that I have out-liv'd
   My life, and unreliev'd   40
Must (soul-lesse shadow !) so live on,
Though life be dead, and my joys gone.

¶

Fair and yong light ! my guide to holy
Grief and soul-curing melancholy ;
Whom living here I did still shun
As sullen night-ravens do the Sun,
And lead by my own foolish fire
Wandred through darkness, dens and mire.
How am I now in love with all
That I term'd then meer bonds and thrall,
And to thy name, which still I keep,
Like the surviving turtle, weep !   10
O bitter curs'd delights of men !
Our souls diseases first, and then
Our bodies ; poysons that intreat
With fatal sweetness, till we eat ;
How artfully do you destroy,
That kill with smiles and seeming joy ?
If all the subtilties of vice
Stood bare before unpractic'd eyes,
And every act she doth commence
Had writ down its sad consequence,   20
Yet would not men grant, their ill fate
Lodged in those false looks, till too late.
O holy, happy, healthy heaven,
Where all is pure, where all is even,
Plain, harmless, faithful, fair and bright,
But what Earth breaths against thy light !
How blest had men been, had their *Sire*
Liv'd still in league with thy chaste fire,

5–8, *the last four lines on the original page* 43, *are repeated on page* 44
as follows :

        And led by my own foolish fire,
        Wandred through darkness dens and mire.
        How am I now in love withal
        That I term'd then mere bonds and thrall,

Nor made life through her long descents,
A slave to lustful Elements!   30
I did once read in an old book
Soil'd with many a weeping look,
That the seeds of foul sorrows be
The finest things that are, to see.
So that fam'd fruit which made all dye
Seem'd fair unto the womans eye.
If these supplanters in the shade
Of Paradise, could make man fade,
How in this world should they deter
This world, their fellow-murtherer!   40
And why then grieve we to be sent
Home by our first fair punishment,
Without addition to our woes
And lingring wounds from weaker foes?
Since that doth quickly freedom win,
For he that's dead, is freed from sin.

O that I were winged and free
And quite undrest just now with thee,
Where freed souls dwel by living fountains
On everlasting, spicy mountains!   50
  Alas! my God! take home thy sheep;
  This world but laughs at those that weep.

The Stone.

Josh. chap. 24. ver. 27.

  I have it now:
But where to act, that none shall know,
Where I shall have no cause to fear
  An eye or ear,
   What man will show?
If nights, and shades, and secret rooms,
  Silent as tombs,
Will nor conceal nor assent to
My dark designs, what shall I do?
Man I can bribe, and woman will   10
Consent to any gainful ill,
But these dumb creatures are so true,
No gold nor gifts can them subdue.

Hedges have ears, said the old *sooth,*
And ev'ry bush is somethings booth ;
This cautious fools mistake, and fear
Nothing but man, when ambush'd there.

But I (Alas !)
Was shown one day in a strange glass
That busie commerce kept betwcen   20
God and his Creatures, though unseen.

They hear, see, speak,
And into loud discoveries break,
As loud as blood.   Not that God needs
Intelligence, whose spirit feeds
All things with life, before whose eyes,
Hell and all hearts stark naked lyes.
But * he that judgeth as he hears,
He that accuseth none, so steers
His righteous course, that though he knows   30
All that man doth, conceals or shows,
Yet will not he by his own light
(Though both all-seeing and all right,)
Condemn men ; but will try them by
A process, which ev'n mans own eye
Must needs acknowledge to be just.
Hence sand and dust
Are shak'd for witnesses, and stones
Which some think dead, shall all at once
With one attesting voice detect   40
Those secret sins we least suspect.
For know, wilde men, that when you erre
Each thing turns Scribe and Register,
And in obedience to his Lord,
Doth your most private sins record.

The *Law* delivered to the *Jews,*
Who promis'd much, but did refuse
Performance, will for that same deed
Against them by a *stone* proceed ;
Whose substance, though 'tis hard enough,   50
Will prove their hearts more stiff and tuff.

* *John chap.* 5. *ver.* 30. 45.

But now, since God on himself took
What all mankinde could never brook,
If any (for he all invites)
His easie yoke rejects or slights,
The *Gospel* then (for 'tis his word
And not himself * shall judge the world)
Will by loose *Dust* that man arraign,
As one then dust more vile and vain.

* *St. John, chap.* 12. *ver.* 47, 48.

The dwelling-place.

S. John, chap. 1. *ver.* 38, 39.

What happy, secret fountain,
    Fair shade, or mountain,
Whose undiscover'd virgin glory
Boasts it this day, though not in story,
Was then thy dwelling? did some cloud
Fix'd to a Tent, descend and shroud
My distrest Lord? or did a star
Becken'd by thee, though high and far,
In sparkling smiles haste gladly down
To lodge light, and increase her own?   10
My dear, dear God! I do not know
What lodgd thee then, nor where, nor how;
But I am sure, thou dost now come
Oft to a narrow, homely room,
Where thou too hast but the least part,
My God, I mean *my sinful heart.*

The Men of War.

S. Luke, chap. 23. *ver.* 11.

If any have an ear
*Saith holy * John, then let him hear.*
He that into Captivity
Leads others, shall a Captive be.
Who with the sword doth others kill,
A sword shall his blood likewise spill.
Here is the patience of the Saints,
And the true faith, which never faints.

* *Revel. cap.* 13. *ver.* 10.

Were not thy word (dear Lord !) my light,
How would I run to endless night,   10
And persecuting thee and thine,
Enact for *Saints* my self and mine.
But now enlighten'd thus by thee,
I dare not think such villany ;
Nor for a temporal self-end
Successful wickedness commend.
For in this bright, instructing verse
Thy Saints are not the Conquerers ;
But patient, meek, and overcome
Like thee, when set at naught and dumb.   20
Armies thou hast in Heaven, which fight,
And follow thee all cloath'd in white,
But here on earth (though thou hast need)
Thou wouldst no legions, but wouldst bleed.
The sword wherewith thou dost command
Is in thy mouth, not in thy hand,
And all thy Saints do overcome
By thy blood, and their Martyrdom.
But seeing Soldiers long ago
Did spit on thee, and smote thee too ;   30
Crown'd thee with thorns, and bow'd the knee,
But in contempt, as still we see,
I'le marvel not at ought they do,
Because they us'd my Savior so ;
Since of my *Lord* they had their will,
The servant must not take it ill.

Dear *Jesus* give me patience here,
And faith to see my Crown as near
And almost reach'd, because 'tis sure
If I hold fast and slight the *Lure*.   40
Give me humility and peace,
Contented thoughts, innoxious ease,
A sweet, revengeless, quiet minde,
And to my greatest haters kinde.
Give me, my God ! a heart as milde
And plain, as when I was a childe ;
That when *thy Throne is set*, and all
These *Conquerors* before it fall,

23 hast] hadst *LGB*

I may be found (preserv'd by thee)
Amongst that chosen company,   50
Who by no blood (here) overcame
But the blood of the *blessed Lamb*.

The Ass.

St. Matt. 21.

Thou! who didst place me in this busie street
Of flesh and blood, where two ways meet:
The *One* of goodness, peace and life,
The *other* of death, sin and strife;
Where frail visibles rule the minde,
And present things finde men most kinde:
Where obscure cares the *mean* defeat,
And splendid vice destroys the *great*;
As thou didst set no law for me,
But that of perfect liberty,   10
Which neither tyres, nor doth corrode,
But is a *Pillow*, not a *Load*:
So give me grace ever to rest,
And build on it, because the best;
Teach both mine eyes and feet to move
Within those bounds set by thy love;
Grant I may soft and lowly be,
And minde those things I cannot see;
Tye me to faith, though above reason,
Who question power, they speak treason: 20
Let me thy Ass be onely wise
To carry, not search mysteries;
Who carries thee, is by thee lead,
Who argues, follows his own head.
To check bad motions, keep me still
Amongst the dead, where thriving ill
Without his brags and conquests lies,
And truth (opprest here) gets the prize.
At all times, whatsoe'r I do,
Let me not fail to question, who   30
Shares in the *act*, and puts me to't?
And if not thou, let not me do't.
Above all, make me love the poor,
Those burthens to the rich mans door,

Let me admire those, and be kinde
To low estates, and a low minde.
If the world offers to me ought,
That by thy book must not be sought,
Or though it should be lawful, may
Prove not expedient for thy way;   40
To shun that peril, let thy grace
Prevail with me to shun the place.
Let me be wise to please thee still,
And let men call me what they will.
    When thus thy milde, instructing hand
Findes thy poor *foal* at thy command,
When he from wilde is become wise,
And slights that most, which men most prize;
When all things here to thistles turn
Pricking his lips, till he doth mourn   50
And hang the head, sighing for those
Pastures of life, where the Lamb goes:
O then, just then! break or untye
These bonds, this sad captivity,
This leaden state, which men miscal
Being and life, but is dead thrall.
And when (O God!) the Ass is free,
In a state known to none but thee;
O let him by his *Lord* be led,
To living springs, and there be fed   60
Where light, joy, health and perfect peace
Shut out all pain and each disease;
Where death and frailty are forgotten,
And bones rejoyce, which once were broken!

The hidden Treasure.

S. *Matt.* 13. 44.

*What can the man do that succeeds the * King?*
Even what was done before, and no new thing.
Who shews me but one grain of sincere light?
False stars and fire-drakes, the deceits of night

* *Ecclesiastes, chap.* 2. 12.

---

39 though] thought *1655*   48 prize; *LGCB* : prize *1655*

Set forth to fool and foil thee, do not boast;
Such Coal-flames shew but Kitchin-rooms at most.
And those I saw search'd through; yea those and all
That these three thousand years time did let fall
To blinde the eyes of lookers-back, and I
Now all is done, finde all is vanity.   10
Those secret searches, which afflict the wise,
Paths that are hidden from the *Vulturs* eyes
I saw at distance, and where grows that fruit
Which others onely grope for and dispute.
    The worlds lov'd wisdom (for the worlds friends think
There is none else) did not the dreadful brink
And precipice it leads to, bid me flie
None could with more advantage use, then I.
    Mans favorite sins, those tainting appetites
Which nature breeds, and some fine clay invites,   20
With all their soft, kinde arts and easie strains
Which strongly operate, though without pains,
Did not a greater beauty rule mine eyes,
None would more dote on, nor so soon entice.
But since these sweets are sowre, and poyson'd here
Where the impure seeds flourish all the year,
And private Tapers will but help to stray
Ev'n those, who *by them* would finde out the day,
I'le seal my eyes up, and to thy commands
Submit my wilde heart, and restrain my hands;   30
I will do nothing, nothing know, nor see
But what thou bidst, and shew'st, and teachest me.
Look what thou gav'st; all that I do restore
But for one thing, though purchas'd once before.

Childe-hood.

I cannot reach it; and my striving eye
Dazles at it, as at eternity.
    Were now that Chronicle alive,
Those white designs which children drive,
And the thoughts of each harmless hour,
With their content too in my pow'r,
Quickly would I make my path even,
And by meer playing go to Heaven.

Why should men love
A Wolf, more then a Lamb or Dove?
Or choose hell-fire and brimstone streams
Before bright stars, and Gods own beams?
Who kisseth thorns, will hurt his face,
But flowers do both refresh and grace,
And sweetly living (*fie on men!*)
Are when dead, medicinal then.
If seeing much should make staid eyes,
And long experience should make wise;
Since all that age doth teach, is ill,
Why should I not love childe-hood still?
Why if I see a rock or shelf,
Shall I from thence cast down my self,
Or by complying with the world,
From the same precipice be hurl'd?
Those observations are but foul
Which make me wise to lose my soul.

And yet the *Practice* worldlings call
Business and weighty action all,
Checking the poor childe for his play,
But gravely cast themselves away.

　Dear, harmless age! the short, swift span,
Where weeping virtue parts with man;
Where love without lust dwells, and bends
What way we please, without self-ends.

An age of mysteries! which he
Must live twice, that would Gods face see;
Which *Angels* guard, and with it play,
Angels! which foul men drive away.

How do I study now, and scan
Thee, more then ere I studyed man,
And onely see through a long night
Thy edges, and thy bordering light!
O for thy Center and mid-day!
For sure that is the *narrow way.*

15 *men!*)] *men!* *1655*

10

20

30

40

The Night.

John 2. 3.

Through that pure *Virgin-shrine,*
That sacred vail drawn o'r thy glorious noon
That men might look and live as Glo-worms shine,
    And face the Moon :
Wise *Nicodemus* saw such light
As made him know his God by night.

Most blest believer he !
Who in that land of darkness and blinde eyes
Thy long expected healing wings could see,
    When thou didst rise,   10
And what can never more be done,
Did at mid-night speak with the Sun !

O who will tell me, where
He found thee at that dead and silent hour !
What hallow'd solitary ground did bear
    So rare a flower,
Within whose sacred leafs did lie
The fulness of the Deity.

No mercy-seat of gold,
No dead and dusty *Cherub,* nor carv'd stone,   20
But his own living works did my Lord hold
    And lodge alone ;
Where *trees* and *herbs* did watch and peep
And wonder, while the *Jews* did sleep.

Dear night ! this worlds defeat ;
The stop to busie fools ; cares check and curb ;
The day of Spirits ; my souls calm retreat
    Which none disturb !
Christs * progress, and his prayer time ;
The hours to which high Heaven doth chime.   30

Gods silent, searching flight :
When my Lords head is fill'd with dew, and all
His locks are wet with the clear drops of night ;
    His still, soft call ;

* *Mark, chap.* 1. 35. *S. Luke, chap.* 21. 37.

_____

27 retreat] retaeat *1655*

His knocking time; The souls dumb watch,
When Spirits their fair kinred catch.

Were all my loud, evil days
Calm and unhaunted as is thy dark Tent,
Whose peace but by some *Angels* wing or voice
    Is seldom rent;   40
Then I in Heaven all the long year
Would keep, and never wander here.

But living where the Sun
Doth all things wake, and where all mix and tyre
Themselves and others, I consent and run
    To ev'ry myre,
And by this worlds ill-guiding light,
Erre more then I can do by night.

There is in God (some say)
A deep, but dazling darkness; As men here   50
Say it is late and dusky, because they
    See not all clear;
O for that night! where I in him
Might live invisible and dim.

Abels blood.

Sad, purple well! whose bubling eye
Did first against a Murth'rer cry;
Whose streams still vocal, still complain
    Of bloody *Cain*,
And now at evening are as red
As in the morning when first shed.
    If single thou
(Though single voices are but low,)
Could'st such a shrill and long cry rear
As speaks still in thy makers ear,   10
What thunders shall those men arraign
Who cannot count those they have slain,
Who bath not in a shallow flood,
But in a deep, wide sea of blood?
A sea, whose lowd waves cannot sleep,
But *Deep* still calleth upon *deep*:
Whose urgent *sound* like unto that
Of many waters, beateth at

The everlasting doors above,
Where souls behinde the altar move,   20
And with one strong, incessant cry
Inquire *How long?* of the most high.
                    Almighty Judge !
At whose just laws no just men grudge ;
Whose blessed, sweet commands do pour
Comforts and joys, and hopes each hour
On those that keep them ; O accept
Of his vow'd heart, whom thou hast kept
From bloody men ! and grant, I may
That sworn memorial duly pay   30
To thy bright arm, which was my light
And leader through thick death and night !
                    I, may that flood,
That proudly spilt and despis'd blood,
Speechless and calm, as Infants sleep !
Or if it watch, forgive and weep
For those that spilt it ! May no cries
From the low earth to high Heaven rise,
But what (like his, whose blood peace brings)
Shall (when they rise) *speak better things*,   40
Then *Abels* doth ! may *Abel* be
Still single heard, while these agree
With his milde blood in voice and will,
Who pray'd for those that did him kill !

Righteousness.

Fair, solitary path ! Whose blessed shades
The old, white Prophets planted first and drest :
Leaving for us (whose goodness quickly fades,)
A shelter all the way, and bowers to rest.

Who is the man that walks in thee ? who loves
Heav'ns secret solitude, those fair abodes
Where turtles build, and carelesse sparrows move
Without to morrows evils and future loads ?

Who hath the upright heart, the single eye,
The clean, pure hand, which never medled pitch ?   10
Who sees *Invisibles*, and doth comply
With hidden treasures that make truly rich ?

33 I,] I *1655*   40 *things,* M: *things. 1655* : *things LGCB*   6 Heav'ns]
Heav ns *1655*   7 carelesse] carelese *1655*

He that doth seek and love
　　The things above,
Whose spirit ever poor, is meek and low ;
　　Who simple still and wise,
　　Still homewards flies,
Quick to advance, and to retreat most slow.

　　Whose acts, words and pretence
　　Have all one sense,   20
One aim and end ; who walks not by his sight :
　　Whose eyes are both put out,
　　And goes about
Guided by faith, not by exterior light.

　　Who spills no blood, nor spreds
　　Thorns in the beds
Of the distrest, hasting their overthrow ;
　　Making the time they had
　　Bitter and sad
Like *Chronic* pains, which surely kill, though slow.   30

　　Who knows earth nothing hath
　　Worth love or wrath,
But in his *hope* and *Rock* is ever glad.
　　Who seeks and follows peace,
　　When with the ease
And health of conscience it is to be had.

　　Who bears his cross with joy
　　And doth imploy
His heart and tongue in prayers for his foes ;
　　Who lends, not to be paid,   40
　　And gives full aid
Without that bribe which Usurers impose.

　　Who never looks on man
　　Fearful and wan,
But firmly trusts in God ; the great mans measure
　　Though high and haughty must
　　Be ta'en in dust,
But the good man is Gods peculiar treasure.

30 pains *LGCB* : prayers *1655* (*from* 39 ?)

Who doth thus, and doth not
These good deeds blot　　　　　　　　　　50
With bad, or with neglect ; and heaps not wrath
By secret filth, nor feeds
Some snake, or weeds,
Cheating himself ; That man walks in this path.

Anguish.

My God and King ! to thee
I bow my knee,
I bow my troubled soul, and greet
With my foul heart thy holy feet.
Cast it, or tread it ! It shall do
Even what thou wilt, and praise thee too.

My God, could I weep blood,
Gladly I would ;
Or if thou wilt give me that Art,
Which through the eyes pours out the hart,　　10
I will exhaust it all, and make
My self all tears, a weeping lake.

O ! 'tis an easie thing
To write and sing ;
But to write true, unfeigned verse
Is very hard ! O God, disperse
These weights, and give my spirit leave
To act as well as to conceive !

O my God, hear my cry ;
Or let me dye ! ——　　　　　　　　　　20

Tears.

O when my God, my glory brings
His white and holy train,
Unto those clear and living *Springs*,
Where comes no *stain* !

Where all is *light*, and *flowers*, and *fruit*,
And *joy*, and *rest*,
Make me amongst them ('tis my suit !)
The last one, and the least.

And when they all are fed, and have
    Drunk of thy living stream,   10
Bid thy poor Ass (with tears I crave !)
    Drink after them.

Thy love claims highest thanks, my sin
    The lowest pitch :
But if he pays, who *loves much*, then
    Thou hast made beggers rich.

Jacobs Pillow, and Pillar.

I see the Temple in thy Pillar rear'd,
And that dread glory, which thy children fear'd,
In milde, clear visions, without a frown,
Unto thy solitary self is shown.
'Tis number makes a Schism : throngs are rude,
And God himself dyed by the multitude.
This made him put on clouds, and fire and smoke,
Hence he in thunder to thy Off-spring spoke ;
The small, still voice, at some low Cottage knocks,
But a strong wind must break thy lofty rocks.   10

    The first true worship of the worlds great King
From private and selected hearts did spring,
But he most willing to save all mankinde,
Inlarg'd that light, and to the bad was kinde.
Hence Catholick or Universal came
A most fair notion, but a very name.
For this rich Pearl, like some more common stone,
When once made publique, is esteem'd by none.
Man slights his Maker, when familiar grown,
And sets up laws, to pull his honor down.   20
This God foresaw : And when slain by the crowd
(Under that stately and mysterious cloud
Which his death scatter'd) he foretold the place,
And form to serve him in, should be true grace
And the meek heart, not in a Mount, nor at
Jerusalem, with blood of beasts, and fat.
A heart is that dread place, that awful Cell,
That secret Ark, where the milde Dove doth dwell
When the proud waters rage : when Heathens rule
By Gods permission, and man turns a Mule.   30

This litle *Goshen*, in the midst of night,
And Satans seat, in all her Coasts hath light,
Yea *Bethel* shall have Tithes (saith *Israels* stone)
And vows and visions, though her foes crye, None.
Thus is the solemn temple sunk agen
Into a Pillar, and conceal'd from men.
And glory be to his eternal Name!
Who is contented, that this holy flame
Shall lodge in such a narrow pit, till he
With his strong arm turns our captivity.   40

But blessed *Jacob*, though thy sad distress
Was just the same with ours, and nothing less;
For thou a brother, and blood-thirsty too
Didst flye, * whose children wrought thy childrens wo:
Yet thou in all thy solitude and grief,
On stones didst sleep and found'st but cold relief;
Thou from the Day-star a long way didst stand
And all that distance was Law and command.
But we a healing Sun by day and night,
Have our sure Guardian, and our leading light;   50
What thou didst hope for and believe, we finde
And feel a friend most ready, sure and kinde.
Thy pillow was but type and shade at best,
But we the substance have, and on him rest.

* *Obadiah chap.* I. II. *Amos chap.* I. II.

The Agreement.

I wrote it down.   But one that saw
And envyed that Record, did since
Such a mist over my minde draw,
It quite forgot that purpos'd glimpse.
    I read it sadly oft, but still
    Simply believ'd, 'twas not my Quill;

At length, my lifes kinde Angel came,
And with his bright and busie wing
Scatt'ring that cloud, shewd me the flame
Which strait, like Morning-stars did sing,   10
    And shine, and point me to a place,
    Which all the year sees the Suns face.

52 feel] feel, *LGCB*

529

O beamy book ! O my mid-day
Exterminating fears and night !
The mount, whose white Ascendents may
Be in conjunction with true light !
    My thoughts, when towards thee they move,
    Glitter and kindle with thy love.

Thou art the oyl and the wine-house :
Thine are the present healing leaves,   20
Blown from the tree of life to us
By his breath whom my dead heart heaves.
    Each page of thine hath true life in't,
    And Gods bright minde exprest in print.

Most modern books are blots on thee,
Their doctrine chaff and windy fits :
Darken'd along, as their scribes be,
With those foul storms, when they were writ ;
    While the mans zeal lays out and blends
    Onely self-worship and self-ends.   30

Thou art the faithful, pearly rock,
The Hive of beamy, living lights,
Ever the same, whose diffus'd stock
Entire still, wears out blackest nights.
    Thy lines are rays, the true Sun sheds ;
    Thy leaves are healing wings he spreads.

For until thou didst comfort me,
I had not one poor word to say :
Thick busie clouds did multiply,
And said, I was no childe of day ;   40
    They said, my own hands did remove
    That candle given me from above.

O God ! I know and do confess
My sins are great and still prevail,
Most heynous sins and numberless !
But thy *Compassions* cannot fail.
    If thy sure mercies can be broken,
    Then all is true, my foes have spoken.

But while time runs, and after it
Eternity, which never ends,   50

Quite through them both, still infinite
Thy Covenant by *Christ* extends ;
    No sins of frailty, nor of youth
    Can foil his merits, and thy truth.

And this I hourly finde, for thou
Dost still renew, and purge and heal :
Thy care and love, which joyntly flow
New Cordials, new *Cathartics* deal.
    But were I once cast off by thee
    I know (my God !) this would not be.   60

Wherefore with tears (tears by thee sent)
I beg, my faith may never fail !
And when in death my speech is spent,
O let that silence then prevail !
    O chase in that *cold calm* my foes,
    And hear my hearts last private throws !

So thou, who didst the work begin
(For *I till* drawn came not to thee*)
Wilt finish it, and by no sin
Will thy free mercies hindred be.   70
    For which, O God, I onely can
    Bless thee, and blame unthankful man.

        * *St. John*, *chap.* 6. *ver.* 44. 65.

The day of Judgement.

O day of life, of light, of love !
The onely day dealt from above !
A day so fresh, so bright, so brave
Twill shew us each forgotten grave,
And make the dead, like flowers, arise
Youthful and fair to see new skies.
All other days, compar'd to thee,
Are but lights weak minority,
They are but veils, and Cypers drawn
Like Clouds, before thy glorious dawn.   10
O come, arise, shine, do not stay
        Dearly lov'd day !
The fields are long since white, and I
With earnest groans for freedom cry,

My fellow-creatures too say, *Come!*
And stones, though speechless, are not dumb.
When shall we hear that glorious voice
   Of life and joys?
That voice, which to each secret bed
   Of my Lords dead,   20
Shall bring true day, and make dust see,
The way to immortality.
When shall those first white Pilgrims rise,
Whose holy, happy Histories
(Because they sleep so long) some men
Count but the blots of a vain pen?
   Dear Lord! make haste,
Sin every day commits more waste,
And thy old enemy, which knows
His time is short, more raging grows. 30
Nor moan I onely (though profuse)
Thy Creatures bondage and abuse;
But what is highest sin and shame,
The vile despight done to thy name;
The forgeries, which impious wit
And power force on Holy Writ,
With all detestable designs
That may dishonor those pure lines.
O God! though mercy be in thee
The greatest attribute we see,   40
And the most needful for our sins;
Yet, when thy mercy nothing wins
But meer disdain, let not man say
Thy arm doth sleep; but write this day
Thy judging one: Descend, descend!
Make all things new! and without end!

Psalm 65.

Sions true, glorious God! on thee
Praise waits in all humility.
All flesh shall unto thee repair,
To thee, O thou that hearest prayer!
But sinful words and works still spread
And over-run my heart and head;
Transgressions make me foul each day,
O purge them, purge them all away!

Happy is he ! whom thou wilt choose
To serve thee in thy blessed house !   10
Who in thy holy Temple dwells,
And fill'd with joy, thy goodness tells !
King of Salvation ! by strange things
And terrible, Thy Justice brings
Man to his duty.   Thou alone
Art the worlds hope, and but thee, none.
Sailers that flote on flowing seas
Stand firm by thee, and have sure peace.
Thou still'st the loud waves, when most wild
And mak'st the raging people mild.   20
Thy arm did first the mountains lay
And girds their rocky heads this day.
The most remote, who know not thee,
At thy great works astonish'd be.

The *outgoings* of the *Even* and *Dawn,*
In *Antiphones* sing to thy Name.
Thou visit'st the low earth, and then
Water'st it for the sons of men,
Thy upper river, which abounds
With fertil streams, makes rich all grounds,   30
And by thy mercies still supplied
The sower doth his bread provide.
Thou water'st every ridge of land
And settlest with thy secret hand
The furrows of it ; then thy warm
And opening showers (restrain'd from harm)
Soften the mould, while all unseen
The blade grows up alive and green.
The year is with thy goodness crown'd,
And all thy paths drop fatness round,   40
They drop upon the wilderness,
For thou dost even the desarts bless,
And hills full of springing pride,
Wear fresh adornments on each side.
The fruitful flocks fill every Dale,
And purling Corn doth cloath the Vale ;
They shout for joy, and joyntly sing,
Glory to the eternal King!

43 hills] hills all *L* : the hills *G*

The Throne.

Revel. chap. 20. *ver.* 11.

When with these eyes clos'd now by thee,
   But then restor'd,
The great and white throne I shall see
   Of my dread Lord :
And lowly kneeling (for the most
   Stiff then must kneel)
Shall look on him, at whose high cost
   (Unseen) such joys I feel.

What ever arguments, or skill
   Wise heads shall use,   10
Tears onely and my blushes still
   I will produce.
And should those speechless beggers fail,
   Which oft have won ;
Then taught by thee, I will prevail,
   And say, *Thy will be done !*

Death.

Though since thy first sad entrance by
   Just *Abels* blood,
'Tis now six thousand years well nigh,
And still thy sov'rainty holds good :
Yet by none art thou understood.

We talk and name thee with much ease
   As a tryed thing,
And every one can slight his lease
As if it ended in a Spring,
Which shades & bowers doth rent-free bring. 10

To thy dark land these heedless go :
   But there was *One,*
Who search'd it quite through to and fro,
And then returning, like the Sun,
Discover'd all, that there is done.

And since his death, we throughly see
            All thy dark way;
Thy shades but thin and narrow be,
Which his first looks will quickly fray:
Mists make but triumphs for the day.   20

As harmless violets, which give
            Their virtues here
For salves and syrups, while they live,
Do after calmly disappear,
And neither grieve, repine, nor fear:

So dye his servants; and as sure
            Shall they revive.
Then let not dust your eyes obscure,
But lift them up, where still alive,
Though fled from you, their spirits hive.   30

The Feast.

O come away,
Make no delay,
      Come while my heart is clean & steddy!
While Faith and Grace
Adorn the place,
      Making dust and ashes ready.

No bliss here lent
Is permanent,
      Such triumphs poor flesh cannot merit;
Short sips and sights   10
Endear delights,
      Who seeks for more, he would inherit.

Come then true bread,
Quickning the dead,
      Whose eater shall not, cannot dye,
Come, antedate
On me that state
      Which brings poor dust the victory.

I victory
Which from thine eye   20
      Breaks as the day doth from the east,

When the spilt dew,
Like tears doth shew
   The sad world wept to be releast.

Spring up, O wine,
And springing shine
   With some glad message from his heart,
Who did, when slain,
These means ordain
   For me to have in him a part.   30

Such a sure part
In his blest heart,
   The well, where living waters spring,
That with it fed
Poor dust though dead
   Shall rise again, and live and sing.

O drink and bread
Which strikes death dead,
   The food of mans immortal being!
Under veyls here   40
Thou art my chear,
   Present and sure without my seeing.

How dost thou flye
And search and pry
   Through all my parts, and like a quick
And knowing lamp
Hunt out each damp,
   Whose shadow makes me sad or sick?

O what high joys
The Turtles voice   50
   And songs I hear! O quickning showers
Of my Lords blood
You make rocks bud
   And crown dry hils with wells & flowers!

For this true ease
This healing peace,
   For this taste of living glory,
My soul and all,
Kneel down and fall
   And sing his sad victorious story.   60

     57 taste] brief taste *L* : fore-taste *G*

O thorny crown
More soft then down !
    O painful Cross, my bed of rest !
O spear, the key
Opening the way !
    O thy worst state, my onely best !

Oh ! all thy griefs
Are my reliefs,
    And all my sins, thy sorrows were !
And what can I,   70
To this reply ;
    What (O God !) but a silent tear ?

Some toil and sow,
That wealth may flow,
    And dress this earth for next years meat ı
But let me heed,
Why thou didst bleed,
    And what in the next world to eat.

Revel. chap. 19. ver. 9.
Blessed are they, which are called unto the marriage Supper of the Lamb !

The Obsequies.

Since dying for me, thou didst crave no more
      Then common pay,
  Some few true tears, and those shed for
      My own ill way ;
With a cheap, plain remembrance still
      Of thy sad death,
Because forgetfulness would kill
      Even lifes own breath :
I were most foolish and unkinde
      In my own sense,   10
Should I not ever bear in minde
If not thy mighty love, my own defense.
Therefore, those loose delights and lusts, which here
      Men call good chear,
  I will close girt and tyed
For mourning sack-cloth wear, all mortified.

Not but that mourners too, can have
        Rich weeds and shrouds ;
For some wore *White* ev'n in thy grave,
And Joy, like light, shines oft in clouds :   20
But thou, who didst mans whole life earn,
Doest so invite, and woo me still,
        That to be merry I want skill,
            And time to learn.
Besides, those Kerchiefs sometimes shed
        To make me brave,
I cannot finde, but where thy head
Was once laid for me in thy grave.
Thy grave ! To which my thoughts shal move
Like Bees in storms unto their Hive,   30
That from the murd'ring worlds false love
Thy death may keep my soul alive.

The Water-fall.

With what deep murmurs through times silent stealth
Doth thy transparent, cool and watry wealth
        Here flowing fall,
        And chide, and call,
As if his liquid, loose Retinue staid
Lingring, and were of this steep place afraid,
        The common pass
        Where, clear as glass,
        All must descend
        Not to an end :   10
But quickned by this deep and rocky grave,
Rise to a longer course more bright and brave.

    Dear stream ! dear bank, where often I
    Have sate, and pleas'd my pensive eye,
    Why, since each drop of thy quick store
    Runs thither, whence it flow'd before,
    Should poor souls fear a shade or night,
    Who came (sure) from a sea of light ?
    Or since those drops are all sent back
    So sure to thee, that none doth lack,   20
    Why should frail flesh doubt any more
    That what God takes, hee'l not restore ?
        16 before] before. *1655*

O useful Element and clear!
My sacred wash and cleanser here,
My first consigner unto those
Fountains of life, where the Lamb goes?
What sublime truths, and wholesome themes,
Lodge in thy mystical, deep streams!
Such as dull man can never finde
Unless that Spirit lead his minde,   30
Which first upon thy face did move,
And hatch'd all with his quickning love.
As this loud brooks incessant fall
In streaming rings restagnates all,
Which reach by course the bank, and then
Are no more seen, just so pass men.
O my invisible estate,
My glorious liberty, still late!
Thou art the Channel my soul seeks,
Not this with Cataracts and Creeks.   40

Quickness.

False life! a foil and no more, when
        Wilt thou be gone?
Thou foul deception of all men
That would not have the true come on.

Thou art a Moon-like toil; a blinde
        Self-posing state;
A dark contest of waves and winde;
A meer tempestuous debate.

Life is a fix'd, discerning light,
        A knowing Joy;   10
No chance, or fit: but ever bright,
And calm and full, yet doth not cloy.

'Tis such a blissful thing, that still
        Doth vivifie,
And shine and smile, and hath the skill
To please without Eternity.

Thou art a toylsom Mole, or less
        A moving mist
But life is, what none can express,
A quickness, which my God hath kist.   20

The Wreath.

Since I in storms us'd most to be
    And seldom yielded flowers,
How shall I get a wreath for thee
    From those rude, barren hours?

The softer dressings of the Spring,
    Or Summers later store
I will not for thy temples bring,
    Which *Thorns*, not *Roses* wore.

But a twin'd wreath of *grief* and *praise*,
Praise soil'd with tears, and tears again   10
Shining with joy, like dewy days,
This day I bring for all thy pain,
Thy causless pain! and sad as death;
Which sadness breeds in the most vain,
(O not in vain!) now beg thy breath;
Thy quickning breath, which gladly bears
Through saddest clouds to that glad place,
Where cloudless Quires sing without tears,
Sing thy just praise, and see thy face.

The Queer.

O tell me whence that joy doth spring
Whose diet is divine and fair,
Which wears heaven, like a bridal ring,
And tramples on doubts and despair?

Whose Eastern traffique deals in bright
And boundless Empyrean themes,
Mountains of spice, Day-stars and light,
Green trees of life, and living streams?

Tell me, O tell who did thee bring
And here, without my knowledge, plac'd,   10
Till thou didst grow and get a wing,
A wing with eyes, and eyes that taste?

Sure, *holyness* the *Magnet* is,
And *Love* the *Lure*, that woos thee down;
Which makes the high transcendent bliss
Of knowing thee, so rarely known.

The Book.

Eternal God ! maker of all
That have liv'd here, since the mans fall ;
The Rock of ages ! in whose shade
They live unseen, when here they fade.

Thou knew'st this *papyr*, when it was
Meer *seed*, and after that but *grass* ;
Before 'twas *drest* or *spun*, and when
Made *linen*, who did *wear* it then :
What were their lifes, their thoughts & deeds
Whither good *corn*, or fruitless *weeds*.   10

   Thou knew'st this *Tree*, when a green *shade*
Cover'd it, since a *Cover* made,
And where it flourish'd, grew and spread,
As if it never should be dead.

   Thou knew'st this harmless *beast*, when he
Did live and feed by thy decree
On each green thing ; then slept (well fed)
Cloath'd with this *skin*, which now lies spred
A *Covering* o're this aged book,
Which makes me wisely weep and look   20
On my own dust ; meer dust it is,
But not so dry and clean as this.
Thou knew'st and saw'st them all and though
Now scatter'd thus, dost know them so.

   O knowing, glorious spirit ! when
Thou shalt restore trees, beasts and men,
When thou shalt make all new again,
Destroying onely death and pain,
Give him amongst thy works a place,
Who in them lov'd and sought thy face !   30

To the Holy Bible.

O book ! lifes guide ! how shall we part,
And thou so long seiz'd of my heart !
Take this last kiss, and let me weep
True thanks to thee, before I sleep.

16 live] liee *1655*   18 *skin*] *skln 1655*

Thou wert the first put in my hand,
When yet I could not understand,
And daily didst my yong eyes lead
To letters, till I learnt to read.
But as rash youths, when once grown strong
Flye from their Nurses to the throng, 10
Where they new Consorts choose, & stick
To those, till either hurt or sick :
So with that first light gain'd from thee
Ran I in chase of vanity,
Cryed dross for gold, and never thought
My first cheap Book had all I sought.
Long reign'd this vogue ; and thou cast by
With meek, dumb looks didst woo mine eye,
And oft left open would'st convey
A sudden and most searching ray 20
Into my soul, with whose quick touch
Refining still, I strugled much.
By this milde art of love at length
Thou overcam'st my sinful strength,
And having brought me home, didst there
Shew me that pearl I sought elsewhere.
Gladness, and peace, and hope, and love,
The secret favors of the Dove,
Her quickning kindness, smiles and kisses,
Exalted pleasures, crowning blisses, 30
Fruition, union, glory, life
Thou didst lead to, and still all strife.
Living, thou wert my souls sure ease,
And dying mak'st me go in peace :
Thy next *Effects* no tongue can tell ;
Farewel O book of God ! farewel !

S Luke chap. 2. ver. 14.

Glory be to God in the highest, and on
Earth peace, good will towards men.

L'Envoy.

O the new worlds new, quickning Sun !
Ever the same, and never done !
The seers of whose sacred light
Shall all be drest in shining white,

And made conformable to his
Immortal shape, who wrought their bliss,
    Arise, arise !
And like old cloaths fold up these skies,
This long worn veyl: then shine and spread
Thy own bright self over each head,   10
And through thy creatures pierce and pass
Till all becomes thy cloudless glass,
Transparent as the purest day
And without blemish or decay,
Fixt by thy spirit to a state
For evermore immaculate.
A state fit for the sight of thy
Immediate, pure and unveil'd eye,
A state agreeing with thy minde,
A state thy birth, and death design'd :   20
A state for which thy creatures all
Travel and groan, and look and call.
O seeing thou hast paid our score,
Why should the curse reign any more?
But since thy number is as yet
Unfinish'd, we shall gladly sit
Till all be ready, that the train
May fully fit thy glorious reign.
Onely, let not our haters brag,
Thy seamless coat is grown a rag,   30
Or that thy truth was not here known,
Because we forc'd thy judgements down.
Dry up their arms, who vex thy spouse,
And take the glory of thy house
To deck their own ; then give thy saints
That faithful zeal, which neither faints
Nor wildly burns, but meekly still
Dares own the truth, and shew the ill.
Frustrate those cancerous, close arts
Which cause solution in all parts,   40
And strike them dumb, who for meer words
Wound thy beloved, more then swords.
Dear Lord, do this ! and then let grace
Descend, and hallow all the place.
Incline each hard heart to do good,
And cement us with thy sons blood,

That like true sheep, all in one fold
We may be fed, and one minde hold.
Give watchful spirits to our guides !
For sin (like water) hourly glides　　　　　　50
By each mans door, and quickly will
Turn in, if not obstructed still.
Therefore write in their hearts thy law,
And lct these long, sharp judgements aw
Their very thoughts, that by their clear
And holy lives, mercy may here
Sit regent yet, and blessings flow
As fast, as persecutions now.
So shall we know in war and peace
Thy service to be our sole ease,　　　　　　60
With prostrate souls adoring thee,
Who turn'd our sad captivity !

　　　　　S. Clemens apud Basil :

　　Ζῆ ὁ Θεὸς, καὶ ὁ κύριος Ἰησοῦς Χριστὸς,
　　καὶ τὸ πνεῦμα τὸ ἅγιον.

　　　58 fast, *M*: fast. *1655* : fast *LGCB*

　　　　　　FINIS.

An Alphabetical
T A B L E,
Containing the several Titles of all
the Hymns or Sacred Poems in
these two Books.

A

	pag.
Abels blood.	523
Admission.	453
Affliction.	459
The Agreement.	528
Anguish.	526
Ascension-day.	481
Ascension hymn.	482
The Ass, Matt. 21.	518

B

Begging.	480
Begging.	500
The Bird.	496
The Book.	540
The Brittish Church.	410
Burial.	427
The Burial of an Infant.	450

C

The Call.	416
Chearfulness.	428
The Check.	443
Childhood.	520
Church service	426
Cock-crowing	488
Content	422
The Constellation.	469
Corruption.	440

D

The daughter of Herodias	503
The Dawning	451
The day of Judgement	402
The day of Judgement	530
Death.	533
Death	399
The Dedication	394
Disorder and frailty	444
Distraction	413
Dressing	455
The Dwelling place, John 1. 38, 39.	516

E

	pag.
Easter day	456
Easter-hymn	457
Private Ejaculations	396
L'Envoy	541
The Evening-watch	425

F

Faith	450
Mans fall and recovery	411
The Favor	492
The Feast	534

G

The Garland	492
The Law and the Gospel	465

H

The Hidden-treasure, Matt. 13. 44.	519
To the holy Bible	540
The Holy Communion	457
Holy Scriptures	441

I

Jacobs Pillow and Pillar, Gen. 28. 18.	527
Jesus weeping, S. Luk. 19. 41.	502
Jesus weeping, S John 11. 35	503
The Jews	499
The Incarnation and Passion	415
Joy	491
Isaacs marriage	408

K

The Knot	506

L

The Lamp.	410
Love and Discipline	463
Love-sick	493

M

	pag.
Man	477
S. Mary Magdalene	507
The Match	434
Mid night	421
Misery	472
The Morning-watch	424
Mount of Olives	414
Mount of Olives	476
The Mutiny	468

N

The Nativity	442
The Night, John 2. 3.	522

O

The Obsequies	536
The Ornament.	507

P

Palm-Sunday	501
The Palm-tree.	490
The Passion	430
Peace	430
The Pilgrimage	464
Praise	454
The Proffer	486
Providence	505
Psalm 65.	531
Psalm 104.	494
Psalm 121.	458
The Pursuit	414

Q

The Quere	539
Quickness	538

R

The Rain-bow, Gen. 9.	509
Regeneration	397
The Relapse	433
Religion	404

	pag.
Repentance	448
The Resolve	434
The Resurrection	400
Retirement	462
The Retreat	419
Righteousness	524
Romans, chap. 8. 19. *for the earnest,* &c.	432
Rules and Lessons.	436

S

The Sap	475
The Search	405
The Seed growing secretly, Mark 4. 26.	510
The shower	412
The shepherds, Luke 2. 10.	470
Sundays	447
The Star	489
The stone, Josh. 24. 27.	514
The Storm	423

T

Tears	526
The Tempest	460
The Throne, Revel. 20. 11.	533
The Timber	497
Trinity Sunday	493

V

Vanity of Spirit	418
Idle verse	446
Vnprofitableness	441

W

The Men of War, Luke 23 11.	516
The Water-fall	537
White-Sunday	485
The World.	466
The Wrath.	539

FINIS.

Romans *etc.*] *no page-number 1655*   *Trinity*] *Yrinity 1655*

HERMETICAL
PHYSICK:

O R,

The right way to pre-
ferve, and to reftore

HEALTH.

BY

That famous and faith-
full Chymift,

HENRY NOLLIVS.

Englifhed by
HENRY UAUGHAN, Gent.

LONDON.

Printed for *Humphrey Mofeley,* and
are to be fold at his fhop, at the
Princes Armes in St. *Pauls Church-
Yard,* 1 6 5 5.

THE
TRANSLATOR
To the ingenious
READER.

If any will be offended with this *Hermeticall* Theorie, I shall
but smile at his frettings, and pitty his ignorance. Those are bad
Spirits, that have the light; and such are all malicious despisers
of true knowledge, who out of meere envie, scribble and rail at all
endeavours; but such as submit to, and Deifie their rigid superstition, and twice sodden Colworts. For my owne part, I honour
the truth where ever I find it, whether in an old, or a new Booke,
in *Galen*, or in *Paracelsus*; and Antiquity, (where I find it gray
with errors) shall have as little reverence from me, as *Novelisme*.
10 *Veritatem tempus manu-ducit.* There is no reason (if they bind
not their owne hands) but the discoveries of Survivers and
Posterity, may and should be more perfect, then the superficiall
searches, and first attempts, or aims rather of their predecessors.
I wish we were all unbiassed and impartiall learners, not the
implicite, groundlesse Proselyts of Authors and opinions, but the
loyall friends and followers of truth. It would not then be impossible, but that we might in a short time attain to that perfection,
which while it is envied in some, will never bee found in all. As
men are killed by fighting, so truth is lost by disputing; for while
20 we study the figments and subtilties of Sophisters, wee cannot
search into the operations and virtues of nature. As many as wil
consider this, it is not improbable, but they may do well. But
despisers, and such as hate to be quietly instructed, must be
punished with silence, lest by seeking their peace, we lose our
owne.

Plautus.

*Qui mali sunt, habeant mala; qui boni, bona; bonos quòd
oderint mali, sunt mali; malos, quod oderint boni, bonos esse
oportet.*

HERMETICALL
PHYSICK &c.

CHAP. I.

Medicine or Physick *is an Art, laying down in certain Rules or Precepts, the right way of preserving and restoring the health of Man-kind.*

The word *Medicine,* hath a manifold sense. First, It is taken for some receipt or medicament. So the *Philosophicall Stone* is termed a Medicine. The Lord hath created Medicines out of the Earth, and the wise man will not abhor them. Secondly, It is taken for the habit, or profession of the Physitian, and then it signifies the faculty of curing existent in some learned and expert 10 Professor. This habit or faculty is delineated, or methodically described and laid down in the Dogmaticall Books of Physicians, that others may learne and practise thereby. Thirdly, It is taken for, and signifies a Physicall System or Treatise, and in this latter sence it is to be understood in this place.

The Object of Medicine or Physick in this latter sence is, Man, not in general, but that man onely who desires to learn the Art of Physick, and is to be informed or instructed by this present Treatise : but the Object of Physick, as it is an habit in the mind of the Physician, is man in general, either for the preserving, or 20 the restoring of his health. The operation, use, and end of Physick, is health ; as the work and end of Physical books, is a rightly principled and instructed Physitian ; so far as instruction goes : It is termed *Hermetical Physicke,* because it is grounded upon *Principles* of true *Philosophy,* as the Physick of *Hermes* was. And for this very reason the true Philosophers applyed themselves wholly to the *Hermetic* science, that they might thereby lay a true foundation of Physick, for the *Hermetic* Phylosophy layes open the most private and abstruse closets of nature, it doth most exquisitely search and find out the natures of health and sickness, it provides 30 most elaborate and effectuall Medicines, teacheth the just Dose of them, and surpasseth by many degrees the vulgar Philosophy, and that faculty which is grounded upon the principles of the common, supposititious knowledge, that is to say, it doth much exceed and outdo the *Galenical Physick.* This appears most evidently, because the *Hermetical Physicians* both can and frequently doe cure those diseases, which the *Galenists* adjudge to be incurable, as the Leprosie, the falling sickness, the Gout, &c. That the Principles of the *Hermetists,* are more certain then those of *Galen,* is sufficiently verified by their performances ; besides, it is a truth which cannot be denyed, that the Certainty and proof of the principles of all Arts, can by no other meanes, be known and tryed but by practise, as *Paracelsus* doth rightly urge *In Præfat. Defensionum, page* 252.

10 Now all the knowledge of the *Hermetists,* proceeds from a laborious manual disquisition and search into nature, but the *Galenists* insist wholly upon a bare received *Theorie* and prescribed Receits, giving all at adventure, and will not be perswaded to inquire further then the mouth of their leader. I call not those *Hermetists,* who know onely to distil a little water from this or that Herb ; nor those, who seeke to extract from other things by their sophistical operations a great treasure of Gold, which onely nature can supply us with : for the most ignorant amongst the people, may make a very useful Distiller, and the other attempt is 20 most commonly the task of Sophisters and Impostors : but I call them *Hermetists,* who observe nature in her workes, who imitate her, and use the same method that she doth, that out of nature, by the mediation of nature, and the assistance of their owne judgements, they may produce and bring to light such rare effectual medicines, as will safely, speedily, and pleasantly cure, and utterly expell the most deplorable diseases. These are the true *Hermetists* : As therefore I doe not approve of all those that would be called *Hermetists,* So neither doe I condemn all those, who diligently and conscientiously practise the *Galenicall Physick* : for some of them are precize and 30 petulant, others are sober & modest : and these latter sort acknowledge the imperfection of their medicines, and therefore they endeavour and take delight to adorne, inlarge, and accomplish their profession with the secrets of *Hermetical Physick* : but the other sort ascribe supreme perfection to that Ethnic, Antichristian writer, and his medicines, and will not for meer envy, or out of a childish depraved ignorance, looke upon the eminency of *Hermetic Philosophy,* nor inquire into the secrets of it, but seek rather by reprehending and carping those things they doe not understand, to magnifie their own way, and with peevish and virulent language, 40 raile at the *Hermetic* professors. Now as I preferre the *Hermetical* science to the medicines of these men : so (their Errours being

9 *Defensionum*] *D fensionum* 1655   21 workes,] workes *1655*

first laid aside,) I unite it with the Physick of the more sober *Galenists*, that theirs by consociation with ours, may become perfect and irreprehensible :

This *Joseph Quercetan*, a most expert Physician, and a learned Philosopher, whom as my master in this science I worthily honour, (for I must confess, that by his instructions (God assisting me,) I benefited very much,) did most happily performe. And many learned men even in this Age design the same thing, especially the professors of Physick in *Marburg*, who by an express and memorable decree of the most illustrious and mighty Prince 10 *William Lantgrave* of *Hassia*, proceed in that very course. And who then can justly blame me, for walking in the same path with such eminent men ? I shall conclude, and give my judgement with learned *Crollius* (a man who for the advancement of the true Physick, was most worthy of a longer life) that whosoever desires to be eminent in the Art of Physick, (and none can be so, that will study onely the *Placets* of one man) must (above all things) be unbiassed and addicted to no Sect, nor any one Author whatso-ever, but passe through them all in pursuit of the sincere truth, and subscribe only unto that, being mindful ever to preserve the 20 same freedome for himself, which *Horace* did.

> *Quo me cunq; rapit tempestas, deferor hospes,*
> *Nullius addictus jurare in verba Magistri.*

> Where-e'r my fancy calls, there I goe still,
> Not sworne a slave to any Masters will.

II.

Health is an incorrupt integrity, and soundnesse of the body pre-served by, and depending upon the strength and virtue of the radical Balsame.

Whence followes this Consequence, that the more strong and 30 virtual the Balsame is, so much the more vegetous and healthful is the body.

III.

The strength and virtue of the Balsame, depends upon the equal and mutual conspiration of the Hypostatical Principles, that by their even and peaceful consistency, the Balsame also may legitimately perform his functions, by which he may advantage and strengthen himself with the received aliment or food which is taken in, and may also (when separation is performed by the stomack,) cast out

*through his proper Emunctories what is not nutritive, and may
further provide that the seeds of diseases (if any lurk in the
flesh, or in the blood, in the disguise of that tincture,) break not
out, and bring suddain destruction to the body, or else may cause
that those ill seeds may by the balsames strength and vigour, be cast
out of the body as superfluous impurities, which cannot consist with
the health of man.*

It is truth therefore which the most noble and learned *Crollius*
speaks in his preface to his *Basilica Chymica*: In what body
10 soever (saith he) the *Hypostatical* principles consist by union, that
body may be judged to be truly sound.

IV.

Medicine *or* Physick, *treats either of the preservation, or of the
restoration of health.*

CHAP. 2.

Of the preservation of Health.

That part of Physick which treates of the preserving of health, is
an Art, which by certaine cautionary Rules, or Precepts, teacheth and prescribeth a certain way and meanes to defend and
20   save people from diseases.

It is by the *Græcians* termed προφυλακτικὴ : To effect what this
Art promiseth, I give these following Precepts.

I.

Lead a pious and an holy life.

For Piety (as the Apostle teacheth) is profitable for all things,
having the promise of this present life, and of that which is to
come. Now all piety consists in this, that we love God with all
our souls, and our Neighbours as our selves. Wonder not therefore, that so many in this age perish so suddainly and so soon.
30 Impiety now bears the sway : true and unfeigned charity hath no
place to abide in; Perjury, Treachery, Tyranny, Usury and
Avarice, or (where these are not,) a vicious, lascivious, and loose
life, are every where in request. The soul, which God made and
ordained to be the nobler essence, and the mistress, is now the
bond-woman, and the servile drudge to the vile body. We daily
see, that one Groom will serve to dresse and look to many Horses,
one sheepheard will keep a thousand sheep, one Herdsman as

many Kine or Oxen: but to dresse and feed one voluptuous body

> *There's need (betwixt his clothes, his bed and bord,)*
> *Of all that Earth and Sea, and Air afford.*

And I would to God that all these would suffice! A most unhappy truth was that of the *Stoic,* He is a servant to many, that serves but one body: for doe but imagine thy selfe placed in the Clouds, or neare the Starres, and from thence to looke down and observe our actions upon earth, thou shalt not see one man quiet, they runne all as busie as Ants over Sea and Land, through 10 Citty and Country, by right and wrong, to become Lordly and rich.

> *With restless cares they wast the night and day,*
> *To compasse great Estates, and get the sway.*

What wouldst thou say at such a sight as this? wouldst not thou cry out with *Seneca, Oh the faith of Go   and men!* how many persons doth one ambitious stomach imploy? If brutes and wild beasts devour or eat one another (unless they be compelled unto it by extream famine) we presently cry out, it is a prodigie: but what thing (I beseech thee) amongst mankind, is more frequent 20 then such prodigies? The Satyrist askes the question,

> ———*When ever did (I pray,)*
> *One Lyon take anothers life away?*
> *Or in what Forrest did a wild Bore by*
> *The tusks of his owne fellow wounded, die?*
> *Tygers with Tygers never have debate,*
> *And Beares amongst themselves abstain from hate.*

> ———*Quando Leoni,*
> *Fortior eripuit vitam leo? quo nemore unquam,*
> *Expiravit Aper, &c.*   30

But men, whom God adorned with rationall soules, kill one another, and those to whom nature, reason, and the faculty of speech, did (above any other creatures) commend love and unity, do by troopes (as it were for spectacle and ostentation,) murther and butcher themselves. Add to this, that (as *Seneca* saith) a Dogge will bark before he bites; stormes will threaten us before they dissolve upon our heads; buildings will crack before they fall, and smoke will give us warning that fire is at hand: but the destruction of man by man is suddain, and without the least notice: nay, the nearer it is, it is by so much the more diligently 40

36 bark before he bites *G*: bite before he barks *1655*

concealed. And what then is one man to another? who smiles, when he hates, salutes and embraceth, when he intends destruction, who under a serene smooth countenance hides poyson, violence and blood-shed. Certainly thou wilt erre, and erre grievously, if thou wilt trust to those faces, that meet thee civilly, and salute thee fairly: they have (indeed) the complexions of men, but the conditions of Devils. Nay, thou wilt meet with some, who (as the same Satyrist hath observed,)

> *Esteem it no point of revenge to kill,*
> 10 *Unless they may drinke up the blood they spill;*
> *Who do believe that hands, & hearts, and heads,*
> *Are but a kind of meat, &c.*

> *——Quorum non sufficit iræ,*
> *Occidisse aliquem, sed pectora, brachia, vultus*
> *Crediderint genus esse cibi, &c.*

But thou wilt reply, that Salvages, Barbarians, and Canibals, may (perhaps) commit such villanies. Art thou no better acquainted with our Saints of *Europe*? that humane society and commerce, that godlinesse and sanctity, which we so much cele-
20 brate and commend our selves for, is nothing else but meere monopolizing, meere deceit, and a mutuall imposture. And amongst us Saints, who (in our owne opinion) are mighty right-eous, tender-hearted and brotherly, there is nothing more usuall, then to have store of *Anthropophagi*, or Men-eaters: for the rich, and the great amongst us, not onely feed upon and live by the sweat, the slaughter, and the blood of the poor and opprest, but esteem them (of all others) their choicest dainties, for they are swallowed without much chewing, and there is none to deliver them: Insomuch that those sheepheards, who were said to flay
30 their sheep, robbing them of their Wool, their skins, and their flesh, and leaving them onely their bare bones, may be truly said to be more merciful then those men. So that man to man, is no more a God, but a Woolf and a Devil. Wonder not then (as I said before,) that so many amongst us dye so suddainly, and so soon for they had rather die sooner, yea and die for ever, then become sober, charitable, and truly pious.

II.

Follow after Sobriety.

For as drunkenness and immoderate feeding oppress and weaken
40 the virtue of the radical balsame: so sobriety preserves from sick-

14 *Occidisse*] *Occid sse 1655*

nesse, and diseases. Sober above most Kings was *Massinissa* the *Numidian,* who standing alwaies, and at his Tent-doore, would in the open field eat his meat without sauce, being contented with dry bread, and military Commons. For which very reason he was so vegetous in old age, that at the years of fourscore and six, he begat a Sonne, and after ninety two, did in a pitched field over-throw the *Carthaginians,* who had broken their league made with him; in which battel he did not onely supply the place of an active, and expert Leader, but performed all the duties of a common Souldier. By the benefit of this virtue of temperance, did M. *Valerius Corvinus* live to be an hundred years old, and retain'd at that age a sound mind in a sound body. And *Socrates* continued all his life long in a perfect undisturbed health: yea, sobriety (if we should fall sick,) will restore us to health. There are some who think, that *Cæsar* used no other remedy to cure his falling sicknesse, which tooke him first at *Corduba* in *Spaine,* so that by a meere spare dyet, hard labours, and tedious watchings, he escaped, and overcame that dangerous and most commonly fatall indisposition.

III.

Eat not greedily, and drink not immoderately.

Nature in Vegetables, doth not swallow down her nutriment, nor take it in ravenously, and all at a time. She doth all things leasurely, and by degrees, that her *motion* may be convenient and useful, or assisting to her *Preservation.* It is thy concernment to imitate Nature, and to do as she doth, when thou dost eat, and when thou dost drink. It is a most foul blemish upon the memory of *Alexander,* that after most of his Victories, he used to riot it with his Officers, inviting them to delicious and sumptuous feasts, in which he used alwaies to drink *Prizes,* and he that could tun in more then all the rest, was rewarded with a Talent: But this intemperate eating and drinking, did cast him into such a violent, suddaine disease, that within three dayes he dyed of it.

IV.

Let thy meat be simple and unarted.

For such victuals (saith the most industrious *Pliny,*) are the most wholesome and agreeable: Nature is but one, therefore she doth most delight in one kinde of meate and drink.   Whence followes this consequence,

Thou shouldest never at one meal feed upon divers sorts of
meats & drinks.

For they are of an Heterogeneous nature, and the fire of Nature, which is but one and the same, cannot work equally upon them all, and prepare (legitimately) a nutriment for his own body, out of divers and differing cibations.   Every thing the nearer it is to unitie, is by so much the more perfect and durable.   There are infinite sorts of Trees which live very long, but they use all of them (without change) onely one kind of nutriment : But if it be so, that thou canst not abstaine from variety of meats, yet be sure (if possibly thou canst) that they have some agreement and correlation amongst themselves : For Contraries, (as *Hippocrates* affirmes) will move sedition and differences, while some of them are sooner, some latter digested and communicated to the body.   *Octavius Augustus,* would never have above three dishes of meat to his supper : Imitate him, and use not too much indulgence towards thy selfe, so shalt thou live the longer and the better.

V.

Accustome not thy selfe suddainly to meats and drinks, which for-
merly thou hast not been used to feed upon, unlesse they be pre-
scribed thee by some expert and learned Physician for thy healths
sake.

For every Change is dangerous.   Nature is simple and alwayes the same : and her manner of operation is simple too, and without change, and she delights altogether in constancy, and simple nutriments : but if thou dost change, she also will suffer the like change.   We see daily, that those birds which are taken, and put into Cages, by changing their naturall dyet, fall into divers diseases, and dye frequently.   A Lamb that is nourished with the milk of a Cow, seldome comes to any improvement, but most commonly dyes.

VI.

Use Antidotes frequently, to preserve thee from poysons, and private
or accidental mischiefes.

Lest thou perish by venemous meats or drinks, or by the aire thou livest in, which may be poysoned as well as thy food.

26 and her *G* : Other *1655*

Mithridates by the frequent use of an Antidote, which from him is still called Mithridate, did so strengthen nature, that no poyson could hurt him : And when he tooke a venemous, deadly confection of purpose to kill himselfe, it could not so much as make him sick : So that being overthrown in battel by his Enemies, and not being able to poyson himselfe, he was forced to command his Armour-bearer to thrust him through, and so dyed. There be divers kinds of Antidotes. I shall onely mention the most effectuall. The first is *Quercetanus*, his confection of *Juniper* and *Vipers*, described by him in his private dispensatory, *page* 349. 10 The second is his blessed *Theriac* : the third, his celestiall *Theriac*, called so by way of Eminency, and described both in the same Book. The fourth is *Crollius* his *Theriac* of *Mummie*, with another very soveraigne, one described by him in his *Basilica Chymica*. Use these Antidotes according to the Philosophers prescriptions, and (God assisting) no poyson shall be able to hurt thee.

VII.

Fly contagious airs, and if the aire thou livest in, be infected, change thy habitation.   20

VIII.

Take Physick in the spring-time, and in the Autumne.

Let us consider the nature of Serpents and Vipers : these in our stated seasons of Spring & Fall, cast off their old skins, and are clothed with new. That Medicine or course of Physick, which in all its circumstances answers to the great world, will work the more easily, the more prosperously, and will have the greatest effect. Seeing therefore that Trees, and all Roots, which in the Winter time seem dead, doe about the entrance of the Spring break forth and bud, putting on greenness, and a renew'd youth- 30 fulnesse and fresh vivacity as it were, therefore the wise *Ancients* did at the very same time (by observing them) take their purging and restorative Physick, and by that meanes (God cooperating with them) did mightily strengthen nature, and multiply their dayes upon earth. Such Physick as this, is the starre of man impregnated with the Physicall tincture. Others use onely the Philosophicall stone. These glorious medicines (whomsoever God shall reveale them to,) may in their just Dose be taken once in every week to the singular comfort, and incredible improvement

37 stone.] stone *1655*

of nature : So the Philosophers tell me. The dose of the universall medicine, is the weight of one graine.

IX.

Vse not too frequently, the permissions of Marriage.

Man for procreations sake, should not abhorre the Concessions and Priviledges of lawfull love, but let him eschew all wantonnesse, and confine his desires to naturall and legitimate, and that too within the bounds of Wedlock : But in this also there must be moderation. *Solons* Law was thrice in the moneth. Emission
10 of seed weakens all bodies : This experience tells us, for men that are addicted to this intemperance, have the most nice and tender constitutions, easily offended, and seldome fruitfull : like Trees, which bearing too much in one year, yeeld nothing but leaves in the next. You are to understand from this *Paragraph,* that seed is two-fold, *Radical,* and *Prolific.* The Radical seed, is the innate balsame of the body, which if it be advantaged with perfect digestion, will yeeld effusion, and a balsame of the same nature as it selfe. In this balsame the body lives as in his proper seed. Hence *Anonymus Leschus,* Tract. 7. instructs us, that so
20 long as there is seed in the body, it lives ; but the seed being consumed, the body dies. It is no wonder then, that so many have perished by this intemperance, who *
going to bed in a vegetous, perfect health,   ** It was not long before*
were found dead next morning. If you   *the publishing of this peece,*
excite a Tree to bear fruit by violent and   *that I was told by a very*
unnaturall means, or by artificiall, as by   *noble Gentleman, that in his late travailes in* France,
kindling fire under his branches in an   *he was acquainted with a young* French *Physician,*
unseasonable time, you will but kill the   *who for a long time had beene suiter to a very hand-*
Tree, and manifest your own indiscretion.   *some Lady, and having at length gained her consent,*
30 *was married to her, but his Nuptial bed proved his Grave, for on the next morning he was found dead. It was the Gentlemans opinion, that this sad accident might be caused by an excessive joy, and for my part I subscribe to it ; for a violent joy hath oftentimes done the worke of death : this comes to passe by an extreame attenuation, and diffusion of the animal spirits, which passing all into the exterior parts, leave the heart destitute, whence followes suffocation and death. Scaliger Exercit. 310. gives the reason of this violent effusion and dissipation of the Spirits : Quia similia maxime cupiunt inter se uniri, ideo spiritus veluti exire conantur ad objectum illud externum gratum ac jucundum, ut videlicet cum eo vniantur, Illudq; sibi maxime simile reddant. If any will*
40 *suspect, that together with this excessive joy, there was a concurrency of the other excess mentioned by my Author, I permit him his liberty, but certainly I thinke he will be deceived.*

3 *frequently*] *freqnently 1655*   12 fruitfull: *G* : fruitfull. *1655*   22 this *G* : the *1655.*   38 *gratum*] *g atum 1655*   41 *liberty*] *lib_rty 1655*

Chap. 3.

Of Diseases in Generall.

Hitherto we have spoken onely of that part of Physick, which teacheth us to preserve health ; It remaines now, that we consider the other part, which treats of the restitution of health.

I.

That part of Physick which teacheth us the restoration of health, is an Art laying down in certaine precepts or rules, a sure & safe way to redeem or free sick persons from diseases. It is termed by the Grecians θεραπευτικὴ.   10

II.

In this we are to consider, first, the disease, and all its circumstances : secondly, the cure of it.

For the true method consists in knowing, first the disease, and afterwards the cure. The Doctrine of diseases, is termed by the *Grecians,* νοσολογία.

III.

Disease or sicknesse, is a privation, or the loss of health.

IV.

Therefore ; because health depends upon the strength and vigour of   20 *the radical balsame, sicknesse must needs proceed from the weaknesse and indisposition of it.*

V.

But when the strength of the Balsame followes the conspiration of the Hypostatical principles, as his proper πάθος *or inclination, then or in that cause the infirmity of the balsame proceeds from the indisposition of the principles.*
Whence followes this consequence.

That those bodies, whose principles agree not amongst them-selves, may be truly judged to be sickly and ill disposed.   30

VI.

Touching the disease, there are two things to be considered. First, The conjoyn'd and apparent cause of the disease, which we shall terme Extrarious. *Secondly, the cause of that Extrarious or con-joyn'd cause.*

27 *indisposition*] *ind sposition 1655* (?)

Chap. 4.

Of the Extrarious or conjoyned and apparent Cause of the Disease.

I.

The conjoyned apparent cause of the disease, I terme* by reason it is a Cause most remote from, and altogether a stranger to, our nature.

* *Extrarious* signifies such a substance, that is quite another thing, and of another disposition than ours is.

II.

This Extrarious Cause is twofold, Substantial and Accidental.

The substantial is so termed, because it is the substantiall Essence, or matter of the disease. The other is termed accidental, by reason that the conjoyned cause signified by it, is an accident, not a substance.

III.

The substantial extrarious Cause, is either an impure tincture, or a Meteor.

IV.

An impure tincture, is an impure spiritual nature, so exactly mixt with the most inward parts of our substance, that at the time of its commixtion, it doth not presently and manifestly hinder nor prejudice the functions of the Balsame, but remaining quiet and inoffensive at first, and for a time, doth afterwards by degrees, discover its enmity and force, and so infects the body.

To this place must be referred; first, those impure seminal tinctures, by which the prolific seed is tainted, and the child that is borne of it, comes to be Hereditarily infected with the Diseases of his parents.

Secondly, the impurity of the body, that proceeds from the bloud, with which the child is fed and nourished in the wombe: from which last impurity, if the substance of the Childe were not vindicated, and free'd by frequent breakings out, by the Measels, and divers other extrusions, and petty indispositions, besides the dayly discharge of it through the proper Emunctories of the body,

5 *conjoyned*] *conjoyned'* *1655*   33 and petty] and petty and *1655*

it were not absurd to conclude, that his whole nature must needs be depraved and overcome by it. Purgations of this kind happen sometimes sooner, sometimes later, according to the strength of the Radicall balsame, which in some is slower, in others quicker and more vigorous ; as we see it exemplified in our very fields, of which some are more barren, some more fruitfull, according to their scituation, and the aspect of the Sun-beames, shining directly and favourably upon some, upon others glancingly, and for a short time, which makes some places more forward, some more back-ward, and their productions, whether flowers, or Hey, or 10 Corne, to differ accordingly, some being very good, some very bad.

V.

A Meteor is either volatile or coagulated, both kindes are Extrarious.

I call it a Meteor, because I would have the Reader to inquire, how the * Meteors of the greater world are generated, and by their Generation, to learn and find out the true Doctrine of the Microcosmical Meteors.

* I promise my English Reader, that (if God will blesse me with health, and his performing assistance) I will shortly communicate to him, (according to the Hermetic principles) a most accurate Treatise of 20 Meteors, their Generation, Causes, qualities, peculiar Regions and Forms: what spirits governe them, and what they signifie or fore-shew.

VI.

The volatile Meteor, is commonly called an Exhalation, and that is either dry or moist.

The dry Exhalation is termed a *Fume*, and the humid a *Vapour* : the fumid Exhalation, because it is a fume arising from a dry body or Principle, is hot, dry, light and subtile, alwayes tending upwards, and is near to a sulphureous fiery nature, which will easily inflame and kindle, and so is set on fire and burns.   Contrarily, a vapour 30 is an humid flux, which if it be deprived by any exterior heat of its owne cold quality and so carried up into the Region of the Air, and there condensed by cold, is presently (because of its thin, Mercurial and aqueous nature,) forced to resume its former state, and is turned againe into the nature of water.   For as we see in the greater world, that those Vapors and Exhalations, which by the heat of the Sun, the influence of the Stars, and by their owne proper internall calidity, are excited and stirred up, doe afterwards afford matter for various, miraculous Meteors, and bodies im- perfectly mixt both in the Region of the Air, and in the bowels of 40 the Earth ; and that those which are of a Mercurial, cold, moist,

29 nature] narure *1655*

and watry nature, doe always produce Clouds, Raine, Hail-stones, Snow, Frost and winds; but those which are sulphureous, hot and dry generate Coruscations, Lightnings, Fire-drakes, Thunder-bolts, and other burning Meteors: so in the lesser world, that is in the body of man, the like, and the very same vapours and Exhalations, afford matter for the generation of many and different kinds of Meteors. Hence it is, that so many and such various sorts of Diseases afflict man-kind. Some of them being Mercurial, cold and moist; others sulphureous, hot and dry: Nor are they so in meer forme and accident, but in substance, that is to say, they are such in their essentiall virtue, and are generated as wel in the inferiour Region, the breast, the stomack, and the belly; as in the superiour, the head and the braine, which parts do exactly quadrate and correspond with the airy Region, and the subterraneous Concavities of the earth. See *Quercetanus, Tetr. page* 45. 46.

VII.

The Coagulated Meteor, is termed Tartar, *of which we shall treat in the following Chapter.*

CHAP. 5.

Of Tartar.

I.

Tartar *is an acrimonious, pricking and corroding, or an aluminous, acid and styptic mucilage, which is bred in the body, and being separated from its proper juyce, is by the supervenient spirit of Salt, according to the various inclination of nature, at a set time, and in those places which are most apt to receive it, collected together, and coagulated; or if that juyce be not separated from it, it putrifies: from whence come worms and other innumerable symptoms.*

Quercetanus in his advice against the Joynt-gout, and the Stone, describes it thus. *Salsuginous* substances, because they have always mixt in them some portion of earth (though the predominant part in them be Liquefactive,) are in the body of man termed *Tartar*; a most apt (in truth) and most significant terme, which was first given them from the Analogy, or similitude that was found betwixt the humours in mans body, yea betwixt his very blood and the substance of wine: which of all the fruits of vegetables, doth most abound with *Tartar*. I doe not meane by

Tartar in this place that substance which is dissolved, and flowes in new Wines, while they are thick and turbid, which being afterwards separated, or (as the common phrase is) settled, doth as the grosser, earthy, and more impure part subside into a feculent substance, found always in the bottome, and called Dregs. Neither doe I mean that *Tartar* onely, whose separation is performed by a long Tract of time, and sticks to the Dregs or Lees of old Wine-pipes. But I meane that *Tartar* also, which is in perpetual liquefaction and commixture with the most refined wines, and which gives them their tincture either red, or any other. 10 This true *Tartar*, either by Evaporation, or simple distillation, or a *Balneum Maris*, is easily discerned to be moderately hot, for the more liquid part of the humour (which was the *Vehiculum*, in which the *Tartar* in its dissolution was contained) being separated from it, the *Tartar* alone remaines in the bottom. This liquid humour, though of red wine, distills all bright and limpid, but the heavier red substance, which I call *Tartar*, stayes all behind: a solid substance, and the more you fetch out of the substantifical humour, it becomes by so much the more hard and the dryer. Nor is this *Tartar* onely in red, or white Wines, but in any other 20 though decocted, and also in the humours of mans body. Nor is it there onely in the Chylus, or nutriment, which answers in proportion to wine newly made (for from the Chylus, as from new wine, divers impure and tartareous dregs are separated,) but also in the very blood, yea in the most pure, and after the very same manner, as we described it to be in wine. And as the Art of distilling (even that which is performed by the most gentle fire) discovers and manifests unto us this kind of *Tartar*: so nature also by her naturall fury both canne and daily doth performe such separations of *Tartar*, by a consumption of the humoural parts 30 of our bodies, out of which the Dogmatical Writers of Physick, suppose the stone to be generated. And it is wonderfull to consider, how many sorts of Diseases by the intervening of obstructions or oppilations, arise out of this meere separation, particularly the joynt-gout, and the stone: which diseases according to the sentiment of these Dogmatists themselves, happen most frequently to those, who have the hottest Livers, and consequently the coldest stomacks: Who ingenerate much crudities and mucous matters, which for want of a through-digestion, may be compared to raw fruits, that failing of their due and perfect maturity, (which 40 is performed by a contemperate heat, that is all concocting and

29 canne *G* : ranne *1655*

digesting,) remaine acid, bitter, sowre and green. These being mixt with, and in the whole Masse of blood, are there by the natural heate againe concocted, and a separation is made of the more crude and tartareous portion, which sticks afterwards to the inward parts, and causing divers obstructions, is at length forcibly carried into the joynts, where it stayes and lodgeth. For every part of the body of man doth naturally delight in, and attract to it, that which is most like to it selfe : the fleshie parts are nourished by that portion of the blood, which is most thinly moist, and
10 mercuriall : the fat and marrowish parts, by that which is most oily, or sulphureous, but the joynts which are parts that be naturally glutinous and mucilaginous, love that portion which hath most likenesse and affinity with their nature ; whence it comes to passe, that this Salsuginous and Tartareous matter is taken in by them. Now, when it happens that these parts in some bodyes, either for their weakness, or an innate hereditary disposition, or some such cause cannot by a proper and particular digestion, inoffensively digest, nor expell this crude and indigested Tarta-reous matter, then is this matter, being of a saltish, viscous nature
20 coagulated in them, and the ligaments of the joynts come to be stuffed up and stiffened with it, whence proceed those acute in-tolerable paines which attend this Disease. And this is the true and genuine conjoyn'd cause of the paines and knottines of the Joynt-gout. The same cause is sometimes lesse acute, sometimes more, according to the nature and condition of the *Tartar.* For as we see that there is in the greater world, a great diversity of Salts, for the Earth yeelds first Salt-gemme, which answers in proportion to Sea-salt, that is onely saltish in tast ; then Salt-nitre which is bitter in tast, and Salt-alum which is austere and Astrin-
30 gent : afterwards Salt of Vitriol, and Salt Armoniac which are acid and hot : and lastly, those corrosive sharp Salts which are termed *Alkali,* with others that are sweet and pleasant as Sugar : so in the lesser world, that is in the body of man, there is generated a Tartar or Salt, which being dissolved, causeth onely a saltish humour, which the Dogmatical Physicians term saltish phlegme, in plaine termes, a salt water or humour. There is also generated, a nitrous or bitter Salt, which mixeth with the Urine, and causeth bitter Choler ; and a vitriolated acid salt which predominates in acid phlegme and melancholy. In like manner there be also alumi-
40 nous and austere kinds of *Tartar,* and other sorts which resemble the acrimonie of Salt, as it is manifestly seen by the various affec-

35 phlegme] phegme *1655*

tions of contractures and astrictions of the sinews, and the many
perilous troubles of acrimonious humours in Dysenteries, and divers
Ulcers as well inward as outward, all which are caused by the
many and different kindes of Salts, which are generated in the
body. For why should not this be done by those things which
are most like to doe it, and most significant, and which do most
properly and fully expresse the natures and diversities of Causes,
having their derivation and appositenes from the very fountains of
nature, who is the best Interpretress of her own concernments.
These Salts (believe me) doe better expresse and discover unto us
the essences and distinctions of Tartareous or saltish diseases, then
those four humours which are commonly termed the Sanguine, the
Phlegmatic, the Bilious, and the Melancholy, both because that
these latter termes, signifie nothing unto us of the essence or
matter of the Disease, and also because that those Dogmatists
themselves, Hallucinate and stagger very much both in the forma-
tion or aptnesse, and in the application of their said termes.

II.

Tartar *is two-fold, Adventitious and Innate.*

III.

Adventitious Tartar, *proceeds from meat and drinke, and the Im-*
pressions of the Firmament.

Every thing that we eat and drinke, hath in it a Mucilaginous,
reddish and sandy Tartar, very noxious to the health of man.
Nature receives nothing for her own use, but what is pure. The
stomack, which is an instrument of the *Archæus* of man, or an
internall, innate Chymist, and implanted there by God, presently
upon the reception of that which is chew'd and swallowed down,
separates the impure, Tartareous part from the pure nutriment:
If the stomack be vigorous, especially in its faculty of separation,
the pure portion passeth presently into all the members to nourish
and preserve the body, and the impure goes forth into the
Draught : if the stomack be weake, the impure portion is through
the *Misaraic* veines conveyd to the Liver, where a second
digestion or separation is made. Here the Liver separates againe
the pure from the impure, the *Rubie* from the *Chrystall*, that is to
say, the *Red* from the *White* : The Red is the nutriment of all the
members the heart, the brain, &c. The white, or that which is
no nutriment, is driven by the Liver to the Reyns and it is Urine,

2 , and] and, *1655*

which is nothing else but Salt, which being exprest from the Mercuriall portions, by the violence of the separation, is forced to a dissolution: It is dissolved into water by the Liver & so cast forth. If the Liver, by reason of its debility, makes no perfect separation, it casts that Mucilaginous and Calculous impurity upon the Reyns, where for want of a right and through separation, it is (according to the concurrency and Method of nature) by the mediation of the spirit of Salt coagulated into Sand, or *Tartar*, either Massie and Solid, or Mucilaginous. This *Tartar* therefore 10 is the Excretion of meat and drinke, which is coagulated in all mens bodies by the spirit of Salt, unless the expulsive faculty by its owne peculiar vigour or virtue, can command it into the Excrements, and so cast it out by dejection.

IV.

There are four kinds of this Adventitious Tartar, *which proceed originally from the four distinct fruits or Cibations which we receive from the four Elements.*

The first kind proceeds from the use of those things that grow out of the Earth, as from all sorts of Pulse, Grains, Fruits, Herbs 20 and Roots, upon which we feed.

The second proceeds from those nutriments which we take out of the Element of Water, as from fish, shel-fish, &c.

The third is from the flesh of Birds and beasts, &c.

The fourth comes from the Firmament, which the spirit of Wine, in respect of its subtilty, doth most resemble. This kind of *Tartar* is of a most forcible impression, while the Air being primarily infected with the vapours of the Earth, the water and the firmament doth afterwards annoy us: as wee frequently see in those acute and pernitious Astral Diseases, the Pleurisie, the 30 Plague, the Prunella, &c.

V.

Tartar *innate, is that which is cogenerated with man in his mothers wombe.*

VI.

Besides these impure Tinctures and Meteors, there is another substantial Extrarious cause, which cannot be reduced to a certaine kind.

To this must be referred, those *Insecta's* or quick Creatures which sometimes (though rarely) are generated in the body, as 40 Snakes, divers worms, &c.

Secondly, those things must be referred hither, which by inchantment and the mediation of evill spirits, are invisibly and insensibly conveyed into the bodies of men and Women.

Thirdly, We are to reduce to this Aphorisme or Canon all Splinters, Bullets, or other weapons, which being violently thrust or shot into the body, lie deeply in the flesh, or under the skin.

VII.

We have now done with the Substantial Extrarious Cause. To the Accidental, I shall referre all disproportions of Limbs, Gibbosities, Luxations, Wounds, and fractures of bones.   10

CHAP. 6.

Of God, the first and supreme Cause of the Extrarious Cause.

Having now done with the Extrarious or conjoyned and apparent cause of the disease, I shall consider the cause of that Extrarious Cause.

I.

This Cause I shall divide into six heads or branches. The first of which is God.   2. Excesse and defect of Necessaries.   3. Fire. 4. Hereditary impurity.   5. Imagination.   6. Violent Illation. Of these I shall treat in their order; and first of GOD.   20

Man, because he is made in the Image of God, is bound also to live according to his *Will.* I mean his will revealed and laid down in the Ten Commandements, and the holy Scriptures, namely in those Bookes onely which were left unto us, and which (without scruple) we have received from the holy Prophets, and the Apostles of the Lord and Saviour : but when we transgresse and violate this Law and will of our maker, then doth God send upon us condigne punishments, amongst which *Diseases* are numbred in the very Booke of the Law. For thus saith the Lord : If ye shall despise my statutes, or if your soules abhor my judgements, 30 so that ye will not do my Commandements, but that ye break my Covenants : I also will do this unto you, I will even appoint over you terrour, consumption and the burning ague, that shall consume the eyes, and cause sorrow of heart. I will also smite thee in the knees and the legges with a sore botch, that cannot be healed, from the sole of thy foot unto the top of the Head. I will make the Pestilence cleave unto thee, untill it hath consumed

36 the Head] thy head *G*

thee from off the Land which thou possessest. And in another place, The Lord shall smite thee with a Consumption, with a Feavour, and with an inflammation and extream burning, and with the Sword, and with Blasting, and with Mildew: and they shall pursue thee untill thou perish. And the Heaven that is over thy head, shall be brass, and the Earth that is under thee shal be Iron. The Lord shall make the Raine of thy Land powder and dust, from heaven shall it come down upon thee, untill thou be destroyed. *Levitic.* Cap. 29. 16. *Deuteron.* 28.
10 And in the new Testament, that everlasting and blessed Physitian, the Holy *JESUS*, who came not to destroy, but to save the world; after he had healed the impotent man, who had beene sick of his infirmity eight and thirty years, he dismissed him not without this loving and gracious caution: Behold, thou art made whole, sinne no more, lest a worse thing come unto thee. S. *John* Chap. 5. 14. and S. *Paul* also in his first Epistle to the *Corinthians*, rebuking that new and sinfull custome (which had crept then into that Church) of prophaning the Lords holy Supper, with their own intemperate feasts, objects to them, that sharp visitation by
20 Diseases, which (for that very abuse) God had punished them with: For this cause (saith he) many are weak and sickly among you, and many sleep: for some of them had beene punished with death. Thus is the just and all-seeing God, the first and supreme cause of the Extrarious cause.

Chap. 7.

Of the excesse and the defect of necessaries, which is the second cause of the Extrarious cause.

Excess of Necessaries, is to be considered, first in Victuals, where the offence is threefold. 1. In superfluousness. 2. In
30 variety. 3. In our manner of receiving them. We offend in superfluousness, when that which is to nourish us is taken in too great a quantity: whence follow frequent and unwholsome evaporations and belchings, which so fill and oppresse the vessels and Organs of the spirits, that they are hindered in their functions; or the meat with its weight and quantity so indisposeth us, that the inordinate operation and digestion is retarded. Innumerable are the Diseases and molestations which proceed from this particular intemperance.

1 thou] thon *1655*   15 whole,] whole *1655*   28 Excess] Fxcess *1655*
30 variety] vairety *1655*

We offend in variety, when at one dinner or supper, we eate many and divers kinds of Meats and Drinkes, for these having a great dissimilitude and enmity amongst themselves, cause divers inconveniences by their various dissents and unequall digestion.

We offend in the manner of receiving, when we eate hastily, or swallow our meat before it be well chew'd and devour our Drinke like Whales, as those are accustomed who drink healths (as they term them) at Meales, taking off whole Bowles and Tankards ἀπνευστί, without so much as breathing time, and thinke the excess very fashionable & praiseworthy.   10

Another Excess in Necessaries, happens about taking of rest and watching : When the Animal spirits by too much sleep, are by degrees habituated into a certaine dulness, so that they perform their functions sluggishly, remitting still something of their due vigour, until at length they lose all their activity, and are natural-ized (as it were) into an incurable stupidity. Contrarywise by too much watching they are easily inflamed, so that oftentimes they cause Maniacal fits and phrensies, with divers others most desperate consequences.

A third excess of Necessaries, happens from cold and heat. 20 Excess of heat happens, either when the body is over exercised, or when any other Extraneous heat hath too free an access to it, and the innate fire of nature is beyond measure excited thereby, so that inordinate exhalations are caused in the body, which produce an excessive and dangerous resolution and weakness of parts. Excess of cold happens either by a suddaine Refrigeration, or cooling after Exercise, or when we expose our selves too much to cold weather, which hinders the evaporation of Excrementitious Exhalations by stopping the Pores, and beating them back into the body, where they lodge and remaine : Whence it comes to 30 pass, that being of an Extrarious malignant disposition, they afford matter and foment for many and severall kinds of diseases.

A like excess to this, proceeds frequently from the hardness and thick Callousness of some peoples skins, by which fault (because little or no perspiration is performed) the *secret*, and the *Ambient* Aire of their bodies is intercepted, so that there is no liberty for inspiration or exspiration.

8 ἀπνευστί *M* : ἀπναστῆ *1655*

Defect of Necessaries is first, the want of meat and drink in their due time and proportion. This is either famine or thirst. Secondly, The want of naturall rest, according to the Verse,

Quod caret alterna requie, durabile non est.

The strongest body, and the best
Cannot subsist, without due rest.

Thirdly, The want of Refrigeration or coolness of aire, which by its needfull community and permeation, allayes and tempers the inward heat of the heart.

10 Fourthly, and lastly, the want of due and requisite heat, by which the Excrementitious Exhalations of the body are vented forth, and the animall spirits incited to their peculiar functions.

Chap. 8.

Of Fire, the third Cause of the Extrarious Cause.

By Fire in this place, I understand not onely Kitchin-fire, or any other fire that burns, but also the celestiall fire of the Sun, and the native implanted fire of all the parts of mans body.

I.

Externall fire is the producent of Extrarious Causes by its separative 20 *power or faculty, by which it separates & extracts them from other bodies, & communicates them afterwards to our nature.*

II.

The Internal, innate fire, produceth Extrarious causes, when by digestion it separates the impure part, from that food or matter in which it first resided, whence our natural substance comes to be infected.

So the naturall heat digests our meat, and by the assistance of the innate Salt dissolves it, that man may retain or keep in his body, that which is agreeable to his nature, and joyne it to his 30 essence: but that which is contrariant, he segregates from the other, and casts forth at his proper Emunctories. This Segregated matter, or Excrement, doth oftentimes mightily afflict the body, and that it doth two manner of waies. The first by being retained in the body, or for want of evacuation. The second, by a noysome

12 animall] animal *catchword 1655*   13 CHAP. 8] CHAP. 7 *1655 and*
following chapters 8, *etc.*   16 Sun, and *G*: Sun, and the Sun and *1655*
28 innate] innnate *1655*

fetid Exhalation, and sent ascending from it to the nobler parts, when it is so retained. It offends by retention first, when it is carried (indeed) to the naturall Emunctories, or dejicient parts; but the weakness of the expulsive faculty is so great, that it cannot drive it out. Secondly, When it is left in the very stomack without farther Exclusion. Thirdly, when some subtil poyson, in and together with the nutritive portion or Chylus, doth convey and insinuate it self into the most inward parts of the body: which poyson was first taken in with meat and drink. It happens often (saith the most learned and expert *Quercetanus*) that when 10 the naturall Balsame is tainted by some impurity proceeding from food or nutriment, it doth afterwards give way and occasion for many dangerous symptomes and diseases. This *Paracelsus*, the great Father and leader of the *German* Philosophers, in his Treatise of the *Being, and nature of poyson*, doth most learnedly expound. The Stars also doe frequently powre down into the Aire, and upon the Earth, certaine Astral Emunctions, and Arsenical vapours, with other noxious Excretions and Exudations. See his Treatise of the *Being*, and the power of the Stars over inferiour Bodies. Hence proceed Distraction, Phrensies, Plurisies, the Plague, and 20 frequent, suddaine Dysenteries. Putrified things grow to be noysome and hurtfull, by the meanes of those corrosive Salts and fuliginous Exhalations, which partly by an externall, partly by their own internall heat, are excited out of them and dispersed. Moreover the Excrements of man, when they happen to be retained in the body, are subject to a Re-putrifaction, and frequently doe so, and Wormes are generated out of them: In this Case, the fuliginous, malignant spirits of that foul Masse, ascend to the braine, whence proceed suddaine madnesse, the Vertigo, the Falling-sickness, and divers other lamentable diseases. 30 There are also certaine living Creatures, which (if they be applyed to man) will by their naturall heat, suddainly indispose him, by *emission* of that which is most remote from, and inconsistent with his nature. *Cantharides* are so full of this virulency, that being onely externally applyed, they prove oftentimes pernicious. *Bartholomew Montagnana* reports, that a certain Citizen of *Padua*, applying them onely to one of his knees, did bleed at the Urinary passage, five quarts of blood. He affirms also, that the like inconvenience happened to another, who applyed them to his great Toe, to take off the Leprous scurfe of his Nayls. The 40

1 fetid *G*: f tid *1655*   3 dejicient] deijcient *1655*   15 *nature catchword 1655* : *naturn text 1655*

Basilisk hath such a subtil and violent poyson in his eyes, that his very looks infect and kill. How hurtfull Minerals are, when elevated into Mercuriall vapours, may be read at large in *Paracelsus* his books, *Von den Bergkranckheiten.*

III.

That Extrarious Causes, and divers indispositions, are introduced by common fire, none is ignorant.

Alchymists, Goldsmiths, and *Colliers,* can sufficiently prove this point, who are oftentimes so offended with vehement searching, 10 Sulphureous, Arsenical and Mercurial smoaks, that they fall into desperate and most painfull Diseases. The smoake of *Galbanum,* and *Hartshorne,* will induce the Lethargy.

Chap. 9.

Of Hereditary impurity, which is the fourth Cause of the Extrarious Cause.

I.

Hereditary *infection, is a transplantation of extrarious Causes, performed by impressing a fixt tincture, springing from another fixt salt into the prolific seed, which Parents contribute to the Genera-* 20 *tion of Children.*

Salt alone and onely, is of all the three Principles fixt and firme. Therefore those Diseases which proceed from the indisposition of the Salt, are radically fixt, and for the most part Hereditary, as the *Leprosie,* the *Stone,* the *Joynt-gout,* and the like. But those Diseases which spring from any infirmity of the fluxible and volatile principles, that is to say, from *Mercury* and *Sulphur* (as all manner of Cathars and Feavers do,) cannot so easily infect posterity: for these Diseases neither fix their seeds firmly, nor deeply, because they have not their tinctures so tenaciously imprest. The nature of this 30 kind of fixed Salt or Sulphur, may be perfectly discern'd in the seeds and the roots of Plants: for if you take but some particles of them, and transplant them, those very peeces will take root and grow, and bear fruit: But neither the leaves, nor the flowers in which the volatile Mercury & Sulphur have their seat, will do so. Now the fixed Salt is alwaies conserved in the root, and in some pithy stalks & Siens, or Graffes: but the fixed Sulphur is in the

4 *Bergkranckheiten M:* Bergfrancfheiten 1655   18 *another*] anotber 1655

seed. And this is the reason that the transplantation of all *Vegetals*, is performed by these onely : but by the Mercuriall parts, which easily fade and wither, it cannot be done ; nor by those parts, which have onely in them a volatile Sulphur, as the flowers, and the leaves of some Vegetables. See *Quercetan*, in his advice against the joynt-gout, and the stone.

Therefore (saith the same *Quercetanus*) whatever lodgeth in the body of the parents, that with a firm, spiritual, impure, and malignant tincture can affect or infect the radical Balsame, the vital seed, and the very root or fundamentall of humane nature : 10 that same impurity (whatever it be) doth by an Hereditary transplantation pass into, and infect the Children. But if these impure seeds of Diseases, have not taken such a deep root, nor so far corrupted the radicall Balsame : or if by the helpe of nature, and her internall Balsame, there is a separation made of them ; or if by the ministry of Art, and externall, specifical Balsames of Physick, they are effectually allayed and weakned, or are come to their proper terme and utmost duration, so that their virulency and force is quite spent and broken : in any of these Causes, Gouty and Leprous persons, doe not alwaies beget Gouty and 20 Leprous Children. For by these means, the roots of Diseases, even the most fixt and malignant are eradicated, impure seeds are purified, and the morbid tincture by long traduction becomes quite extinct. This Eradication of hereditary Diseases, and Purification of diseased seed comes to passe by the benefit and assistance of good *Seed-plots*, that is, by the excellent, wholesome temperament of the *Matrix*, in vegetous and healthy women : whence it happens, that the Fathers seed, though tainted with some morbific indisposition, is by the laudable vigour of the mothers radical *Balsame* amended, so that Arthritical and Calcu- 30 lous Fathers beget Children, which all their life-time continue healthy and unattempted by such Diseases. Yea, they beget such Children, as are not obnoxious or liable to such indispositions. In like manner also it happens, that a vegetous, healthy Father, contributing good seed, may have a sickly, impure issue, troubled with hereditary infirmities, the Fathers seed attracting to it the malignant propriety of those Diseases which possessed the Mother. Thus good Corne, if it be cast into a bad soile, will degenerate into Tares, or yeeld a very bad and a thin Crop: but sow it againe in good ground, and it will recover its former goodnesse 40 and perfection.

33 indispositions. *G*: indispositions *1655*

C H A P. 10.

Of Imagination, the fifth Cause of the Extrarious Cause.

I.

Imagination *is a Star, excited in the firmament of man, by some externall Object.*

II.

When the Imagination is inflamed, or at the height, then strange passions and defections follow.

III.

It is inflamed first, when it feigns some object to it selfe, and longs for it, but cannot enjoy it.

Hence it comes to passe, that pregnant or breeding women (whose imagination is most vehement, because of the Starre of the Child, which upon some singular longing, doth most powerfully move them,) doe by the force of an inflamed or exalted imagination (when they faile to come by that Object they long for) impresse into the very child, the perfect forme or figure of it ; yea, it oftentimes causeth miscarriage, and the death of the Child, as may be seen in this following History. A certaine woman great with child, seeing a Baker carrying Bread into the Oven with his Doublet off, longed for a peece of the Bakers shoulder, and when any other meat was offered unto her, or brought in to her sight, she would presently fall to vomit. Her Husband distrest betwixt love and pitty, offered such a large summe of money to the Baker, that he consented, & suffered her to bite off two morsels of his flesh, but being not able to endure the pain the third time, the woman presently fell in Labour, and was delivered of three boyes, whereof two were alive, and the third dead. *Mizaldus* in his first Century, relates it out of *Langius.* To this first Division, must be referred those unfortunate Aspirers, who affecting some great knowledge or science, and missing to attain to it, by reason of a blockish stupidity, or imbecillity of apprehension, come to be distracted and stark mad.

IV.

Secondly, The Imagination comes to be inflamed, when by some unexpected Object or Accident, a man or woman is suddainly frighted.

Such Accidents prove oftentimes very pernicious. A causeless, imaginary fear in times of infection, hath cast many into the

36 *comes to*] *comes tomes to 1655*

Plague, and the Plague hath beene their death. There lives at *Gueilburg,* a certaine Bakers wife, who being young with Child, went into the adjoyning Woods or Forrest, to gather sticks, and being very intent in gathering with her face towards the ground, a Citizen of that place comming suddainly at her, did so fright her, that (not knowing well what to doe,) she struck one hand into the other, and continued rubbing them together with a very strong compression for a good while. This woman was shortly after delivered of a Son with one hand onely, which Childe I my selfe saw, and taught there in the publick free-Schoole. In the like manner, some men that have been frighted by Phantasms, and spiritual Apparitions in the night time, have instantly fallen into grievous diseases, and some have dyed. Others by the excesse and violence of the horrour, had the hairs of their heads changed from the native colour, into a quite contrary, especially that part which they chanced to touch at the time they were so frighted. I my self have known two, who affirmed, that such a change did happen to them upon the like occasion : the one had halfe his Beard turned gray, the other had part of the haires of his head turned perfect white, the rest retaining still their first colour.

V.

Thirdly, The imagination is inflamed, when the stomack is offended by some object of sence.

Such perturbations happen often, and men are frequently inclined to vomit, when they looke earnestly upon those Ejectments which another hath cast up.

VI.

Fourthly, The imagination is inflamed, when any person imagines or fancies, that paine or trouble he is in, to be intolerable for him, and incurable.

Hence it comes to passe, that men despairing of their health or redemption, contrive their owne death, and make themselves away.

Chap. II.

Of violent Illation, which is the sixth and last cause of the extrarious Cause.

Violent Illation is performed two wayes, Corporally, and Spiritually.

12 Apparitions *G* : Apparition *1655*   34 CHAP.] CAHP. *1655*

I.

Corporally, when a man or woman is wounded, thrust, or shot, or fallen, or their bones broken.

II.

Spiritually, when by the meanes and ministry of evill spirits, a man or woman is either blinded, or maimed, or any extraneous visible matter, is invisibly and without manifest violence, conveyed into, and lodged in their bodies, or when they are by any other preternatural wayes and meanes set upon and afflicted.

10   That such things may and have been done, we shall prove by the truth of this following relation. In the year of our Lord, 1539. there lived in the village of *Fugesta*, within the Bishoprick of *Eisteter*, a certaine Husbandman, named *Ulrich Neusesser*, who was grievously pained in the Hypochondriacal Region, with most violent and sharp stitches; whose fury and persistance made him send for a Chirurgion, and (incision being made) there was found, and taken out of his side, an Iron Naile, which lay under the skin, without the least external symptome, or discoloration of the part. This notwithstanding, the pain ceased not, but was dayly 20 exasperated, and did more and more increase: whereupon this miserable man resolving with himselfe, that there could be no cure for him but death, snatched a knife out of the hand of his attendant, and did therewith cut his own throat. Upon the third day after, when his body was to be drest for buriall, there were present, *Eucherius, Rosenbader* of *Weisenburg,* and *John* of *Ettenstet,* (a Town in the Dukedome of *Bavaria,*) both Chirurgions, who in the presence of as many persons as came to the Funeral, did cut up the Body, and in the fore-part of his belly, betwixt the Cartilages and the Navill, towards the side-region there were 30 found, and taken out, and seen by them all (a prodigious and wonderfull sight!) a round and long peece of wood, foure knives of steel made partly with edges, and partly with teeth like a saw, and two peeces of sharp and rough Iron, each of them being more then a span in length, and underneath all these, a great lock of haire wrapt close together and made up in the forme of a Ball. *Mizaldus* in his sixth Century, relates this sad History out of *Langius.*

---

7 afflicted] aff i ted *1655*   19 This notwithstanding, *G*: This, notwithstanding *1655*   23 own] own own *1655*

Chap. 12.

Of the cure of Diseases.

Hitherto we have known the Disease by his Causes : It remains now that we teach the Cure of it ; and this we shall doe onely by certain generall Rules or Precepts.   But lest we should proceed without method, we shall divide this Chapter concerning the Cure, into seven Sections.

We shall teach, 1. What, and how manifold the Cure is. 2. How a Physician ought to be qualified. 3. Of what sort, kind or quality, the medicines or meanes of the Cure ought to be. 4. Out 10 of what things those Remedies must be sought and taken. 5. Why Medicines sometimes cannot restore and introduce health. 6. How the Remedies or Medicaments ought to be administred. 7. How the sick man must carry or dispose of himselfe, while he is in a course of Physick.

Section 1.

What, and how manifold the Cure is.

I.

The cure of Diseases, is an operation by which a sick person is restored to his former health, and his sicknesse (what ever it be) 20 quite expelled, and radically extirpated.

II.

The cure or healing of all Diseases, (that I may in this place make use of the most apposite, significant termes of Severinus, *out of* Crollius) *is twofold.*

1. Universal, *which is an absolute Extirpation of every radical morbid impurity, whether hereditary, or from the sinister use of food, or by the force of externall impression.*

This universall Cure is performed by a naturall medicinall Balsame, consentaneous to the nature of man, which resolves, 30 discusseth and consumes the Seminary tinctures of all impurities and diseases : but corroborates, confirms, and conserves the innate humane Balsame ; for (as *Paracelsus* teacheth) so long as the radicall humour keepes in its due quantity and proportion, no Disease or indisposition can be perceived.   And in this way of

3 Disease] Diseases *1655*   5 generall] generall *1655*

Cure, the pluralities, particularities, and orderly Rules of Symptoms and Prognosticks, have no place, for all Diseases (what ever they be) are universally & perfectly cured by this one universall medicine. It is not without reason then, that *Raymund Lullie* affirms, that this onely one, supreme, universall medicine (to which, and in which the virtues of all other particular and specificall medicines are reduced and included) may be safely administred unto all sick persons, without inquiring what Disease they are sick of. For wise nature, by an instinct from her selfe, 10 hath given unto this her favourite-medicine, the prerogative and power to cure, and absolutely to exterminate all naturall infirmities whatsoever; yea, and to rectifie and restore her own selfe, when disordered and weakned. There be four chief kinds of Diseases, which if once confirmed, or inveterate, can be expelled by no medicine, but the universall, namely the Falling-sicknesse, the Gout, the Dropsie, and the Leprosie. To these *Paramount* Diseases, all other inferiour sicknesses, as to their proper fountaines and originalls, have relation and affinity. This universall medicine, is a Jewel much to be wished for and worthy the looking after; 20 but few are they whom God blesseth with his favourite-secret. *Lullius* adviseth all Physicians, that diligently and faithfully labour for to search and looke after it : because it is the infallible remedy against all infirmities, and the greatest and most proper restorative and comforter of the spirits in their functions : For in this medicine (as in their onely and proper subject) there is a reall and universall collection and conjunction of all the operative, effectuall virtues of generall Physick, coacted and united together by a natural method, consent and design : which virtues are otherwise, (according to the ordinary course and dispensation of 30 nature) confusedly dispersed and distributed amongst and through
* *Animalls, Vege-* her * three great Families; and he that hath
tals, and Minerals. such an Antidote against all bodily Diseases, hath the gift of God, which is an incorrupt, incomparable, and invaluable treasure in this life : What ever infirmity cannot be healed by this competent, natural medicine, we may boldly and safely conclude, that the finger of the great God of nature is in the Cause. But the paine (when we find it to proceed from his righteous hand,) is by much the more tolerable, and we ought to beare it patiently, and thankfully, until the Almighty Physician 40 himselfe will be pleased to heal us, by those wayes and means which his divine and unerring wisdome shall judge the best.

3 perfectly] perfecty *1655*   8 Disease] Dis a e *1655* (?)   26 universall] universal *catchword 1655*

III.

2. Next to the universall, is the particular cure, by which the roots of diseases, and the Seminal tinctures themselves, are not alwayes taken away ; but the bitter fruits of them, the Symptoms, Paroxismes, and paines, are oftentimes prevented, mitigated, and so supprest, that they cannot come to their exaltation, or the worst passe, as the common phrase is. By this Cure, the Physicall evacuation of Excrements is instituted, and some considerable succours are communicated to opprest nature by the friendly, consentaneous spirits of those medicines that are administred ; 10 *which spirits can onely rightly know, and penetrate into the secret lodges and topicall residencies of the radicall morbific impurity.*

Now, though this particular Cure performs no more, than we have told you in the definition of it, yet is it not therefore to be slighted, nor rejected ; for it doth oftentimes in the most desperate diseases, doe the work of the universal, because the most mercifull God hath discovered unto us certain secret-natural universals, of which some containe in them the nature of the whole Heaven, others of the whole Air, and some againe of the whole earth, by whose help most Diseases are easily known and cured. 20 Moreover specifical, appropriate medicines, when they are rightly refined and spiritualized, will emulate the virtue of the universal, by consuming radical impurities & strengthning the virtue of the innate humane Balsame. Seeing then that we want the universal, it will be happy for us, if we may attaine to the true knowledge of (at least) the particular, subordinate, specifical and individual kinds and means of cures.

Section 2.

How a Physician ought to be qualified.

I.

30

Every Physician that desires to cure sick persons well and happily, must be a sound Christian, and truly religious and holy.

For true and perfect medicines, and the knowledge of them, can no where be had, but from God, whom we can serve by no other means in this life, but onely by piety, and piety hath included in it fervent and incessant supplications unto God, hearty and frequent thanksgivings for his gracious and free benefits, with sincere and actuall love towards our Neighbours. God is so infinitely good and kind, that he doth dayly give, and offer both

to the *good* and to the *bad*, all those things which are necessary
both for their *sustenance* and their *health* : but that we use those
gifts to the glory of God, and the good of our Neighbours, piety
alone is the onely cause. Therefore, if thou desirest to select,
and extract convenient and effectuall Medicines out of those
Myriads of Creatures, which by the secret power of their Creator,
dayly flow upon thee, & appear about thee, *Fear God, and love
thy Neighbour as thy selfe.* This being done, I affirm it to thee,
thou shalt find those things which will fill thee with joy. Thou
10 maist easily apprehend by what I say, that he is unworthily
permitted to be a Physician, whose practise hath no other aim
then Covetousness and Usury, and abuseth the gifts of God
(I mean his medicinal favours and discoveries,) to hoord up for
himselfe the riches of this world. They are all impostors, and
faithlesse Mountebanks, who professe Physick, and its great
ornament Chymistry, out of such a sordid, uncharitable, and
unjust design.

II.

*He must be the servant, not the Master of nature, and according to
20   the sentiment of* Hippocrates *and* Galen, *he must be a profound
Philosopher, and expert, or well vers'd in the Art of healing.*

He must be throughly seen in *Philosophy*, because there be
two sorts of Philosophers. The one (who are in truth but Philosophers by name,) after the common Doctrine of the Schooles,
inquire onely into the Elementary qualities of sublunary bodies :
but the other sort (who are the true Philosophers indeed) search
into the most secret operations, proprieties, and performances of
nature : her most private Closets, and Sanctuaries, are ever open
unto these ; whence it comes to passe, that they have a perfect
30 experimentall knowledge by the light of Nature, and are indeed
true Physicians : For the innate naturall faculty of all productions
of the earth, is, by the Chymical dexterity of these latter sort of
Philosophers, vindicated from the drossie adherencies of the
matter, and united with the firmamentall virtue, or occult quality,
which is caused and communicated to them, by the influence of
the Stars. This Art of refining, and uniting inferiours to their
superiours, makes a compleat and a successeful Physician.

III.

*He must be an Alchymist skilfull in all spagirical operations, to
40   separate the pure from the impure, the drossie and venemous parts*

8 *as thy*] *as tby 1655*

of his medicinall Ingredients, from the usefull and sanative, and one that knowes exactly how to prepare, and when to administer Chymical medicines for the restoration of his Patients.

For as Gold is seven times purified, so a Physician ought to try and refine all his Physicall Materials by the ministry of fire, which separates the good from the bad. Also he ought to have in some things, a certain and confirmed knowledge acquired by long experience, and a diligent daily inspection into the works of nature; for true Philosophy is nothing else, but a Physicall practise or triall, communicating daily to industrious and learned operators, most usefull and various conclusions and medicines. And after all the coyl of Academical licenciated Doctors, he onely is the true Physician, created so by the light of Nature, to whom Nature her selfe hath taught and manifested her proper and genuine operations by Experience.

Section 3.

Of Medicines, what their qualities should be, and how prepared.

I.

Physicall Remedies or Medicines, should both expell the disease, and strengthen nature.

Hence came that infallible Rule of Physicians, *Contraries* are cured by their *Contraries*. For *Contraries*, by the consent of all Philosophers, expell and drive out one another, therefore it is necessary, that those Medicines which take away the Disease, be repugnant and contrary to the Disease: and for the same reason, they must be auxiliaries and consentaneous to our nature. Upon which very consideration, that famous principle of the *Hermetists* is grounded: *Every like is cured by its like.* Therefore *Medicines*, as they respect, or look to the Hypostatical principles, ought also to have some correspondence with the nature of the disease, but in their Energie and effect, they must be adversant and quite opposite. Thus the stone which proceeds from *Tartar*, or coagulated Salt, is cured by Salt, but it must be Analytical or resolvent salt. The Joynt-gout also which proceeds from Tartareous, sharp and corrosive Salts, is cured by lenitive and consolidating Salts. In like manner, sulphureous Diseases must be cured by their proper and specificall sulphurs: but to inflammatory sulphur, that causeth Feavers, we must oppose acid, Vitriolated sulphur, which is a most effectuall cooler, and will coagulate and allay those incensed sulphureous spirits. Whence followes this Consequence.

That some Medicines may be corrosive, without any danger or prejudice.

But with this Caution, that they be so qualified, as not to work upon the innate, radical Balsame, but only upon that Extrarious malignant matter, which is the conjoyn'd and apparent cause of the Disease.

II.

It is requisite, that of Medicines, some be Spagyrically prepared, and some otherwise.

For Chymical remedies must not be used at all times, nor in all Causes, but onely then, when our internal natural Alchymist is insufficient of himselfe to separate the pure from the impure, and perfectly to extract out of compound Medicines, that noble Essence in which the force and virtue, or spirit of the medicament, is chiefly resident : or when there is a necessity in fixed and rooted Diseases, to use minerall remedies, that confirmed and obstinate Maladies may be set upon, and brought under by such powerfull and active Medicines that will not be baffled. It is otherwise a foolish and needlesse imployment, to separate that by Chymistry, which nature her selfe will performe with more ease and dexterity. And Nature knowes better what is most convenient for her, then any Physician : for she makes use of her own proper fire, and Magnet, which attracts both from Physick and food, that which is congeneous, and most like to her selfe : whereas an Artist on the contrary, doth not at all times use the like fire, nor exactly in the same degree to perform his operations. For which cause, the true Hermetical Physicians, do not at all times administer Minerals ; but most commonly when they exhibit Minerals, they make use also of Medicines extracted out of Vegetables, or to quicken the operation of these latter, they give a competent and safe quantity of the former.

III.

All Medicines must be specificall and appropriated to the Disease.

That is to say, they must have in them by the gift of God, such a virtue, that is peculiarly proper, and designed (as it were) to remove those diseases against which they are administred. Whether they be universally so gifted, or particularly for some one sort of disease. That body, or subject in nature, which will be easily corrupted, cannot be medicinall for all diseases : and this is the reason, that out of such bodies, the true Philosophers extract onely specifical Antidotes, whose power or virtue is effectual onely against some particular kind of disease. That thou maist have some knowledge of those materials or ingredients which are requisite and proper to make such specifical Medica- ments, thou must diligently read the Bookes of the *Hermetists,* 10 *De signaturis rerum,* That is to say, Of those impressions and Characters, which God hath communicated to, and marked (as I may say) all his Creatures with. These Bookes thou must carefully peruse, and all others which teach us the true and solid practise of Physick. But if it would please God to blesse thee with the universal Medicine, these studies, and all other cures whatsoever, might be safely pretermitted. This glorious uni- versal Medicine (without all doubt) is to be extracted out of such a subject, whose innate Balsame preserves both it *Selfe,* and the *Body* in which it exists from all corruption. This body is so 20 adequate, and temperated with such a just and even proportion of all the foure Elements, that the qualities of no one of them, can ever possibly corrupt it. If thou conceivest it may be had in another kind of subject, thou dost but play the fool and deceive thy selfe. What ever Nature hath, that she can give us; what she hath not, she neither will, nor can afford. To the wise man one word is enough. I speake out of the true light of nature : My Studies also hitherto cannot find any other *Fundamental* of an universal Medicine.

Section 4.   30

Out of what things Medicines must be sought.

I.

They must be sought. 1. Out of the Word of God. 2. Out of Nature : and in nature, out of Vegetals, Animals, and Minerals.

In this search, we must first pray for Gods assistance ; and in the next place, we must attend to the instructions of the wise Ancients. If thou couldst finde out such a thing as would purge and rectifie nature in the great world so effectually that ever after she would remaine sound and unimpaired, so that nothing of her Homogeneous essence and perfection, could be saved from her by any Extraneous fire, then (without doubt) both the way to, and the miraculous Energie of this onely true and undeceiving medicine were in thy hands.

Section 5.

Why Medicines cannot alwayes restore sick Persons to their former health.

Oswaldus Crollius, a truly learned and expert Physician, in his
10 Preface to his *Basilica Chymica*, doth most fully and judiciously handle this point. His words are these. It is observed sometimes, that sick persons by the most convenient and effectuall Medicines, cannot be healed for some one or more of these eight subsequent reasons.

The first is, because their appointed time or terme of life is come, which by no humane wit or Medicine can be prolonged. For there is no remedy upon earth, by which our corruptible bodies can be freed from death, the decreed penalty, and the wages of our sinnes : But there is one thing, which (if we add
20 holinesse to it,) will keep back and restrain corruption, renew youth, and lengthen our short life, as heretofore in the *Patriarchs.*

* The terme of life is moveable, not fixed: conditionall, not positive, as appears by that commandement, which S. Paul observed to be the first with a promise; and by many other reasons, which cannot be inserted in this place. Now though our life may be shortned and * prolonged ; yet because of the punishment for sinne, we must by the immutable decree of the eternal Law, unavoydably die : for a conjunction of different Natures, and things (suppose a Spirit and a Body) must necessarily induce a dissolution, else we should state a Pythagorical Metempsuchosis, or a revertency in
30 ages as Plato did. And in this Case the use of our universall and supreme Medicine, will prove as vaine and ineffectuall, as an old womans *Recipe*, because the Marriage of souls and bodyes, ordained by an inevitable necessity for divorcement and separation, can by no industry of Artists, nor Ayds of nature be rendred perpetuall ; for the statute Lawes of the present things, and their great Law-giver, are inviolable. It is impious therefore to seeke, and impossible to find out such a Medicine, that will carry us alive beyond those bounds, which the very Father of life will not have us to transpasse.

The second reason is, Because that sick persons are tootoo often brought to such a lamentable passe by the ignorance of unlearned Physicians, and their pernicious *Recipe's*, that the best and most virtual medicines can doe them no good, their bodies being utterly poysoned, and made immedicable by those fatal Tormentors and Executioners of mankind. In this desperate Case (most commonly) is the Chymicall Physician called upon ; but then would I have him to call to mind, that saying of *Trophilus* in *Plutarch*, which affirms that man onely to be the compleat Physician, τὰ δυνατὰ, ἔφη καὶ τὰ μὴ δυνατὰ, δυνάμενος ἀναγινω- 10 σκειν : and not to cast away (out of vaine-glory,) their soveraigne and undeserved medicines, to salve the credit of such detestable villaines, whose infamy is past cure : οὐ γὰρ μετανοεῖν, ἀλλὰ προνοεῖν χρὴ τὸν ἄνδρα τὸν σοφὸν : Let them beware also, that they suffer not their Medicaments to be mingled with the sluttish and venemous compositions of others, lest the ill consequence of such doings be laid to their charge, and the success or good event (if any comes to passe,) be arrogated by, and ascribed unto those impudent and clamorous impostors ; for such a perverse and execrable envy possesseth these Medicasters, that to disgrace those that are more 20 learned and expert than themselves, and to keep up their owne decaying repute, they will (if they can have that opportunity) cast those Patients which are curable and towards recovery, into an incurable and hopelesse condition. Hence it comes to pass, that amongst the common sort of people, (who suffer most by them) they are publiquely saluted by the most apposite Title of *Profest Poysoners.*

The third reason is, Because the Physician is called upon too late, when nature is quite mastred or orecome, and the disease hath got his full sway ; otherwise if convenient or proper medicines 30 were seasonably, (that is to say, in a time of prevention, by resisting the beginnings and first attempts of diseases) administred, no doubt but (with Gods blessing and assent) the consequence and effect would be happinesse and health.

The fourth reason is, because the sick person will not punctually observe the Physicians prescriptions : for it happens too often, that Diseased people charge the Physician or his Medicines, with those ill events which by some omission or irregularity (contrary to that golden Law of the *Locrenses* in *Ælianus*,) they have drawne upon themselves. 40

10 ἀναγινωσκειν] ἀναγινασκειν *1655*   30 medicines] medines *1655*

The fifth reason is, because the nature or peculiar propriety of some persons, are not inclinable or adapted to health, as we see some timber to be so tough and knotty, and out of a certaine natural defect, to degenerate into such an untowardnesse, that by no force or Art it can be cleft or wrought : And it happens very frequently, that the time chosen for healing, together with the indisposition of the Stars, oppose the Cure : for what ever Disease is unseasonably, that is to say, immaturely heal'd, the party will be ever after subject to a relapse, because it is the seasonablenesse
10 or fulnesse of time, that (like harvest) gives a firme and a fixed health. A ripe Pear will fall off the Tree spontaneously, but if we seeke to have it off, while it is green, we must either bruise the tree by shaking it, or with more violence break off the bough. Therefore, if these considerations be neglected, especially in the Cure of *Astral* diseases, we shall but lose our labour, and come off with prejudice. Physicians also must religiously provide, that the remedies they give, prove not worse then the Disease, therefore let them never advise their Patients to any impious course, nor consent to doe those things, which by salving the sore, destroy the
20 soule and the body too : let it be their chiefe care not to hurt, if they cannot help. By doing so, they will keep a good conscience, which is a continuall feast, but for a bad one there is no medicine.

The sixth reason is, because the disease is come to that pitch or confirmation, from whence there can be no regress by the Laws of nature, as in perfect, absolute, and confirmed bituminous, massie, sandy, and stony coagulations : for in such consummated Diseases, no medicines can availe : nor in a native deafnesse or blindness : for what nature her selfe hath once deprived us off, that cannot be restored by any Artists, no more then corporall dispro-
30 portions and birth-maimes, or transpositions can be amended.

The seventh Cause or Reason is, the sordid, tenacious parcimonie of some rich Patients, which makes the Physician (for no Money is better disbursed, nor more honestly gotten) discontented and carelesse : sometimes also the diffidence, incredulity, and suspition of Patients, (though the Physician be never so faithful and diligent,) hinders the operation of the Medicine, and is a great impediment to the Physician himself.

The eighth and last reason is, the wisdome and the goodnesse of God, who (without further toleration) takes away the Patient,
40 lest being recovered, he should commit more, and more heynous offences against his Maker, his Neighbour, and himself, to the

30 transpositions] tianspositions *1655* (?)

utter misery and perdition of his soul. For every disease is an expiatory penance, and by this divine affliction, correction and rod of judgement is the patient called upon, and required to amend his life : or else by this fatherly visitation and imposition of the Crosse, which every child of God (in imitation of his blessed Sonne) must patiently bear, he is purposely exercised to be an example of piety, submission, and perfection unto others ; for God doth oftentimes permit some particular persons to be afflicted with many and grievous Diseases, whom the cheerefulness and health of the flesh, with their dayly continuation in sins (if left without 10 rebuke,) had cast at length into some desperate spirituall malady, to the manifest hazard of their eternal welfare : for health, without holinesse, and a penitent resentment of our frequent infirmities, is no token of Gods mercy, but rather of damnation, and the portion of this life. Moreover, sinnes by weakning the forces and activities of the soule, make her impotent and unfit to govern the body ; so that the principall part being sick and unapt to rule, the bodily faculties are profusely wasted and abused, and so death is hastned on, and with it a total and a finall destruction. At least by this yoke and bridle of sicknesse, as by a wholsome kind of 20 purgatory, men will be retained in the ordinary offices of piety, and (though they be but few, who are effectually reclaimed or converted by it,) yet this detainment of their health, (which if still left to them, they had still abused,) will in some measure restrain and cut off from them, both the liberty and the power of sinning. Hitherto the most learned *Crollius.*

Thou wilt now (perhaps) object, that seeing all Diseases are not curable, it is consequently absurd, to terme any Medicine universal. I answer, That it is termed universall, not becaus it takes away all diseases at all times & in all Causes, for that it cannot do ; but 30 because it being but one, can expell and cure all those diseases, which by all other particular or specifical Medicines whatsoever can, or have been healed and eradicated ; yea, and some diseases which by no appropriated particular medicine can be healed, as the Gout, the Falling-sicknesse, the Dropsie, the Leprosie, &c. Therefore it is termed universal, because it hath in it really and effectually, all the manifest and occult virtues of all other specifical medicines, & that eminently, or by way of transcendency, so that all other medicines are subordinate and accomptable unto this.

13 of] of of *1655*   29 That it *M*: That *1655*   36 really *M*: real *1655*

Section 6.

How Medicines ought to be administred to the sick, and after what
manner the Physician must be-
have himself in their administration, and generally
in his practise.

I.

Every professor of Physick, when he is furnished with convenient,
10 *effectuall, and rightly prepared medicines, before he enters into*
practise, must be conversant with, and acquire the friendship
of some learned and well experienced Physician, whose advise and
assistance in his first attempts, he must make use of, not omitting
his own observations.

For in the multitude of Counsellours there is safety, and a more
exact judgement is given of the Patients present condition, and
the wayes and meanes to restore him are better and surer laid.
By this Course, that opprobrious *German* Proverb, which sticks
too fast to some young Adventurers, (*Ein newer Arzt, Ein newer*
20 *Kirch-hoff:* A new Physician must have a new Church-yard,)
would be easily refuted and quite abolished. This very Course
(after serious and needful considerations) I did heretofore propose
to my selfe, and to effect it throughly, I procured and entred
into mutuall and friendly Covenants with a certaine Doctor of
Physick, who was not unlearned: and that I might by this meanes
proceed farther in my Chymical discoveries, I conversed with him
by frequent Letters, and other more familiar wayes: And this I
did, because I supposed him (at that time) to be a true Philosopher, but I could never receive one line from him, that was not
30 wholly dictated by the spirit of pride and arrogancy. At length,
when it fortuned, that (after a most loving invitation, I could not
for very moving, and extraordinary reasons, attend upon him) he
rail'd at me (though altogether innocent,) with most horrid impre-
cations, and virulent language, terming me an unsanctified villaine,
and laboured by all meanes to vilifie my studies and person, that
by such clamorous and publique discouragements, he might force
me to desist, and give over my profession. But none of these
things shall move me: for God will yet give me such friends, with
whom I may freely deliberate, and advise about Physical opera-
40 tions, and the healing of the sick: too much knowledge is oftentimes foolishness. True Philosophers walk wholly in the plaine

19 *Arzt*] *Arkt 1655*   28 Philosopher] Philososopher *1655*

path of nature. What profits learning, where pride beares the
sway, and blinds the owner? I have ever judged, the modest
knowledge to be the most divine. It is true indeed, we are not
all equalls : but let him that hath more of the light, walke in that
shining path with modesty. I confesse indeed, and it is true, that
he was my superiour by many degrees, but had he beene moved to
this harsh-dealing, by a meer conceit of his superiority in learning,
perhaps he would not have cast me off so as he hath done. God
resisteth the proud, and gives grace even to the humble. Yea,
the most wise, and the blessed *JESUS,* did humble himselfe in 10
the very forme of a servant, that he might familiarly live and
converse with the most obscure and inferiour sort of people : and
he was not ashamed, nor disdained to teach those poore spirits,
not a sublunary, transient knowledge, but the glorious and permanent mysteries of the Kingdome of heaven. I love still the learning of so eminent a person because others whom I love, commend
it unto me : But that great knowledge, which he abuseth to an
injurious scorn and undervaluing of me, I heartily hate. God
Almighty (it may be) for some secret respects, which his all-
discerning spirit onely knowes, would not suffer me to impart any 20
longer, (as we were mutually bound,) my private affaires unto him.
Therefore from henceforth let him live to himselfe, onely I would
have him understand by this which is published, that his vehement and bitter Letters made me very sad. But to returne to
what we have proposed in the Contents of this Section ; A Physician that would practise successfully, must

First and before all things find out the disease, and what the cause
  of it is.

For in vain wilt thou either seek or apply remedies, if the cause
of the disease be not perfectly knowne unto thee : the beginning 30
of the Cure, is a right knowledge of the Disease : but the disease
cannot be known, without knowing the cause : For then are we
confident, that we know the matter and effect, when we have
discovered the cause or efficient of it.

II.

He must appiy and appropriate his remedies to the root and originall
  apparent cause of the disease, and not otherwise.

III.

He must administer no Medicines, whose forces or operative virtues
  in taking away the disease, he is not throughly acquainted with, 40

40 *acquainted*] *acquaintd 1655*

unlesse he be well assured that they cannot indanger nor prejudice a person that is in health: by such trials he may safely and profitably discern what his Medicines can, and what they cannot effect.

IV.

He must administer nothing that hath in it a manifest poyson, unlesse the venome be first wholly and actually separated or taken out.

V.

10 *He must before the administration of his Medicines, remove all impediments that are likely to oppose or weaken their virtues; and this must be done either by himself, or by another, viz. by a Surgeon.*

He must let blood, take away all luxations, set broken bones, &c. And afterwards apply his Medicines inwardly or outwardly, or both wayes, as need requires.

VI.

He must prescribe such a Dyet both of Meat and Drinke, as will be agreeable to his Patients present exigencie, and for the furtherance 20 *or assistance of nature, and the restoration of health.*

VII.

He must carefully observe a just Dose in all his Medicines, with respect had to their operations, and to the strength of the Patient.

VIII.

He must never administer any of his Medicines, without sanctifying them in, and with the blessed name of JESUS CHRIST. Whatsoever ye doe (saith the Apostle of the Gentiles) in word or deed, doe all in the name of the Lord JESUS, giving thankes to God and the Father by him. Colos. 3. 17.

30 ## Section. 7.

How the sick man should behave himself, while he is in a course of Physick.

I.

Let the sick person acknowledge, that he hath deserved, and drawn upon himselfe, the just anger of God by his frequent sinnes: and that it is by his righteous permission, that he is visited with sick-nesse.

II.

Let him by an unfeigned penitence, and a godly sorrow reconcile him- 40 *selfe unto God through the merits of his Saviour, putting on an*

39 *himselfe*] *him-* | *himselfe 1655*

holy resolution to become a new man ; and afterwards let him
draw near to the throne of Grace, and intreat God for mercy,
and his healing assistance.

III.

After reconciliation and invocation of the divine Aide, let him send
for the Physician, and Physick being taken, let him not doubt of
Gods mercy, and his own recovery.

That is to say, let him certainly believe that there is communicated
and infused (by the gift of God) into the medicine which he hath
taken, such an innate vertue, as is effectual and proper to expell 10
his Disease.   If he doth this, the event will be answerable to his
faith, and the Medicine will in all circumstances work successfully.
A firm credulity, chearfull hope and true love and confidence
towards the Physician, and the Medicine, (saith that great Philosopher *Oswaldus Crollius,*) conduce as much to the health of the
Patient, yea sometimes more, then either the remedy, or the
Physician.   Naturall faith (I meane not the faith of Grace which
is from Christ, but the *imaginative faith,* which in the day that
the first man was created, was then infused and planted in him
by God the Father, and is still communicated to his posterity,) is 20
so powerfull, that it can both expell and introduce Diseases : as
it manifestly appeares in times of infection, when man by his owne
private imagination, out of meere feare and horrour, generates
a *Basiliscum Cœli,* which infects the Microcosmical Firmament by
means of the Imaginants superstition, according as the Patients
faith assists, or resists.   To the faithfull all things are possible,
for faith ascertaines all those things which are uncertaine : God
can by no meanes be reach'd and injoy'd of us, but onely by
faith : whosoever therefore believes in God, he operates by the
power of God, and to God all things are possible.   But how this 30
is performed, no humane wit can find out : This onely we can
say, that faith is an operation or work not of the Believer but of
him in whom he believes.   Cogitations or thoughts, surpasse the
operations of all Elements and Stars : for while we imagine and
believe, such a thing shall come to passe, that faith brings the
worke about, and without it is nothing done.   Our faith that it
will be so, makes us imagine so : imagination excites a Star, that
Star (by conjunction with Imagination) gives the effect or perfect
operation.   To believe that there is a medicine which can cure
us, gives the spirit of Medicine : that spirit gives the knowledge 40
of it and the Medicine being known, gives health.   Hence it

appeares, that a true Physician, whose operations are natural, is born of this faith, and the spirit (I meane this spirit of nature, or star of medicine,) furthers and assists him, according to his faith. It happens oftentimes, that an illiterate man performes those cures by this imaginative faith, which the best Physicians cannot doe with the most soveraigne medicines. Sometimes also, this bare perswasion or imaginative faith heales more, and more effectually, then any virtue in the exhibited Medicine, as it was manifestly found of late years, in that famous *Panacea,* or *All-heal* 10 of *Amwaldus,* and since his time, in that new medicinall spring, which broke out this present yeare in the Confines of *Misnia* and *Bohemia,* to which an incredible number of sick persons doe daily resort. No other cause can be rendred of these *Magnalia,* or rare Physical operations, then the firme and excessive affection of the Patient ; for the power, which worketh thus, is in the Spirit of the receiver, when taking the medicine without any fear or hesitation, he is wholly possessed and inspired (as it were) with an actual desire and beliefe of health : for the rationall soule, when stirred up, and enkindled by a vehement imagination, overcomes nature, and by 20 her own effectuall affections, renewes many things in her own body or mansion, causing either health or sicknesse, and that not onely in her own body, but Extraneously, or in other bodies. The efficacy of this naturall faith, manifested it selfe in that woman with the bloody Issue, and in the Centurion. Hitherto are the words of *Crollius.*

IV.

When the Patient is delivered from his disease, and restored to his former health, let him heartily and solemnly give all the glory to the Supreme, All-mighty Physician : let him offer the sacrifice of Thankes-giving, and acknowledge the goodness and the tender 30 *mercies of the Lord. And let not the Physitian forget to performe his duty, by a thankeful and solemn acknowledgement of Gods gracious concessions, by choosing and enabling him to be his unworthy instrument to restore the sick. And this he must do, not onely because it is his duty, and a most deserved and obliged gratitude, but also out of a wise Christian caution, to avoid those judgements which are poured upon the negligent and ungratefull, by the most just jealousie of the irresistible and everlasting GOD ; unto whom alone be rendred by Angels and Men, and by all his creatures,* All Praise and Glory, and 40 perpetual thanks in this the Temporall, and in the eternall Being. *Amen.*

FINIS.

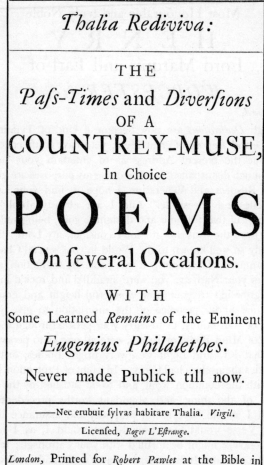

Thalia Rediviva:

THE

Pass-Times and *Diversions*

OF A

COUNTREY-MUSE,

In Choice

POEMS

On several Occasions.

WITH

Some Learned *Remains* of the Eminent

Eugenius Philalethes.

Never made Publick till now.

———Nec erubuit sylvas habitare Thalia. *Virgil.*

Licensed, *Roger L'Estrange.*

London, Printed for *Robert Pawlet* at the Bible in
Chancery-lane, near *Fleetstreet,* 1 6 7 8.

TO THE
Most Honourable and truly Noble
HENRY
Lord Marquis and Earl of
WORCESTER, &c.

My Lord,

Though *Dedications* are now become a kind of Tyranny over
the Peace and Repose of great Men; yet I have confidence I shall
so manage the present Address as to entertain your Lordship
without much disturbance; and because my purposes are govern'd
by deep Respect and Veneration, I hope to find your Lordship
more facile and accessible. And I am already absolv'd from
a great part of that fulsome and designing guilt, being sufficiently
remov'd from the causes of it: for I consider, my Lord! that you
10 are already so well known to the World in your several Characters,
and advantages of Honour; it was yours by traduction, and the
adjunct of your Nativity, you were swaddl'd and rock'd in't, bred
up and grew in't to your now wonderful height and eminence:
that for me under pretence of the inscription to give you the
heraldry of your family, or to carry your person through the fam'd
Topicks of Mind Body, or Estate, were all one as to perswade the
World that Fire and Light were very bright Bodies, or that the
Luminaries themselves had Glory. In point of Protection I beg to
fall in with the common wont, and to be satisfied by the reason-
20 ableness of the thing, and abundant worthy precedents; and
although I should have secret prophecy and assurance that the
ensuing Verse would live eternally, yet would I, as I now do,
humbly crave it might be fortifi'd with your Patronage; for so the
Sextile Aspects and Influences are watch'd for, and applied to the
actions of Life, thereby to make the Scheme and good Auguries
of the Birth pass into Fate, and a success infallible.

My Lord! By a happy obliging Intercession, and your own
consequent Indulgence, I have now recourse to your Lordship;
hopeing, I shall not much displease by putting these Twin
30 Poets into your Hands. The Minion and Vertical Planet of the
Roman Lustre and Bravery was never better pleased, than

when he had a whole Constellation about him : not his finishing
Five several Wars to the promoting of his own Interest, nor particularly the prodigious success at *Actium*, where he held in chase
the Wealth, Beauty and Prowess of the East; not the Triumphs
and absolute Dominions which followed, all this gave him not half
that serene Pride and Satisfaction of Spirit as when he retir'd
himself to umpire the different Excellencies of his insipid Friends,
and to distribute Lawrels among his Poetick Heroes : If now upon
the Authority of this, and several such Examples I had the
Ability and Opportunity of drawing the Value and strange Worth 10
of a Poet, and withall of applying some of the Lineaments to the
following pieces; I should then do my self a real Service, and
attone in a great measure for the present insolence.   But best of
all will it serve my Defence and Interest to appeal to your Lordships own conceptions and image of *Genuine* Verse; with which
so just, so regular Original, if these Copies shall hold proportion
and resemblance, then am I advanced very far in your Lordships
pardon : the rest will entirely be supplied me by your Lordships
Goodness, and my own awful Zeal of being,

My Lord!   20

Your Lordships most
obedient, most humbly
devoted Servant

J. W.

7 insipid] inward *MS. alteration in Bodleian copy*

To the Reader.

The Nation of Poets *above all Writers has ever challeng'd perpetuity of Name, or as they please by their Charter of Liberty to call it,* Immortality. *Nor has the World much disputed their claim, either easily resigning a Patrimony in it self not very substantial; or, it may be, out of despair to controule the authority of Inspiration and Oracle. Howsoever the price as now quarrell'd for among the* Poets *themselves is no such rich bargain: 'tis only a vanishing interest in the Lees and Dreggs of Time, in the Rear of those Fathers and Worthies in the Art, who if they know anything of the heats*
10 *and fury of their Successors must extreamly pity them.*

I am to assure, that the Author has no portion of that aiery happiness to lose by any injury or unkindness which may be done to his Verse: his Reputation is better built in the sentiment of several judicious Persons, who know him very well able to give himself a lasting Monument, by undertaking any Argument of note in the whole Circle of Learning.

But even these his Diversions have been valuable with the matchless Orinda, *and since they deserv'd her esteem and commendations; who so thinks them not worth the publishing, will put himself in the*
20 *opposite Scale, where his own arrogance will blow him up.*

I. W.

To Mr. Henry Vaughan *the Silurist : upon these and his former* Poems.

Had I ador'd the Multitude, and thence
Got an Antipathy to wit and sence,
And hugg'd that Fate, in hope the World would grant
'Twas *good Affection* to be Ignorant :
Yet the least Ray of thy bright fancy seen
I had converted, or excuseless been.
For each Birth of thy Muse to after-times
Shall expiate for all this Ages Crimes.
First shines thy *Amoret*, twice crown'd by thee :
Once by thy Love, next by thy Poetrie,   10
Where thou the best of Unions dost dispense
Truth cloath'd in Wit, and Love in Innocence.
So that the muddie Lover may learn here,
No Fountains can be sweet, that are not clear.
There *Juvenal*, by thee reviv'd declares
How flat man's Joys are, and how mean his Cares ;
And wisely doth upbraid the World, that they
Should such a value for their ruine pay.
 But when thy sacred Muse diverts her Quill
The Landskip to design of *Sions* Hill,   20
As nothing else was worthy her, or thee :
So we admire almost t' Idolatrie.
What savage Breast would not be rap'd to find
Such Jewels in such Cabinets enshrin'd ?
Thou fill'd with joys (too great to see or count :)
Descend'st from thence, like *Moses* from the Mount,

---

 4 be *KP*: the *1678*   13 muddie Lover] muddiest Lovers *KP*
15 by thee reviv'd] reviv'd by thee *KP* 17 wisely doth upbraid] generally
upbraids *KP 1664*: generously (gen'rously *1710*) upbraids *KP* 1667-1710
20 *Sions*] *Leon*'s *KP*

And with a candid, yet unquestion'd awe
Restor'st the Golden Age, when Verse was Law.
Instructing us, thou so secur'st thy Fame,
That nothing can disturb it, but my name.   30
Nay I have hopes, that standing so near thine
'Twill loose its dross, and by degrees refine.
Live ! till the disabused World consent
All Truths of Use, of Strength or Ornament
Are with such Harmony by thee display'd
As the whole World was first by number made ;
And from the charming rigour thy Muse brings
Learn, there's no pleasure but in serious things !

Orinda

Upon the Ingenious Poems of his Learned Friend, Mr. Henry Vaughan the Silurist.

Fairly design'd ! to charm our *Civil* Rage
With *Verse*, and plant *Bayes* in an *Iron* Age.
But hath steel'd *Mars* so ductible a Soul,
That *Love* and *Poesie* may it controule ?
Yes : brave *Tyrtæus*, as we read of old,
The *Grecian* Armies, as he pleas'd cou'd *mold* ;
They march'd to his high *Numbers*, and did fight
With that *instinct* and *rage*, which he did write.
When he fell *lower*, they would strait *retreat*,
Grow soft and calm : and temper their bold heat.   10
Such *Magick* is in *Vertue* !   See hear a young
Tyrtæus too, whose sweet persuasive Song
Can lead our *Spirits* any way, and move
To all *Adventures* : either *War* or *Love*.

Then veil the bright *Etesia*, that choice *She*,
Lest *Mars*, (*Timander's* Friend) his Rival be.
So fair a *Nymph*, drest by a *Muse* so neat,
Might warm the *North*, and thaw the frozen *Gete*.

Tho. Powel, D.D.

To the ingenious Author of Thalia Rediviva.

Ode I.

Where Reverend Bards of old have sate
And sung the pleasant enterludes of Fate,
   Thou takest the hereditary shade
   Which Natures homely Art had made,
And thence thou giv'st thy Muse her swing, and she
     Advances to the Galaxie ;
There with the sparkling *Cowley* she above
Does hand in hand in graceful Measures move.
   We groveling Mortals gaze below,
     And long in vain to know   10
   Her wondrous paths, her wondrous flight
     In vaine ; alas ! we grope,
   In vain we use our earthly Telescope,
   We'r blinded by an intermedial night :
     Thine *Eagle-Muse* can only face
     The fiery Coursers in their race,
   While with unequal paces we do try
To bear her train aloft, and keep her company.

II.

     The loud harmonious *Mantuan*
Once charm'd the world, and here's the *Uscan* Swan   20
     In his declining years does chime,
And challenges the last remains of Time.
     Ages run on, and soon give o're,
     They have their Graves as well as we,
     Time swallows all that's past and more,
Yet time is swallow'd in eternity :
This is the only profits Poets see.
There thy triumphant Muse shall ride in state
     And lead in Chains devouring Fate ;
     Claudian's bright Phœnix she shall bring   30
     Thee an immortal offering ;
   Nor shall my humble tributary Muse
   Her homage and attendance too refuse,
     She thrusts her self among the Crowd
And joyning in th' applause she strives to clap aloud.

12 vaine *GC* : raine *1678*

III.

Tell me no more that Nature is severe
    Thou great Philosopher!
Lo she has laid her vast Exchequer here.
    Tell me no more that she has sent
    So much already she is spent;   40
Here is a vast *America* behind
Which none but the great Silurist could find.
    Nature her last edition was the best,
    As big, as rich as all the rest
      So will we here admit
      Another world of Wit.
No rude or savage fancy here shall stay
    The travailing Reader in his way,
But every coast is clear: go where he will
Vertu's the road *Thalia* leads him still: 50
Long may she live, and wreath thy sacred head
For this her happy resurrection from the dead.

                    N. W. Jes. Coll. *Oxon.*

To my worthy Friend, Mr. Henry Vaughan *the Silurist.*

See what thou wert! by what Platonick round
Art thou in thy first youth and Glories found!
Or from thy Muse does this Retrieve accrue,
Do's she which once inspir'd thee, now renew!
Bringing thee back those Golden years which time
Smooth'd to thy Lays, and polisht with thy Rhyme.
Nor is't to thee alone she do's convey
Such happy change, but bountiful as day
On whatsoever Reader she do's shine
She makes him like thee, and for ever thine.   10

And first thy manual op'ning gives to see
Ecclipse and suff'rings burnish Majesty,
Where thou so artfully the draught hast made
That we best read the lustre in the shade,
And find our Sov'raign greater in that shroud:
So Lightning dazzles from its night and cloud;
So the *first Light himself* has for his Throne
Blackness, and Darkness his Pavilion.

    7 is't] i'st *1678*   11 manual] manu'al *1678*

Who can refuse thee company, or stay,
By thy next charming summons forc'd away,   20
If that be force which we can so resent
That only in its joys 'tis violent :
Upward thy *Eagle* bears us e're aware
Till above Storms and all tempestuous Air
We radiant Worlds with their bright people meet,
Leaving this little *All* beneath our feet.
But now the pleasure is too great to tell,
Nor have we other bus'ness than to dwell
As on the hallow'd Mount th' Apostles meant
To build and fix their glorious banishment.   30
Yet we must know and find thy skilful Vein
Shall gently bear us to our homes again ;
By which descent thy former flight's impli'd
To be thy extasie and not thy pride.
And here how well do's the wise *Muse* demeane
Her self, and fit her song to ev'ry Scene !
Riot of Courts, the bloody wreaths of War,
Cheats of the Mart, and clamours of the Bar,
Nay, life it self thou dost so well express
Its hollow Joyes, and real Emptiness,   40
That *Dorian* Minstrel never did excite,
Or raise for dying so much appetite.

Nor does thy other softer Magick move
Us less thy fam'd *Etesia* to love ;
Where such a *Character* thou giv'st that shame
Nor envy dare approach the Vestal Dame :
So at bright Prime *Idea's* none repine,
They safely in th' *Eternal Poet* shine.

Gladly th' *Assyrian Phœnix* now resumes
From thee this last reprizal of his Plumes ;   50
He seems another more miraculous thing
Brighter of Crest, and stronger of his Wing ;
Proof against Fate in spicy Urns to come,
Immortal past all risque of Martyrdome.

Nor be concern'd, nor fancy thou art rude
T' adventure from thy Cambrian solitude,
Best from those lofty Cliffs thy *Muse* does spring
Upwards, and boldly spreads her Cherub-wing.

      51 another] anothet *1678*

So when the *Sage* of *Memphis* would converse
With boding Skies, and th' Azure Universe,   60
He climbs his starry Pyramid, and thence
Freely sucks clean prophetique influence,
And all Serene, and rap't and gay he pries
Through the Æthereal volum's Mysteries,
Loth to come down, or ever to know more
The *Nile's* luxurious, but dull foggy shore.

                                        I. W. A.M. Oxon.

Choice P O E M S on several occasions.

To his Learned Friend and Loyal Fellow-Prisoner, Thomas Powel of Cant. Doctor of Divinity.

If sever'd Friends by *Sympathy* can joyn,
And absent *Kings* be honour'd in their *coin* ;
May they do both, who are so curb'd ! but we
Whom no such *Abstracts* torture, that can see
And pay each other a full self-return,
May laugh, though all such *Metaphysics* burn.
   'Tis a kind Soul in *Magnets*, that attones
Such two hard things as *Iron* are and *Stones*,
And in their dumb *compliance* we learn more
Of Love, than ever Books could speak before.   10
For though *attraction* hath got all the name,
As if that *power* but from one side came,
Which both unites ; yet, where there is no *sence*,
There is no *Passion*, nor *Intelligence* :
And so by consequence we cannot state
A Commerce, unless both we animate.
For senseless things, though ne'r so call'd upon,
Are deaf, and feel no Invitation ;
But such as at the last day shall be shed
By the great Lord of Life into the Dead.   20
   'Tis then no *Heresie* to end the strife
With such rare Doctrine as gives *Iron* life.
   For were it otherwise (which cannot be,
And do thou judge my bold Philosophie :)
Then it would follow that if I were dead,
Thy love, as now in life, would in that Bed
Of Earth and darkness warm me, and dispense,
Effectual informing Influence.
Since then 'tis clear, that Friendship is nought else
But a Joint, kind propension : and excess   30

The pagination of 1678 begins with the next poem

In none, but such whose equal easie hearts
Comply and meet both in their *whole* and *parts* :
And when they cannot meet, do not forget
To mingle Souls, but secretly reflect
And some third place their Center make, where they
Silently mix, and make an unseen stay :
Let me not say (though *Poets* may be bold,)
Thou art more hard than *Steel*, than *Stones* more cold,
But as the *Mary-gold* in Feasts of Dew
And early Sun-beams, though but thin and few   40
Unfolds its self, then from the Earths cold breast
Heaves gently, and salutes the hopeful *East* :
So from thy quiet *Cell*, the retir'd Throne
Of thy fair thoughts, which silently bemoan
Our sad distractions, come : and richly drest
With reverend mirth and manners, check the rest
Of loose, loath'd men ! why should I longer be
Rack't 'twixt two Ev'ls ? *I see and cannot see.*

Thalia Rediviva.

The King Disguis'd.

Written about the same time that Mr. John
Cleveland *wrote his.*

A King and no King ! Is he gone from us,
And stoln alive into his Coffin thus ?
This was to ravish Death, and so prevent
The Rebells treason and their punishment.
He would not have them damn'd, and therefore he
Himself deposed his own Majesty.
Wolves did pursue him, and to fly the Ill
He wanders (Royal Saint !) in sheep-skin still.
Poor, obscure shelter ! if that shelter be
Obscure, which harbours so much Majesty.   10
Hence prophane Eyes ! the mysterie's so deep,
Like *Esdras* books, the vulgar must not see't.

    Thou flying Roll, written with tears and woe,
Not for thy Royal self, but for thy Foe :
Thy grief is prophecy, and doth portend,
Like sad *Ezekiel's* sighs, the Rebells end.
Thy robes forc'd off, like *Samuel's* when rent,
Do figure out anothers Punishment.
Nor grieve thou hast put off thy self a while,
To serve as Prophet to this sinful Isle ;   20
These are our days of *Purim*, which oppress
The Church, and force thee to the Wilderness.
But all these Clouds cannot thy light confine,
The Sun in storms and after them, will shine.
Thy day of life cannot be yet compleat,
'Tis early sure ; thy shadow is so great.

    But I am vex'd, that we at all can guess
This change, and trust great *Charles* to such a dress.
When he was first obscur'd with this coarse thing,
He grac'd *Plebeians*, but prophan'd the King.   30
Like some fair Church, which Zeal to Charcoals burn'd,
Or his own Court now to an Ale-house turn'd.

15 portend, *G C* : portend. *1678*

But full as well may we blame Night, and chide
His wisdom, who doth light with darkness hide:
Or deny Curtains to thy Royal Bed,
As take this sacred cov'ring from thy Head.
Secrets of State are points we must not know;
This vizard is thy privy Councel now,
   Thou Royal Riddle, and in every thing
The true white Prince, our Hieroglyphic King!   40
Ride safely in his shade, who gives thee Light:
And can with blindness thy pursuers smite.
O may they wander all from thee as farr
As they from peace are, and thy self from Warr!
And wheresoe're thou do'st design to be
With thy (now spotted) spottles Majestie,
Be sure to look no Sanctuary there,
Nor hope for safety in a temple, where
Buyers and Sellers trade: O strengthen not
With too much trust the Treason of a Scot!   50

The Eagle

'Tis madness sure; And I am in the *Fitt*,
To dare an *Eagle* with my *unfledg'd* witt.
For what did ever *Rome* or *Athens* sing
In all their *Lines*, as loftie as his wing?
He that an Eagles *Powers* would rehearse
Should with his plumes first feather all his Verse.
   I know not, when into thee I would prie,
Which to admire, thy *Wing* first: or thine *Eye*;
Or whether Nature at thy birth design'd
More of her *Fire* for thee, or of her *Wind*.   10
When thou in the clear *Heights* and upmost *Air*
Do'st face the Sun, and his dispersed Hair,
Ev'n from that distance thou the *Sea* do'st spie
And sporting in its deep, wide Lap the *Frie*.
Not the least *Minoe* there, but thou can'st see;
Whole Seas are narrow spectacles to thee.
   Nor is this Element of water here
Below, of all thy miracles the sphere.

43 wander *GC*: wonder *1678*

If Poets ought may add unto thy store,
Thou hast in Heav'n of wonders many more.　　20
For when just *Jove* to Earth his thunder bends
And from that bright, eternal Fortress sends
His louder vollies : strait this Bird doth fly
To *Ætna*, where his Magazine doth lye :
And in his active Talons brings him more
Of ammunition, and recruits his store.
Nor is't a low, or easie *Lift*. He soares
'Bove *Wind* and *Fire*; gets to the *Moon*, and pores
With scorn upon her duller face; for she
Gives him but shadows and obscurity.　　30
Here much displeas'd, that any thing like night
Should meet him in his proud and loftie flight,
That such dull *Tinctures* should advance so farr,
And rival in the glories of a star :
Resolv'd he is a nobler Course to try
And measures out his voyage with his Eye.
Then with such furie he begins his flight,
As if his *Wings* contended with his sight.
Leaving the Moon, whose humble light doth trade
With *Spotts*, and deals most in the *dark* and *shade* :　　40
To the day's Royal *Planet* he doth pass
With daring Eyes, and makes the Sun his glass.
Here doth he plume and dress himself, the Beams
Rushing upon him, like so many Streams ;
While with direct looks he doth entertain
The thronging flames, and shoots them back again.
And thus from star to star he doth repaire
And wantons in that pure and peaceful air.
Sometimes he frights the starrie *Swan*, and now
Orion's fearful *Hare* and then the Crow.　　50
Then with the *Orbe* it self he moves, to see
Which is more swift th' *Intelligence* or *He*.
Thus with his wings his body he hath brought
Where man can travell only in a thought.
　I will not seek, rare bird, what *Spirit* 'tis
That mounts thee thus ; I'le be content with this ;
To think, that Nature made thee to express
Our souls bold *Heights* in a material dress.

To Mr. M. L. *upon his reduction of the* Psalms *into Method.*

SIR,

You have oblig'd the *Patriarch.*   And tis known
He is your Debtor now, though for his own.
What he wrote, is a *Medley.*   We can see
Confusion trespass on his Piety.
Misfortunes did not only Strike at him ;
They charged further, and oppress'd his pen.
For he wrote as his *Crosses* came, and went
By no safe *Rule,* but by his *Punishment.*
His *quill* mov'd by the *Rod* ; his witts and he   10
Did know no *Method,* but their *Misery.*
    You brought his *Psalms* now into *Tune.*   Nay, all
His measures thus are more than musical.
Your *Method* and his *Aires* are justly sweet,
And (what's *Church-musick* right) like *Anthems* meet.
You did so much in this, that I believe
He gave the *Matter,* you the *form* did give.
And yet I wish you were not understood,
For now *'tis a misfortune to be good* !
    Why then, you'l say, all I would have, is this ;   20
None must be good, because the time's amiss.
For since wise Nature did ordain the *Night,*
I would not have the *Sun* to give us Light.
Whereas this doth not take the *Use* away :
But urgeth the *Necessity* of day.
Proceed to make your pious work as free,
Stop not your seasonable charity.
Good works despis'd, or censur'd by bad times,
Should be sent out to aggravate their Crimes.
They should first *Share* and then *Reject* our store :   30
Abuse our *Good,* to make their *Guilt* the more.
'Tis *Warr* strikes at our *Sins,* but it must be
A *Persecution* wounds our *Pietie.*

To the pious memorie of C. W. Esquire *who finished his Course here, and made his Entrance into Immortality upon the* 13 *of* September, *in the year of* Redemption 1653.

Now, that the publick Sorrow doth subside,
And those slight tears which *Custom* Springs, are dried ;
While all the rich & *out-side-Mourners* pass
Home from thy *Dust* to empty their own *Glass* :
I (who the throng affect not, nor their state :)
Steal to thy grave undress'd, to meditate
On our sad loss, accompanied by none,
An obscure mourner that would weep alone.
  So when the world's great Luminary setts,
Some scarce known Star into the *Zenith* gets,   10
Twinkles and curls a weak but willing spark :
As Gloworms here do glitter in the dark.
Yet, since the dimmest flame that kindles there,
An humble love unto the light doth bear,
And true devotion from an Hermits Cell
Will Heav'ns kind King as soon reach and as well
As that which from rich Shrines and Altars flyes
Lead by ascending Incense to the Skies :
'Tis no malicious rudeness, if the might
Of love makes dark things wait upon the bright,   20
And from my sad retirements calls me forth
The Just Recorder of thy death and worth.
  Long did'st thou live (if length be measured by
The tedious Reign of our Calamity :)
And Counter to all storms and changes still
Kept'st the same temper, and the self same will.
Though trials came as duly as the day,
And in such mists, that none could see his way :
Yet thee I found still virtuous, and saw
The Sun give Clouds : and *Charles* give both the Law.   30
When private Interest did all hearts bend
And wild dissents the public peace did rend :
Thou neither won, nor worn wer't still thy self ;
Not aw'd by force, nor basely brib'd with pelf.
  What the insuperable stream of times
Did dash thee with, those *Suff'rings* were, not *Crimes.*

So the bright *Sun* Ecclipses bears ; and we
Because then passive, blame him not, should he
For inforc'd shades, and the *Moon's* ruder veile
Much nearer us, than him ; be Judg'd to fail?   40
Who traduce thee, so erre.   As poisons by
Correction are made Antidotes, so thy
Just Soul did turn ev'n hurtful things to Good ;
Us'd bad Laws so, they drew not Tears, nor Blood.
Heav'n was thy Aime, and thy great rare Design
Was not to Lord it here, but there to shine.
Earth nothing had, could tempt thee.   All that e're
Thou pray'dst for here, was *Peace* ; and *Glory* there.
For though thy Course in times long progress fell
On a sad age, when Warr and open'd Hell   50
Licens'd all Artes and Sects, and made it free
To thrive by fraud and blood and blasphemy :
Yet thou thy just Inheritance did'st by
No sacrilege, nor pillage multiply ;
No rapine swell'd thy state : no bribes, nor fees
Our new oppressors best Annuities.
Such clean, pure hands had'st thou !   And for thy heart
Man's secret region and his noblest part ;
Since I was privy to't, and had the Key
Of that faire Room, where thy bright Spirit lay :   60
I must affirm, it did as much surpass
Most I have known, as the clear Sky doth glass.
Constant and kind, and plain and meek and Mild
It was, and with no new Conceits defil'd.
Busie, but sacred thoughts (like *Bees*) did still
Within it stirr, and strive unto that Hill,
Where redeem'd Spirits evermore alive
After their Work is done, ascend and *Hive*.
No outward tumults reach'd this inward place,
'Twas holy ground : where peace, and love and grace   70
Kept house : where the immortal restles life
In a most dutiful and pious strife
Like a fix'd *watch*, mov'd all in order, still ;
The *Will* serv'd God, and ev'ry *Sense* the Will !
   In this safe state death mett thee.   Death which is
But a kind Usher of the good to bliss.

41 thee, so] thee so, *GC*   53 did'st] di'dst *1678*

Therefore to Weep because thy Course is run,
Or droop like Flow'rs, which lately lost the *Sun* :
I cannot yield, since faith will not permitt,
A *Tenure* got by *Conquest* to the *Pitt.*   80
For the great Victour fought for us, and Hee
Counts ev'ry dust, that is lay'd up of thee.
Besides, Death now grows decrepit and hath
Spent the most part both of its time and wrath.
That thick, black night which mankind fear'd, is torn
By *Troops* of Stars, and the bright day's *Forlorn.*
The next glad news (most glad unto the Just !)
Will be the Trumpet's summons from the dust.
Then Ile not grieve ; nay more, I'le not allow
My Soul should think thee absent from me now.   90
Some bid their Dead *good night !* but I will say
Good morrow to dear Charles ! for it is day.

In Zodiacum Marcelli Palingenii.

It is perform'd ! and thy great *Name* doth run
Through ev'ry *Sign* an everlasting *Sun.*
Not Planet-like, but *fix'd* ; and we can see
Thy *Genius* stand still in his *Apogie.*
For how canst thou an *Aux* eternal miss,
Where ev'ry *House* thine *Exaltation* is ?
Here's no *Ecclyptic* threatens thee with night,
Although the wiser few take in thy light.
They are not at that glorious *pitch*, to be
In a *Conjunction* with *Divinitie.*   10
Could we partake some oblique *Ray* of thine,
Salute thee in a *Sextile*, or a *Trine*,
It were enough ; but thou art flown so high,
The *Telescope* is turn'd a Common Eye.
Had the grave *Chaldee* liv'd thy Book to see,
He had known no *Astrologie*, but thee ;
Nay more, (for I believ't,) thou shouldst have been
Tutor to all his Planets, and to him.
Thus whosoever reads thee, his charm'd sense
Proves captive to thy *Zodiac's* influence.   20
Were it not foul to erre so, I should look
Here for the *Rabbins* universal Book :

And say, their fancies did but dream of thee,
When first they doted on that mystery.
Each line's a *via lactea*, where we may
See thy fair steps, and tread that happy way
Thy *Genius* lead thee in.   Still I will be
Lodg'd in some *Sign*, some *Face* and some *Degree*
Of thy bright *Zodiac*,   Thus I'le teach my *Sense*
To move by that, and thee th' *Intelligence*.   30

To Lysimachus, *the Author being with him in* London.

Saw not, *Lysimachus*, last day, when wee
Took the pure Air in its simplicity,
And our own too : how the trim'd *Gallants* went
Cringing, & past each step some Complement?
What strange, phantastic *Diagrams* they drew
With Legs and Arms ; the like we never knew
In *Euclid, Archimed* : nor all of those
Whose learned lines are neither Verse nor Prose?
What store of *Lace* was there? how did the *Gold*
Run in rich *Traces*, but withall made bold   10
To measure the proud *things*, and so deride
The *Fops* with that, which was part of their pride?
How did they point at us, and boldly call,
As if we had been Vassals to them all,
Their poor *Men-mules* sent thither by hard fate
To yoke our selves for their *Sedans* and State?
Of all ambitions, this was not the least,
Whose drift translated man into a beast.
What blind discourse the *Heroes* did afford?
This *Lady* was their Friend, and such a *Lord*.   20
How much of *Blood* was in it? one could tell
He came from *Bevis* and his *Arundel* ;
Morglay was yet with him, and he could do
More feats with it, than his old Grandsire too.
   Wonders my Friend at this? what is't to thee,
Who canst produce a nobler Pedigree,
And in meer truth affirm thy Soul of kin
To some bright *Star*, or to a *Cherubin?*
When these in their profuse *moods* spend the night
With the same sins, they drive away the light,   30

Thy learned *thrift* puts her to use ; while she
Reveals her firy Volume unto thee ;
And looking on the separated skies
And their clear Lamps with careful thoughts & eyes
Thou break'st through Natures upmost rooms & bars
To Heav'n, and there conversest with the Stars.

    Well fare such harmless, happy *nights* that be
Obscur'd with nothing but their *privacie* :
And missing but the false world's *glories,* do
Miss all those *vices,* which attend them too !   40
Fret not to hear their ill-got, ill-giv'n praise ;
Thy darkest nights outshine their brightest dayes.

On Sir Thomas Bodley's *Library ; the Author being then in* Oxford.

Boast not proud *Golgotha* : that thou can'st show
The ruines of mankind, and let us know
How fraile a thing is flesh ! though we see there
But empty Skulls, the *Rabbins* still live here.
They are not dead, but full of *Blood* again,
I mean the *Sense,* and ev'ry *Line* a *Vein.*
Triumph not o're their Dust ; whoever looks
In here, shall find their *Brains* all in their Books.

    Nor is't old *Palestine* alone survives,
Athens lives here, more than in *Plutarch's* lives.   10
The stones which sometimes danc'd unto the strain
Of *Orpheus,* here do lodge his muse again.
And you the *Roman* Spirits, learning has
Made your lives longer, than your Empire was.
Cæsar had perish'd from the World of men,
Had not his *Sword* been rescu'd by his *pen.*
Rare *Seneca* ! how lasting is thy breath ?
Though *Nero* did, thou could'st not bleed to Death.
How dull the expert Tyrant was, to look
For that in thee, which lived in thy Book ?   20
Afflictions turn our *Blood* to *Ink,* and we
Commence when *Writing,* our *Eternity.*
Lucilius here I can behold, and see
His *Counsels* and his *Life* proceed from thee.
But what care I to whom thy *Letters* be ?
I change the *Name,* and thou do'st write to me ;

And in this Age, as sad almost as thine,
Thy stately *Consolations* are mine.
Poor Earth ! what though thy viler dust enrouls
The frail Inclosures of these mighty Souls ?   30
Their graves are all upon Record ; not one
But is as bright, and open as the Sun.
And though some part of them obscurely fell
And perish'd in an unknown, private Cell :
Yet in their books they found a glorious way
To live unto the Resurrection-day.
    Most noble *Bodley* ! we are bound to thee
For no small part of our *Eternity*.
Thy treasure was not spent on *Horse* and *Hound*,
Nor that new Mode, which doth old *States* confound.   40
Thy legacies another way did go :
Nor were they left to those would spend them so.
Thy safe, discreet Expence on us did flow ;
Walsam is in the mid'st of *Oxford* now.
Th' hast made us all thine *Heirs* : whatever we
Hereafter write, 'tis thy *Posterity*.
This is thy *Monument* ! here thou shalt stand
Till the times fail in their last grain of Sand.
And wheresoe're thy silent *Reliques* keep,
This *Tomb* will never let thine honour sleep.   50
Still we shall think upon thee ; all our fame
Meets here to speak one *Letter* of thy name.
Thou can'st not dye ! here thou art more than safe
Where every *Book* is thy large *Epitaph*.

The importunate Fortune, written to Doctor Powel *of* Cantre.

For shame desist, why should'st thou seek my fall ?
It cannot make thee more Monarchical.
Leave off ; thy Empire is already built ;
To ruine me were to inlarge thy guilt,
Not thy Prerogative.   I am not he
Must be the measure to thy victory.
The Fates hatch more for thee ; 'twere a disgrace
If in thy Annals I should make a Clause.

28 Consolations are] *Bodleian copy inserts* (*MS*) all *between these two words*

The future Ages will disclose such men,
Shall be the glory, and the end of them.   10
Nor do I flatter. So long as there be
Descents in Nature, or Posterity,
There must be Fortunes ; whether they be good,
As swimming in thy Tide and plenteous Flood,
Or stuck fast in the shallow Ebb, when we
Miss to deserve thy gorgeous charity.
Thus, Fortune, the great World thy period is ;
Nature and you are *Parallels* in this.
   But thou wilt urge me still. Away, be gone ;
I am resolv'd, I will not be undone.   20
I scorn thy trash and thee: nay more, I do
Despise my self, because thy Subject too.
Name me Heir to thy malice, and I'le be ;
Thy hate's the best Inheritance for me.
I care not for your wondrous *Hat* and *Purse* :
Make me a *Fortunatus* with thy Curse.
How careful of my self then should I be,
Were I neglected by the world and thee ?
Why do'st thou tempt me with thy dirty Ore,
And with thy Riches make my Soul so poor ?   30
My Fancy's pris'ner to thy Gold and thee,
Thy favours rob me of my liberty.
I'le to my Speculations. Is't best
To be confin'd to some dark narrow chest
And Idolize thy Stamps, when I may be
Lord of all Nature, and not slave to thee ?
The world's my Palace. I'le contemplate there,
And make my progress into ev'ry Sphere.
The Chambers of the *Air* are mine ; those three
Well furnish'd *Stories* my possession be.   40
I hold them all *in Capite*, and stand
Propt by my Fancy there. I scorn your Land,
It lies so far below me. Here I see
How all the Sacred Stars do circle me.
Thou to the *Great* giv'st rich Food, and I do
Want no Content ; I feed on *Manna* too.
They have their *Tapers* ; I gaze without fear
On flying *Lamps*, and flaming *Comets* here.
Their wanton flesh in *Silks* and *Purple* Shrouds,
And Fancy wraps me in a *Robe* of *Clouds*.   50

There some delicious beauty they may woo,
And I have *Nature* for my Mistris too.
    But these are mean ; the *Archtype* I can see,
And humbly touch the *hem* of Majestie.
The power of my Soul is such, I can
Expire, and so *analyse* all that's man.
First my dull Clay I give unto the *Earth*,
Our common Mother, which gives all their birth.
My growing Faculties I send as soon
Whence first I took them, to the humid *Moon*.   60
All Subtilties and every cunning Art
To witty *Mercury* I do impart.
Those fond Affections which made me a slave
To handsome Faces, *Venus* thou shalt have.
And saucy Pride (if there was ought in me,)
Sol, I return it to thy Royalty.
My daring Rashness and Presumptions be
To *Mars* himself an equal Legacy.
My ill-plac'd Avarice (sure 'tis but small ;)
Jove, to thy Flames I do bequeath it all.   70
And my false *Magic,* which I did believe,
And mystic Lyes to *Saturn* I do give.
My dark Imaginations rest you there,
This is your grave and Superstitious Sphære.
    Get up my disintangled Soul, thy fire
Is now refin'd & nothing left to tire,
Or clog thy wings.   Now my auspicious flight
Hath brought me to the *Empyrean* light.
I am a sep'rate *Essence*, and can see
The *Emanations* of the Deitie,   80
And how they pass the *Seraphims*, and run
Through ev'ry *Throne* and *Domination*.
So rushing through the Guard, the Sacred streams
Flow to the neighbour Stars, and in their beams
(A glorious Cataract !) descend to Earth
And give Impressions unto ev'ry birth.
With Angels now and Spirits I do dwell.
And here it is my Nature to do well,
Thus, though my Body you confined see,
My boundless thoughts have their *Ubiquitie*.   90

87, 88 dwell. . . . well,] dwell, . . . well. *GC*

And shall I then forsake the *Stars* and *Signs*
To dote upon thy dark and cursed *Mines*?
Unhappy, sad exchange! what, must I buy
Guiana with the loss of all the skie?
Intelligences shall I leave, and be
Familiar only with mortalitie?
Must I know nought, but thy Exchequer? shall
My purse and fancy be Symmetrical?
Are there no Objects left but one? must we
In gaining that, lose our Varietie?   100
    Fortune, this is the reason I refuse
Thy Wealth; it puts my Books all out of use.
'Tis poverty that makes me wise; my mind
Is big with speculation, when I find
My purse as *Randolph's* was, and I confess
There is no Blessing to an Emptiness!   -
The *Species* of all things to me resort
And dwell then in my breast, as in their port.
Then leave to Court me with thy hated store,
Thou giv'st me that, to rob my Soul of more.   110

To I. Morgan *of* White-Hall Esq; *upon his sudden Journey and succeeding Marriage.*

So from our cold, rude World, which all things tires
To his warm *Indies* the bright sun retires.
Where in those provinces of Gold and spice
Perfumes his progress: *pleasures* fill his Eyes.
Which so refresh'd in their return convey
Fire into *Rubies*, into *Chrystalls* day;
And prove, that *Light* in kinder Climates can
Work more on senseless *Stones*, than here on *man*.
    But you, like one ordain'd to shine, take in
Both *Light* and *Heat*: can *Love* and *Wisdom* spin   10
Into one thred, and with that firmly tye
The same bright Blessings on posterity;
Which so intail'd, like *Jewels* of the Crown,
Shall with your *Name* descend still to your own.
    When I am dead, and malice or neglect
The worst they can upon my dust reflect,
(For *Poets* yet have left no names, but such
As men have *envied*, or *despis'd* too much;)

You above both (and what *state* more excells
Since a just Fame like *Health,* nor *wants,* nor *swells?*)   20
To after ages shall remain Entire,
And shine still spottles, like your planets Fire.
No single lustre neither ; the access
Of your fair *Love* will yours adorn and bless ;
Till from that bright *Conjunction,* men may view
A *Constellation* circling her and you :
   So two sweet *Rose-buds* from their *Virgin-beds*
First peep and blush, then kiss and couple heads ;
Till yearly blessings so increase their store
Those two can number two and twenty more,   30
And the fair *Bank* (by heav'ns free bounty Crown'd)
With choice of *Sweets* and *Beauties* doth abound ;
Till time, which *Familys* like *Flowers* far spreads ;
Gives them for *Garlands* to the best of heads.
Then late posterity (if chance, or some
Weak *Eccho,* almost quite expir'd and dumb
Shall tell them, who the *Poet* was, and how
He liv'd and lov'd thee too ; which thou do'st know)
Strait to my grave will *Flowers* and *spices* bring
With *Lights* and *Hymns,* and for an *Offering*   40
There vow this truth ; That *Love* (which in old times
Was censur'd *blind,* and will contract worse Crimes
If hearts mend not ;) did for thy sake in me
Find both his *Eyes,* and all foretell and see.

FIDA : *Or The Country-beauty* : *to* Lysimachus.

Now I have seen her ; And by *Cupid*
The young *Medusa* made me stupid !
A face, that hath no Lovers slain,
Wants forces, and is near disdain.
For every *Fop* will freely peep
At Majesty that is asleep.
But she (fair Tyrant !) hates to be
Gaz'd on with such impunity.
Whose prudent Rigor bravely bears
And scorns the trick of whining tears :   10

43 not ;)] not; *1678*   3 slain *GC* : stain *1678*

Or sighs, those false All-arms of grief,
Which kill not, but afford relief.
Nor is it thy hard fate to be
Alone in this Calamity,
Since I who came but to be gone,
Am plagu'd for meerly looking on.

    Mark from her forhead to her foot
What charming *Sweets* are there to do't.
A *Head* adorn'd with all those glories
That *Witt* hath shadow'd in quaint stories :   20
Or *pencill* with rich colours drew
In imitation of the true.

    Her *Hair* lay'd out in curious *Setts*
And *Twists*, doth shew like silken *Nets*,
Where (since he play'd at *Hitt* or *Miss* :)
The God of *Love* her pris'ner is,
And fluttering with his skittish Wings
Puts all her locks in Curls and Rings.

    Like twinkling Stars her *Eyes* invite
All gazers to so sweet a light,   30
But then two *arched Clouds* of brown
Stand o're, and guard them with a frown.

    Beneath these rayes of her bright Eyes
Beautie's rich *Bed* of *blushes* lyes.
Blushes, which lightning-like come on,
Yet stay not to be gaz'd upon ;
But leave the *Lilies* of her Skin
As fair as ever, and run in :
Like swift *Salutes* (which dull *paint* scorn,)
Twixt a *white* noon, and *Crimson* Morne.   40

    What *Corall* can her *Lips* resemble ?
For hers are warm, swell, melt and tremble :
And if you dare contend for *Red*,
This is *alive*, the other *dead*.

    Her equal *Teeth* (above, below :)
All of a *Cise*, and *Smoothness* grow.
Where under close restraint and awe
(Which is the Maiden, Tyrant law :)
Like a cag'd, sullen *Linnet*, dwells
Her *Tongue*, the *Key* to potent spells.   50

49 dwells] dwells. *1678*

Her *Skin*, like heav'n when calm and bright,
Shews a rich *azure* under *white*,
With *touch* more soft than heart supposes,
And *Breath* as sweet as new blown *Roses*.

Betwixt this *Head-land* and the *Main*,
Which is a rich and flowry *Plain* :
Lyes her fair *Neck*, so fine and slender
That (gently) how you please, 'twill bend her.

This leads you to her *Heart*, which ta'ne
Pants under *Sheets* of whitest *Lawn*,   60
And at the first seems much distrest,
But nobly treated, lyes at rest.

Here like two *Balls* of new fall'n snow,
Her *Breasts*, Loves native *pillows* grow ;
And out of each a *Rose-bud* Peeps
Which *Infant* beauty sucking, sleeps.

Say now my *Stoic*, that mak'st soure faces
At all the *Beauties* and the *Graces*,
That criest *unclean !* though known thy self
To ev'ry coorse, and dirty shelfe :   70
Could'st thou but see a *piece* like this,
A piece so full of *Sweets* and *bliss* :
In *shape* so rare, in *Soul* so rich,
Would'st thou not swear she is a witch ?

Fida forsaken.

Fool that I was ! to believe blood
While swoll'n with greatness, then most good ;
And the false thing, forgetful man :
To trust more than our true God, *Pan*,
Such swellings to a dropsie tend,
And meanest things such great ones bend.

Then live deceived ! and *Fida* by
That life destroy fidelity.
For living wrongs will make some wise,
While death chokes lowdest Injuries :   10
And skreens the *faulty*, making Blinds
To hide the most unworthy minds.

And yet do what thou can'st to hide
A bad trees fruit will be describ'd.
For that foul guilt which first took place
In his dark heart, now damns his face:
And makes those Eyes, where life should dwell,
Look like the pits of Death and Hell.

Bloud, whose rich *purple* shews and seals
Their faith in *Moors*, in him reveals   20
A blackness at the heart, and is
Turn'd *Inke*, to write his faithlesness.
Only his lips with bloud look *red*,
As if asham'd of what they sed.

Then, since he wears in a dark skin
The shadows of his hell within,
Expose him no more to the light,
But thine own *Epitaph* thus write.
Here burst, and dead and unregarded
Lyes Fida's *heart! O well rewarded!*   30

To the Editor of the matchless Orinda.

Long since great witts have left the Stage
Unto the *Drollers* of the age,
And noble numbers with good sense
Are like good works, grown an offence.
While much of verse (worse than old story,)
Speaks but *Jack-Pudding*, or *John-Dory*.
Such trash-admirers made us poor,
And *Pyes* turn'd *Poets* out of door.
For the nice Spirit of rich verse
Which scorns absurd and low commerce,   10
Although a flame from heav'n, if shed
On *Rooks* or *Daws*: warms no such head.
Or else the Poet, like bad priest,
Is seldom good, but when opprest:
And wit, as well as piety
Doth thrive best in adversity;
For since the thunder left our air
Their *Laurels* look not half so fair.
However 'tis 'twere worse than rude
Not to profess our gratitude   20

And debts to thee, who at so low
An Ebbe do'st make us thus to flow:
And when we did a Famine fear,
Hast blest us with a fruitful year.
So while the world his absence mourns
The glorious Sun at last returns,
And with his kind and vital looks
Warms the cold Earth and frozen brooks:
Puts drowsie nature into play
And rids impediments away,   30
Till Flow'rs and Fruits and spices through
Her pregnant lap get up and grow.
But if among those sweet things, we
A miracle like that could see
Which nature brought but once to pass:
A *Muse*, such as *Orinda* was,
Phœbus himself won by these charms
Would give her up into thy arms;
And recondemn'd to kiss his *Tree*,
Yield the young *Goddess* unto thee.   40

Upon sudden news of the much lamented death of *Judge* Trevers.

Learning and *Law* your *Day* is done,
And your *work* too; you may be gone!
Trever, that lov'd you, hence is fled:
And *Right*, which long lay *Sick*, is *dead*.
Trever! whose rare and envied *part*
Was both a wise and winning heart,
Whose sweet civilitys could move
Tartars and *Goths* to noblest love.
      Bold *Vice* and *blindness* now dare act,
And (like the *gray groat*,) pass, though crack't;   10
While those sage lips lye dumb and cold,
Whose words are well-weigh'd and tried gold.
O how much to descreet desires
Differs pure *Light* from foolish *fires*!
But nasty *Dregs* out last the *Wine*,
And after Sun-set *Gloworms* shine.

4 *Sick*,] *Sick* 1678 (?)

To Etesia (*for* Timander,) *the first Sight.*

What smiling *Star* in that fair Night,
Which gave you *Birth* gave me this *Sight*,
And with a kind *Aspect* tho keen
Made me the *Subject*: you the *Queen*?
That sparkling *Planet* is got now
Into your Eyes, and shines below;
Where nearer force, and more acute
It doth dispence, without dispute,
For I who yesterday did know
Loves fire no more, than doth cool Snow   10
With one bright look am since undone;
Yet must adore and seek my Sun.
    Before I walk'd free as the wind,
And if but stay'd (like it,) unkind.
I could like daring Eagles gaze
And not be blinded by a face;
For what I saw, till I saw thee,
Was only not deformity.
Such shapes appear (compar'd with thine,)
In *Arras*, or a tavern-sign,   20
And do but mind me to explore
A fairer piece, that is in store.
So some hang *Ivy* to their Wine,
To signify, there is a *Vine*.
    Those princely Flow'rs (by no storms vex'd,)
Which smile one day, and droop the next:
The gallant *Tulip* and the *Rose*,
Emblems which some use to disclose
Bodyed *Idea's*: their weak grace
Is meer imposture to thy face.   30
For nature in all things, but thee,
Did practise only *Sophistry*;
Or else she made them to express
How she could vary in her dress:
But thou wert form'd, that we might see
Perfection, not Variety.
    Have you observ'd how the Day-star
Sparkles and smiles and shines from far:
Then to the gazer doth convey
A silent, but a piercing Ray?   40

So wounds my love, but that her Eys
Are in *Effects*, the better Skys.
A brisk bright *Agent* from them Streams
Arm'd with no arrows, but their beams,
And with such stillness smites our hearts,
No noise betrays him, nor his darts.
He working on my easie Soul
Did soon persuade, and then controul;
And now he flyes (and I conspire)
Through all my blood with wings of fire,   50
And when I would (which will be never)
With cold despair allay the fever:
The spiteful thing *Etesia* names,
And that new-fuells all my flames.

The Character, *to* Etesia

Go catch the *Phœnix*, and then bring
A *quill* drawn for me from his wing.
Give me a Maiden-beautie's *Bloud*,
A pure, rich *Crimson*, without mudd:
In whose sweet *Blushes* that may live,
Which a dull verse can never give.
Now for an untouch'd, spottles *white*,
For blackest things on paper write;
Etesia at thine own Expence
Give me the *Robes* of innocence.   10
    Could we but see a *Spring* to run
Pure *Milk*, as sometimes Springs have done,
And in the *Snow-white* streams it sheds
Carnations wash their *bloudy* heads.
While ev'ry *Eddy* that came down
Did (as thou do'st,) both *smile* and *frown*.
Such objects and so fresh would be
But dull Resemblances of thee.
    Thou art the dark worlds Morning-star,
Seen only, and seen but from far;   20
Where like Astronomers we gaze
Upon the glories of thy face,
But no acquaintance more can have,
Though all our lives we watch and Crave.
Thou art a world thy self alone,
Yea three great worlds refin'd to one.

Which shews all those, and in thine Eyes
The shining *East*, and *Paradise*.
 Thy Soul (a *Spark* of the first *Fire*,)
Is like the *Sun*, the worlds desire ;   30
And with a nobler influence
Works upon all, that claim to sense ;
But in *Summers* hath no *fever*,
And in frosts is chearful ever.
 As *Flowr's*, besides their curious *dress*
Rich *odours* have, and *Sweetnesses*.
Which tacitely infuse desire
And ev'n oblige us to admire :
Such and so full of innocence
Are all the *Charms*, thou do'st dispence ;   40
And like fair *Nature*, without *Arts*
At once they seize, and please our hearts.
O thou art such, that I could be
A lover to Idolatry !
I could, and should from heav'n stray,
But that thy life shews mine the way,
And leave a while the *Diety*,
To serve his *Image* here in thee.

To Etesia *looking from her Casement at the full* Moon.

See you that beauteous *Queen*, which no age tames ?
Her Train is *Azure*, set with *golden* flames.
My brighter *fair*, fix on the *East* your Eyes,
And view that bed of Clouds, whence she doth rise.
Above all others in that one short hour
Which most concern'd me, she had greatest pow'r.
This made my *Fortunes* humorous as wind,
But fix'd *Affections* to my constant mind.
She fed me with the *tears* of *Starrs*, and thence
I suck'd in *Sorrows* with their *Influence*.   10
To some in *smiles*, and store of *light* she broke :
To me in sad *Eclipses* still she spoke.
She bent me with the motion of her *Sphere*,
And made me feel, what first I did but fear.
 But when I came to Age, and had o'regrown
Her Rules, and saw my freedom was my own,

6 me C : in 1678

I did reply unto the Laws of Fate,
And made my Reason, my great Advocate:
I labour'd to inherit my just right;
But then (O hear *Etesia* !) lest I might   20
Redeem my self, my unkind Starry Mother
Took my poor Heart, and gave it to another.

To Etesia *parted from him, and looking back.*

O Subtile Love ! thy Peace is War;
It wounds and kills without a scar:
It works unknown to any sense,
Like the Decrees of Providence,
And with strange silence shoots me through;
The *Fire* of Love doth fall like *Snow*.
   Hath she no *Quiver*, but my Heart?
Must all her Arrows hit that part?
Beauties like Heav'n, their Gifts should deal
Not to destroy us, but to heal.   10
   Strange *Art* of Love ! that can make sound,
And yet exasperates the wound;
That *look* she lent to ease my heart,
Hath pierc't it, and improv'd the smart.

In Etesiam lachrymantem.

O dulcis luctus, risuque potentior omni!
   Quem decorant lachrymis Sydera tanta suis.
Quam tacitæ spirant auræ ! vultusque nitentes
   Contristant veneres, collachrymantque suæ !
Ornat gutta genas, oculisque simillima gemma:
   Et tepido vivas irrigat imbre rosas.
Dicite Chaldæi *! quæ me fortuna fatigat,*
   Cum formosa dies & sine nube perit?

To Etesia *going beyond Sea.*

Go, if you must ! but stay—and know
And mind before you go, my vow.
   To ev'ry thing, but *Heav'n* and *you*,
With all my Heart, I bid Adieu !
Now to those happy *Shades* I'le go
Where first I saw my beauteous Foe.

   In Etesiam 8 *periit M*: *peruit 1678*: *perit GC*

I'le seek each silent *path*, where we
Did walk, and where you sate with me
I'le sit again, and never rest
Till I can find some *flow'r* you prest.   10
That near my dying Heart I'le keep,
And when it wants *Dew*, I will weep:
Sadly I will repeat past Joyes,
And Words, which you did sometimes voice:
I'le listen to the *Woods*, and hear
The *Eccho* answer for you there.
But famish'd with long absence I
Like *Infants* left, at last shall cry,
And Tears (as they do *Milk*) will sup
Until you come, and take me up.   20

Etesia *absent.*

Love, the Worlds Life! what a sad death
Thy absence is? to lose our breath
At once and dye, is but to live
Inlarg'd, without the scant reprieve
Of *Pulse* and *Air*: whose dull *returns*
And narrow *Circles* the Soul mourns.
    But to be dead alive, and still
To wish, but never have our will:
To be possess'd, and yet to miss;
To wed a true but absent bliss:
Are lingring tortures, and their smart   10
Dissects and racks and grinds the Heart!
As Soul and Body in that state
Which unto us seems separate,
Cannot be said to live, until
Reunion; which dayes fulfill
And slow-pac'd seasons: So in vain
Through hours and minutes (Times long *train*,)
I look for thee, and from thy sight,
As from my Soul, for life and light.   20
For till thine Eyes shine so on me,
Mine are fast-clos'd and will not see.

Translations.

Some *Odes* of the Excellent and Knowing *Severinus*, Englished.

Metrum 12. *Lib.* 3.

Happy is he, that with fix'd Eyes
The Fountain of all goodness spies!
Happy is he, that can break through
Those Bonds, which tie him here below!
  The *Thracian* Poet long ago
Kind *Orpheus*, full of tears and wo
Did for his lov'd *Euridice*
In such sad Numbers mourn, that he
Made the *Trees* run in to his mone,
And *Streams* stand still to hear him grone.   10
The *Does* came fearless in one throng
With *Lyons* to his mournful Song,
And charm'd by the harmonious sound
The *Hare* stay'd by the quiet *Hound*.
  But when *Love* heightned by *despair*
And deep *reflections* on his *Fair*
Had swell'd his Heart, and made it rise
And run in Tears out at his Eyes:
And those sweet *Aires*, which did appease
Wild Beasts, could give their Lord no ease;   20
Then vex'd, that so much grief and Love
Mov'd not at all the gods above,
With desperate thoughts and bold intent,
Towards the *Shades* below he went;
For thither his fair Love was fled,
And he must have her from the dead.
There in such *Lines*, as did well suit
With sad *Aires* and a Lovers *Lute*,
And in the richest Language drest
That could be thought on, or exprest,   30
Did he complain, whatever *Grief*,
Or *Art*, or *Love* (which is the chief,

30 exprest, *GC* : exprest. *1678*

And all innobles,) could lay out ;
In well-tun'd woes he dealt about.
And humbly bowing to the *Prince*
Of Ghosts, begg'd some Intelligence
Of his *Euridice*, and where
His beauteous *Saint* resided there.
Then to his *Lutes* instructed grones
He sigh'd out new melodious mones ;   40
And in a melting charming *strain*
Begg'd his dear *Love* to life again.
   The *Music* flowing through the shade
And darkness, did with ease invade
The silent and attentive Ghosts ;
And *Cerberus*, which guards those coasts
With his lowd barkings, overcome
By the sweet *Notes*, was now struck dumb.
The *Furies*, us'd to rave and howl
And prosecute each guilty Soul,   50
Had lost their rage, and in a deep
Transport did most profusely weep.
Ixion's wheel stopt, and the curst
Tantalus almost kill'd with thirst,
Though the *Streams* now did make no haste,
But waited for him, none would taste.
That *Vultur*, which fed still upon
Tityus his liver, now was gone
To feed on *Air*, and would not stay
Though almost famish'd, with her prey.   60
  Won with these wonders, their fierce Prince
At last cry'd out, *We yield ! and since*
Thy merits claim no less, take hence
Thy Consort for thy Recompence.
But, Orpheus, *to this law we bind*
Our grant, you must not look behind,
Nor of your fair Love have one Sight,
Till out of our Dominions quite.
   Alas ! what laws can Lovers awe ?
Love is it self the greatest Law !   70
Or who can such hard bondage brook
To be in Love, and not to Look ?
Poor *Orpheus* almost in the light
Lost his dear Love for one short sight ;

And by those Eyes, which Love did guide,
What he most lov'd unkindly dyed!
   This tale of *Orpheus* and his *Love*
Was meant for you, who ever move
Upwards, and tend into that light,
Which is not seen by mortal sight.   80
For if, while you strive to ascend,
You droop, and towards Earth once bend
Your seduc'd Eyes, down you will fall
Ev'n while you look, and forfeit all.

Metrum 2. Lib. 3.

What fix'd *Affections*, and lov'd *Laws*
(Which are the hid, magnetic *Cause* ;)
Wise *Nature* governs with, and by
What fast, inviolable *tye*
The whole Creation to her ends
For ever provident she bends:
All this I purpose to rehearse
In the sweet *Airs* of solemn Verse.
   Although the *Lybian Lyons* should
Be bound with chains of purest Gold,   10
And duely fed, were taught to know
Their keepers voice, and fear his blow:
Yet, if they chance to taste of bloud,
Their rage which slept, stirr'd by that food
In furious roarings will awake,
And fiercely for their freedom make.
No chains, nor bars their fury brooks,
But with inrag'd and bloody looks
They will break through, and dull'd with fear
Their keeper all to pieces tear.   20
   The *Bird*, which on the *Woods* tall boughs
Sings sweetly, if you Cage or house,
And out of kindest care should think
To give her honey with her drink,
And get her store of pleasant meat,
Ev'n such as she delights to Eat:
Yet, if from her close prison she
The *shady-groves* doth chance to see,

2 (Which . . . *Cause* ;)] (which . . . *Cause*; *1678*

Straitway she loaths her pleasant food
And with sad looks longs for the *Wood*.   30
The wood, the wood alone she loves!
And towards it she looks and moves:
And in sweet *notes* (though distant from,)
Sings to her first and happy home!

   That *Plant*, which of it self doth grow
Upwards, if forc'd, will downwards bow;
But give it freedom, and it will
Get up, and grow erectly still.

   The *Sun*, which by his prone descent
Seems westward in the Evening bent,   40
Doth nightly by an unseen way
Haste to the *East*, and bring up day.

   Thus all things long for their first State,
And gladly to't return, though late.
Nor is there here to any thing
A *Course* allow'd, but in a *Ring*;
Which, where it first *began*, must *end*:
And to that *Point* directly tend.

Metrum 6 Lib. 4.

Who would unclouded see the Laws
Of the supreme, eternal *Cause*,
Let him with careful thoughts and eyes
Observe the high and spatious *Skyes*.
There in one league of Love the *Stars*
Keep their old peace, and shew our wars.
The *Sun*, though flaming still and hot,
The cold, pale *Moon* annoyeth not.
Arcturus with his *Sons* (though they
See other stars go a far way,   10
And out of sight,) yet still are found
Near the *North-pole*, their noted bound.
Bright *Hesper* (at set times) delights
To usher in the dusky nights:
And in the *East* again attends
To warn us, when the day ascends,
So alternate *Love* supplys
Eternal Courses still, and vies
Mutual kindness; that no Jars
Nor discord can disturb the Stars.   20

The same sweet *Concord* here below
Makes the fierce *Elements* to flow
And *Circle* without quarrel still,
Though temper'd diversly ; thus will
The *Hot* assist the *Cold* : the *Dry*
Is a friend to *Humidity*.
And by the *Law* of *kindness* they
The like relief to them repay.
The *fire*, which active is and bright,
Tends upward, and from thence gives light.   30
The *Earth* allows it all that space
And makes choice of the lower place ;
For things of weight hast to the Center
A fall to them is no adventure.
  From these kind *turns* and *Circulation*
Seasons proceed and *Generation*.
This makes the *Spring* to yield us flow'rs,
And melts the Clouds to gentle show'rs.
The *Summer* thus matures all seeds
And ripens both the Corn and weeds.   40
This brings on *Autumn*, which recruits
Our old, spent store with new fresh fruits.
And the cold *Winters* blustring Season
Hath snow and storms for the same reason.
This *temper* and wise *mixture* breed
And bring forth ev'ry living *seed*.
And when their *strength* and *substance* spend
(For while they *live*, they drive and tend
Still to a *change*,) it takes them hence
And shifts their *dress* ; and to our sense   50
Their *Course* is over, as their *birth* :
And hid from us, they turn to Earth.
  But all this while the *Prince* of life
Sits without *loss*, or *change*, or *strife* :
Holding the *Rains*, by which all move ;
(And those his *wisdom*, *power*, *Love*
And *Justice* are ;) And still what he
The *first life* bids, that needs must be,
And live on for a time ; that done
He calls it back, meerly to shun   60
The mischief, which his *creature* might
Run into by a further flight.

For if this dear and tender sense
Of his preventing providence
Did not restrain and call things back :
Both heav'n and earth would go to wrack.
And from their great *preserver* part,
As *blood* let out forsakes the *Heart*
And perisheth ; but what returns
With fresh and Brighter spirits burns.   70
   This is the *Cause* why ev'ry living
Creature affects an *endless being*.
A *grain* of this bright *love* each thing
Had giv'n at first by their great King ;
And still they creep (drawn on by this :)
And look back towards their *first bliss*.
For otherwise, it is most sure,
Nothing that liveth could *endure* :
Unless it's Love turn'd retrograde
Sought that *first life*, which all things made.   80

Metrum 3. Lib. 4

If old tradition hath not fail'd,
Ulysses, when from *Troy* he sail'd,
Was by a tempest forc'd to land
Where beauteous *Circe* did command.
Circe, the daughter of the Sun,
Which had with *Charms* and *Herbs* undone
Many poor strangers, and could then
Turn into Beasts, the bravest Men.
Such *Magic* in her potions lay
That whosoever past that way   10
And drank, his shape was quickly lost ;
Some into *Swine* she turn'd, but most
To *Lyons* arm'd with teeth and claws ;
Others like *Wolves*, with open Jaws
Did howl ; But some (more savage) took
The *Tiger's* dreadful shape and look.
   But wise *Ulysses* by the *Aid*
Of *Hermes*, had to him convey'd
A *Flow'r*, whose virtue did suppress
The force of charms, and their success.   20

While his *Mates* drank so deep, that they
Were turn'd to *Swine*, which fed all day
On *Mast*, and humane food had left;
Of shape and voice at once bereft.
Only the *Mind* (above all charms,)
Unchang'd, did mourn those monstrous harms.
  O worthless *herbs*, and weaker *Arts*
To change their *Limbs*, but not their *Hearts*!
Mans *life and vigor* keep within,
Lodg'd in the *Center*, not the *Skin*.   30
Those piercing charms and poysons, which
His *inward parts* taint and bewitch,
More fatal are, than such, which can
Outwardly only spoile the man.
Those change his *shape* and make it foul;
But these deform and kill his soul.

Metrum 6. Lib. 3.

All *sorts* of men, that live on Earth,
Have one *beginning* and one *birth*.
For all things there is one *Father*,
Who *lays out* all, and all doth *gather*.
He the warm Sun with rays adorns,
And fils with brightness the Moon's horns.
The azur'd heav'ns with stars he burnish'd
And the round world with creatures furnish'd.
But *Men* (made to inherit all,)
His *own Sons* he was pleas'd to call,   10
And that they might be so indeed,
He gave them *Souls* of divine seed.
A noble *Offspring* surely then
Without distinction, are all men.
  O why so vainly do some boast
Their *Birth* and *Blood*, and a great *Hoste*
Of Ancestors, whose *Coats* and *Crests*
Are some rav'nous *Birds* or *Beasts*!
If *Extraction* they look for
And *God*, the great *Progenitor*:   20
No man, though of the meanest state
Is *base*, or can *degenerate*;
Unless to *Vice* and *lewdness* bent
He leaves and *taints* his true *descent*

The old man of Verona out of Claudian.

Fælix, qui propriis ævum transegit in arvis,
Una domus puerum &c.

Most happy man! who in his own sweet *fields*
Spent all his time, to whom one *Cottage* yields
In *age* and *youth* a lodging : who grown *old*
Walks with his *staff* on the same *soil* and *mold*
Where he did creep an *infant*, and can tell
Many fair years spent in one quiet *Cell*!
No *toils* of fate made him from home far known,
Nor forreign *waters* drank, driv'n from his own.
No loss by *Sea*, no wild *lands* wastful war
Vex'd him ; not the brib'd *Coil* of *gowns* at bar.　　10
Exempt from *cares*, in *Cities* never seen
The fresh *field-air* he loves, and rural *green*.
The years set *turns* by *fruits*, not *Consuls* knows ;
Autumn by apples : *May* by blossom'd boughs.
Within one hedg his *Sun* doth set and rise,
The world's wide day his short Demeasnes comprise.
Where he observes some known, concrescent *twig*
Now grown an *Oak*, and old, like him, and big.
Verona he doth for the *Indies* take,
And as the *red Sea* counts *Benacus* lake.　　20
Yet are his *limbs* and *strength* untir'd, and he
A lusty *Grandsire* three *descents* doth see.
Travel and sail who will, search sea, or shore ;
This man hath *liv'd*, and that hath *wander'd* more.

The Sphere of Archimedes out of Claudian.

Jupiter in parvo cum cerneret æthera vitro
Risit, & ad superos &c.

When *Jove* a heav'n of small glass did behold,
He smil'd, and to the Gods these words he told.
Comes then the power of mans *Art* to this?
In a fraile *Orbe* my work new acted is.
The *poles* decrees, the *fate* of things : *God's* laws
Down by his *Art* old *Archimedes* draws.

10 *gowns GC* : *growns 1678*

Spirits inclos'd the sev'ral *Stars* attend,
And orderly the *living work* they bend.
A feigned *Zodiac* measures out the year,
Ev'ry new *month* a false *Moon* doth appear.   10
And now bold *industry* is proud, it can
Wheel round its *world*, and rule the *Stars* by man.
Why at *Salmoneus* thunder do I stand?
Nature is rivall'd by a *single hand*.

The Phœnix *out of* Claudian.

Oceani summo circumfluus æquore lucus
Trans Indos, Eurumque viret &c,

A grove there grows round with the *Sea* confin'd
Beyond the *Indies,* and the *Eastern* wind.
Which, as the *Sun* breaks forth in his first beam,
Salutes his *steeds,* and hears him whip his *team.*
When with his dewy *Coach* the *Eastern* Bay
Crackles, whence blusheth the approaching day;
And blasted with his burnish'd *wheels*, the night
In a pale dress doth vanish from the light.
   This the blest *Phœnix* Empire is, here he
Alone exempted from mortality,   10
Enjoys a land, where no diseases raign;
And ne'r afflicted, like our world, with pain.
A *Bird* most equal to the Gods, which vies
For length of life and durance, with the skyes;
And with renewed limbs tires ev'ry age,
His appetite he never doth asswage
With common food.   Nor doth he use to drink
When thirsty, on some *River's* muddy brink.
A purer, vital *heat* shot from the Sun
Doth nourish him, and *airy sweets* that come   20
From *Tethis* lap, he tasteth at his need;
On such *abstracted Diet* doth he feed.
   A secret *Light* there streams from both his Eyes
A firy *hue* about his *cheeks* doth rise.
His *Crest* grows up into a glorious *Star*
Giv'n t' adorn his head, and shines so far,
That piercing through the bosom of the night
It rends the darkness with a gladsome light.
His thighs like *Tyrian* scarlet, and his wings
(More swift than *Winds* are,) have skie-colour'd *rings*   30

26 far,] far. *1678*

Flowry and rich : and round about inroll'd
Their utmost *borders* glister all with gold.
Hee's not conceiv'd, nor springs he from the Earth,
But is himself the *Parent,* and the *birth.*
None him begets ; his fruitful death reprieves
Old age, and by his funerals he lives.
For when the tedious *Summer*'s gone about
A thousand times : so many *Winters* out,
So many *Springs* : and *May* doth still restore
Those leaves, which *Autumn* had blown off before ;   40
Then prest with years his vigour doth decline
Foil'd with the number ; as a stately *Pine*
Tir'd out with storms, bends from the top & height
Of *Caucasus,* and falls with its own weight :
Whose part is torn with dayly *blasts,* with *Rain*
Part is consum'd, and part with *Age* again.
So now his Eyes grown dusky, fail to see
Far off, and drops of colder rheums there be
Fall'n slow and dreggy from them ; such in sight
The cloudy *Moon* is, having spent her light.   50
And now his *wings,* which used to contend
With *Tempests,* scarce from the low Earth ascend.
He knows his time is out ! and doth provide
New principles of life ; herbs he brings dried
From the hot hills, and with rich spices frames
A *Pile* shall burn, and *Hatch* him with its flames.
On this the *weakling* sits ; salutes the Sun
With pleasant noise, and prays and begs for some
Of his own fire, that quickly may restore
The youth and vigour, which he had before.   60
Whom soon as *Phœbus* spyes, stopping his rayns,
He makes a stand and thus allayes his pains.
O thou that buriest old age in thy grave,
And art by seeming funerals to have
A new return of life ! whose custom 'tis
To rise by ruin, and by death to miss
Ev'n death it self : a new beginning take,
And that thy wither'd body now forsake !
Better thy self by this thy change !   This sed,
He shakes his *locks,* and from his golden *head*   70

44 *Caucasus*] *Causacus 1678*

Shoots one bright *beam*, which smites with vital fire
The willing bird; to burn is his desire,
That he may live again : he's proud in death,
And goes in haste to gain a better breath.
The spicie heap fir'd with cœlestial rays
Doth burn the aged *Phœnix*, when strait stays
The Chariot of th' amazed *Moon* ; the *pole*
Resists the wheeling, swift *Orbs*, and the whole
Fabric of *Nature* at a stand remains,
Till the old bird a new, young being gains.   80
All stop and charge the faithful flames, that they
Suffer not nature's glory to decay.
   By this time, *life* which in the ashes lurks
Hath fram'd the *Heart*, and taught new *bloud* new *works* ;
The whole *heap* stirs, and ev'ry *part* assumes
Due vigour ; th' *Embers* too are turn'd to *plumes*.
The parent in the Issue now revives,
But young and brisk ; the bounds of both these lives
With very little space between the same,
Were parted only by the middle flame.   90
   To *Nilus* straight he goes to consecrate
His parents ghoste ; his mind is to translate
His dust to *Egypt*.   Now he hastes away
Into a distant land, and doth convey
The ashes in a turf.   Birds do attend
His Journey without number, and defend
His pious flight like to a guard ; the sky
Is clouded with the Army, as they fly.
Nor is there one of all those thousands dares
Affront his leader : they with solomn cares   100
Attend the progress of their youthful king ;
Not the rude hawk, nor th' Eagle that doth bring
Arms up to *Jove*, fight now ; lest they displease ;
The miracle enacts a common peace.
So doth the *Parthian* lead from *Tigris* side
His barbarous troops, full of a lavish pride
In pearls and habit, he adorns his head
With royal tires : his steed with gold is lead.
His robes, for which the scarlet fish is sought,
With rare *Assyrian* needle work are wrought.   110
And proudly reigning o're his rascal bands,
He raves and triumphs in his large Commands.

A City of *Egypt* famous in all lands
For rites, adores the *Sun*, his temple stands
There on a hundred pillars by account
Dig'd from the quarries of the *Theban* mount.
Here, as the Custom did require (they say,)
His happy parents dust down he doth lay ;
Then to the Image of his *Lord* he bends
And to the flames his burden strait commends.   120
Unto the *Altars* thus he destinates
His own Remains : the light doth gild the gates ;
Perfumes divine the *Censers* up do send :
While th' *Indian* odour doth it self extend
To the *Pelusian* fens, and filleth all
The men it meets with the sweet storm.   A gale
To which compar'd, *Nectar* it self is vile :
Fills the seav'n channels of the misty *Nile.*
  O happy bird ! sole heir to thy own dust !
Death, to whose force all other Creatures must   130
Submit, saves thee.   Thy ashes make thee rise ;
'Tis not thy nature, but thy age that dies.
Thou hast seen All ! and to the times that run
Thou art as great a witness, as the Sun.
Thou saw'st the *deluge*, when the sea outvied
The land, and drown'd the mountains with the tide.
What year the stragling *Phaeton* did fire
The world, thou know'st.   And no plagues can conspire
Against thy life ; alone thou do'st arise
Above mortality ; the Destinies   140
Spin not thy days out with their fatal Clue ;
They have no Law, to which thy life is due.

Pious thoughts and Ejaculations.

To his Books.

Bright books ! the *perspectives* to our weak sights :
The clear *projections* of discerning lights.
Burning and shining *Thoughts* ; man's posthume *day* :
The *track* of fled souls, and their *Milkie-way.*
The dead *alive* and *busie*, the still *voice*
Of inlarg'd Spirits, kind heav'ns white *Decoys.*

Who lives with you, lives like those knowing *flow'rs*,
Which in commerce with *light*, spend all their hours:
Which shut to *Clouds*, and *shadows* nicely shun;
But with glad haste unveil to *kiss* the Sun.   10
Beneath you all is dark and a dead night;
Which whoso lives in, wants both health and sight.
    By sucking you, the wise (like *Bees*) do grow
Healing and rich, though this they do most slow:
Because most choicely, for as great a store
Have we of *Books*, as Bees of *herbs*, or more.
And the great task to *try*, then know the good:
To discern *weeds*, and Judge of wholsome *Food*,
Is a rare, scant performance; for *Man* dyes
Oft e're 'tis done, while the *bee* feeds and flyes.   20
But you were all choice *Flow'rs*, all set and drest
By old, sage *florists*, who well knew the best.
And I amidst you all am turn'd a *weed*!
Not wanting knowledge, but for want of heed.
Then thank thy self *wild fool*, that would'st not be
Content to know——what was to much for thee!

Looking back.

Fair, shining *Mountains* of my pilgrimage,
    And flow'ry *Vales*, whose flow'rs were stars:
The *days* and *nights* of my first, happy age;
    An age without distast and warrs:
When I by thoughts ascend your *Sunny heads*,
    And mind those sacred, *midnight* Lights:
By which I walk'd, when curtain'd Rooms and Beds
    Confin'd, or seal'd up others sights;
            O then how bright
            And quick a light   10
    Doth brush my heart and scatter night;
            Chasing that shade
            Which my sins made,
    While I so *spring*, as if I could not *fade*!

How brave a prospect is a bright *Back-side*!
    Where flow'rs and palms refresh the Eye:
And days well spent like the glad *East* abide,
    Whose morning-glories cannot dye!

14 slow:] slow, *LGC*   18 *Food, LGC : Food. 1678 : Food, MS.*
alteration in Bodleian copy.

The Shower.

Waters above! eternal Springs!
The dew, that silvers the *Doves* wings!
O welcom, welcom to the sad :
Give dry dust drink ; drink that makes glad !
Many fair *Ev'nings*, many *Flowr's*
Sweeten'd with rich and gentle showers
Have I enjoy'd, and down have run
Many a fine and shining *Sun* ;
But never till this happy hour
Was blest with such an *Evening-shower*!   10

Discipline.

Fair prince of life, lights living well !
Who hast the keys of death and hell !
If the mule man despise thy day,
Put chains of darkness in his way.
Teach him how deep, how various are
The Councels of thy love and care.
When Acts of grace and a long peace
Breed but rebellion and displease ;
Then give him his own way and will,
Where lawless he may run until   10
His own choice hurts him, and the sting
Of his foul sins full sorrows bring.
If Heav'n and Angels, hopes and mirth
Please not the *mole* so much as Earth :
Give him his *Mine* to dig, or dwell ;
And one sad *Scheme* of hideous hell.

The Ecclipse.

Whither, O whither did'st thou fly
When I did grieve thine holy Eye ?
When thou did'st mourn to see me lost,
And all thy Care and Councels crost.
O do not grieve where e'er thou art !
Thy grief is an undoing smart.
Which doth not only pain, but break
My heart, and makes me blush to speak.
Thy anger I could kiss, and will :
But (O !) thy grief, thy grief doth kill.   10

Discipline] 3 mule] mole *GC* (*cp.* 14)

Affliction.

O come, and welcom! Come, refine ;
For *Moors* if wash'd by thee, will shine.
Man *blossoms* at thy touch ; and he
When thou draw'st blood, is thy *Rose-tree.*
Crosses make strait his *crooked* ways,
And *Clouds* but cool his *dog-star* days.
Diseases too, when by thee blest,
Are both *restoratives* and *rest.*
    Flow'rs that in *Sun-shines* riot still,
Dye scorch'd and sapless ; though *storms* kill.   10
The fall is fair ev'n to desire,
Where in their *sweetness* all expire.
O come, pour on ! what *calms* can be
So fair as *storms*, that appease thee ?

Retirement.

Fresh *fields* and *woods* ! the Earth's fair *face*,
God's *foot-stool*, and mans *dwelling-place.*
I ask not why the first *Believer*
Did love to be a Country liver ?
Who to secure pious content
Did pitch by *groves* and *wells* his tent ;
Where he might view the boundless *skie*,
And all those glorious *lights* on high :
With flying *meteors*, *mists* and *show'rs*,
Subjected *hills, trees, meads* and *Flow'rs* :   10
And ev'ry minute bless the King
And wise Creatour of each thing.
    I ask not why he did remove
To happy *Mamre*'s holy grove,
Leaving the *Citie*'s of the plain
To *Lot* and his successless train ?
All various Lusts in *Cities* still
Are found ; they are the *Thrones* of Ill.
The dismal *Sinks*, where blood is spill'd,
Cages with much uncleanness fill'd.   20
But *rural shades* are the sweet fense
Of piety and innocence.

21 fense] sense *LGC*

They are the *Meek's* calm region, where
Angels descend, and rule the sphere:
Where heav'n lyes *Leiguer,* and the *Dove*
Duely as *Dew,* comes from above.
If *Eden* be on Earth at all,
'Tis that, which we the *Country* call.

The Revival.

Unfold, unfold! take in his light,
Who makes thy Cares more short than night.
The Joys, which with his *Day-star* rise,
He deals to all, but drowsy Eyes:
And what the men of this world miss,
Some *drops* and *dews* of future bliss.
　　Hark! how his *winds* have chang'd their *note,*
And with warm *whispers* call thee out.
The *frosts* are past, the *storms* are gone:
And backward *life* at last comes on.　　　　　10
The lofty *groves* in express Joyes
Reply unto the *Turtles* voice,
And here in *dust* and *dirt,* O here
The *Lilies* of his love appear!

The Day-spring.

Early, while yet the *dark* was gay,
And *gilt* with stars, more trim than day:
Heav'ns *Lily,* and the Earth's chast *Rose*:　} *S. Mark*
The green, immortal B R A N C H arose;　} *c.* 1. *v.* 35.
And in a solitary place
Bow'd to his father his bless'd face.
　　If this calm season pleas'd my *Prince,*
Whose *fullness* no need could evince,
Why should not I poor, silly sheep
His *hours,* as well as *practice* keep?　　　　　10
Not that his hand is tyed to these,
From whom *time* holds his transient *Lease:*
But *mornings,* new Creations are,
When men all night sav'd by his Care,
Are still reviv'd; and well he may
Expect them grateful with the day.

So for that first *drawght* of his hand,
Which finish'd heav'n and sea and land,⎫
The *Sons* of God their thanks did bring, ⎬ Job. *c.* 38.
And all the *Morning-stars* did sing. ⎭ *v.* 7.   20
Besides, as his part heretofore
The *firstlings* were of all, that bore :
So now each day from all he saves,
Their Soul's *first thoughts* and fruits he craves.
This makes him daily shed and shower
His graces at this early hour ;
Which both his Care and Kindness show,
Chearing the good : quickning the slow.
As holy friends mourn at delay,
And think each minute an hour's stay :   30
So his divine and loving *Dove*
With longing throws doth heave and move,
And soare about us, while we sleep :
Sometimes quite through that *lock* doth *peep*,
And shine ; but always without fail
Before the slow Sun can unveile,
In new *Compassions* breaks like light,
And *Morning-looks*, which scatter night.
    And wilt thou let thy *creature* be
When *thou* hast watch'd, asleep to thee ?   40
Why to unwellcome, loath'd surprises
Do'st leave him, having left his vices ?
Since these, if suffer'd, may again
Lead back the *living*, to the *slain*.
O change this *Scourge* ! or, if as yet
None less will my transgressions fit :
Dissolve, dissolve ! death cannot do
What I would not submit unto.

The Recovery.

Fair *Vessell* of our daily light, whose proud
And previous *glories* gild that blushing Cloud :
Whose lively *fires* in swift projections glance
From hill to hill, and by refracted chance
Burnish some neighbour-*rock*, or tree, and then
Fly off in coy and winged *flams* agen :
          If thou this day
          Hold on thy way,

Know, I have got a greater *light* than thine;
A light, whose *shade* and *back-parts* make thee shine.   10
    Then get thee down: then get thee down;
    I have a *Sun* now of my own.

II.

Those nicer livers, who without thy Rays
Stirr not abroad, those may thy lustre praise:
And wanting light (*light*, which no *wants* doth know!)
To thee (weak *shiner*!) like blind *Persians* bow;
But where that *Sun*, which tramples on thy head,
From his own bright, eternal *Eye* doth shed
      One living *Ray*,
      There thy dead day   20
Is needless, and man to a *light* made free,
Which shews what thou can'st neither shew, nor see.
    Then get thee down, Then get thee down;
    I have a *Sun* now of my own.

The Nativity.
Written in the year 1656.

Peace? and to all the world? sure, one
And he the prince of peace, hath none.
He travels to be born, and then
Is born to travel more agen.
Poor *Galile*! thou can'st not be
The place for his Nativity.
His restless mother's call'd away,
And not deliver'd, till she pay.
  A *Tax*? 'tis so still! we can see
The Church thrive in her misery;   10
And like her head at *Bethlem*, rise
When she opprest with troubles, lyes.
Rise? should all fall, we cannot be
In more extremities than he.
Great *Type* of passions! come what will,
Thy grief exceeds all *copies* still.
Thou cam'st from heav'n to earth, that we
Might go from Earth to Heav'n with thee.
And though thou found'st no welcom here,
Thou did'st provide us *mansions* there.   20

A *stable* was thy *Court*, and when
Men turn'd to *beasts*; Beasts would be *Men*.
They were thy *Courtiers*, others none;
And their poor *Manger* was thy *Throne*.
No swadling *silks* thy Limbs did fold,
Though thou could'st turn thy Rays to gold.
No *Rockers* waited on thy birth,
No *Cradles* stirr'd: nor songs of mirth;
But her chast *Lap* and sacred *Brest*
Which lodg'd thee first, did give thee *rest*.   30
    But stay: what light is that doth stream,
And drop here in a gilded beam?
It is thy Star runs *page*, and brings
Thy tributary *Eastern* Kings.
Lord! grant some *Light* to us, that we
May with them find the way to thee.
Behold what mists eclipse the day:
How dark it is! shed down one *Ray*
To guide us out of this sad night,
And say once more, *Let there be Light*.   40

The true Christmas.

So stick up *Ivie* and the *Bays*,
And then restore the *heathen* ways.
Green will remind you of the spring,
Though this great day denies the thing.
And mortifies the Earth and all
But your wild *Revels*, and loose *Hall*.
Could you wear *Flow'rs*, and *Roses* strow
Blushing upon your breasts *warm Snow*,
That very *dress* your lightness will
Rebuke, and wither at the Ill.   10
The brightness of this day we owe
Not unto *Music*, *Masque* nor *Showe*:
Nor gallant *furniture*, nor *Plate*;
But to the *Manger's* mean Estate.
His *life* while here, as well as *birth*,
Was but a check to *pomp* and *mirth*;
And all mans *greatness* you may see
Condemn'd by his *humility*.

26 Rays] rags *LG*   16 check] cheek *1678* (*MS. alteration in Bodleian copy*)

Then leave your open *house* and *noise*,
To welcom him with *holy Joys*, 20
And the poor *Shepherd's* watchfulness :
Whom *light* and *hymns* from Heav'n did bless.
What you *abound* with, cast abroad
To those that *want*, and ease your loade.
Who empties thus, will bring more in ;
But riot is both *loss* and *Sin*.
Dress finely what comes not in sight,
And then you keep your *Christmas* right.

The Request.

O thou ! who did'st deny to me
This world's ador'd felicity,
And ev'ry big, imperious lust,
Which fools admire in sinful Dust ;
With those fine, subtile *twists*, that tye
Their *bundles* of foul gallantry :
Keep still my weak Eyes from the *shine*
Of those gay things, which are not thine,
And shut my Ears against the noise
Of wicked, though applauded *Joys*. 10
For thou in any land hast store
Of shades and Coverts for thy poor,
Where from the busie dust and heat,
As well as storms, they may retreat.
A Rock, or Bush are douny beds,
When thou art there crowning their heads
With secret blessings : or a *Tire*
Made of the *Comforter's* live-fire.
And when thy goodness in the *dress*
Of anger, will not seem to bless : 20
Yet do'st thou give them that rich *Rain*,
Which as it drops, clears all again.
  O what kind *Visits* daily pass
'Twixt thy great self and such poor *grass*,
With what sweet looks doth thy love shine
On those low *Violets* of thine !
While the tall *Tulip* is accurst,
And *Crowns Imperial* dye with thirst.

O give me still those secret meals,
Those rare *Repasts*, which thy love deals! 30
Give me that Joy, which none can grieve,
And which in all griefs doth relieve.
This is the portion thy Child begs,
Not that of rust, and rags and dregs.

Jordanis

Quid celebras auratam undam, Et combusta pyropis
  Flumina, vel Medio quæ serit æthra salo?
Æternùm refluis si pernoctaret in undis
  Phœbus, & incertam sydera suda Tethyn
Si colerent, tantæ gemmæ! nil cærula librem:
  Sorderet rubro in littore dives Eos.
Pactoli *mea lympha macras ditabit arenas,*
  Atq; Universum gutta minuta Tagum
O charum caput! O cincinnos unda beatos
  Libata! O domini balnea Sancta mei! 10
Quod fortunatum voluit spectare Canalem,
  Hoc erat in laudes area parva tuas.
Jordanis *in medio perfusus flumine lavit,*
  Divinoq; tuas ore beavit aquas.
Ah! Solyma *infœlix rivis obsessa prophanis!*
  Amisit Genium porta Bethesda *suum.*
Hic Orientis *aquæ currunt, &* apostata Pharpar,
  Atq; Abana *immundo turbidus amne fluit.*
Ethnica te totam cum fœdavere fluenta,
  Mansit Christicolâ Jordanis *unus aqua.* 20

Servilii Fatum, *sive* Vindicta divina.

Et sic in cythara, *sic in* dulcedine *vitæ*
  Et facti & luctus *regnat* amarities.
Quàm subitò in fastum *extensos atq; effera vultus*
  Ultrici *oppressit* vilis *arena sinu!*
Si violæ, spiransque crocus: si lilium ἄεινον
  Non nisi Justorum nascitur è cinere:
Spinarum, tribuliq; atq; infœlicis avenæ
  Quantus in hoc tumulo & qualis acervus erit?

17 Pharpar] Parphar. *1678*

Dii superi! damnosa piis sub sydera longum
  Mansuris stabilem conciliate fidem! 10
Sic olim in cœlum post nimbos clariùs ibunt,
  Supremo occidui tot velut astra die.
Quippe ruunt horæ, qualisq; in Corpore vixit,
  Talis it in tenebras bis moriturus homo.

De Salmone.

Ad virum optimum, & sibi familiariùs notum: D. *Thomam Poellum*
Cantrevensem: S. S. Theologiæ Doctorem.

Accipe prærapido Salmonem in gurgite captum,
  Ex imo in summas cum penetrásset aquas.
Mentitæ culicis quem forma elusit inanis:
  Picta coloratis plumea musca notis.
Dum captat, capitur; vorat inscius, ipse vorandus;
  Fitq; cibi raptor grata rapina mali.
Alma quies! miseræ merces ditissima vitæ,
  Quàm tutò in tacitis hic latuisset aquis!
Qui dum spumosi fremitus & murmura rivi
  Quæritat, hamato fit cita præda cibo. 10
Quam grave magnarum specimen dant ludicra rerum?
  Gurges est mundus: Salmo, homo: pluma, dolus.

The World.

Can any tell me what it is? can you,
  That wind your thoughts into a *Clue*
To guide out others, while your selves stay in,
                    And hug the Sin?
  I, who so long have in it liv'd,
                    That if I might,
  In truth I would not be repriev'd:
                    Have neither sight,
                    Nor sense that knows
                    These *Ebbs* and *Flows.* 10
  But since of all, all may be said,
  And *likelines* doth but upbraid,
  And mock the *Truth*, which still is lost
In fine *Conceits*, like streams in a sharp frost:

The World] 12 upbraid,] upbraid. *1678*: upbraid *LGC*

I will not strive, nor the *Rule* break
Which doth give Loosers leave to speak.
Then false and foul World, and unknown
     Ev'n to thy own:
Here I renounce thee, and resign
Whatever thou can'st say, is thine.   20
 Thou art not *Truth*; for he that tries
Shall find thee all deceit and lyes.
Thou art not *friendship*; for in thee
'Tis but the *bait* of policy.
Which, like a *Viper* lodg'd in *Flow'rs*,
Its venom through that sweetness pours.
And when not so, then always 'tis
A fadeing *paint*; the short-liv'd bliss
Of *air* and *Humour*: out and in
Like *Colours* in a *Dolphin*'s skin.   30
But must not live beyond *one day*,
Or *Convenience*; then away.
Thou art not *Riches*; for that *Trash*
Which one age hoords, the next doth wash
And so severely sweep away;
That few remember, where it lay.
So rapid *streams* the wealthy *land*
About them, have at their command:
And shifting *channels* here restore,
There break down, what they bank'd before. 40
Thou art not *Honour*; for those gay
Feathers will wear, and drop away;
And princes to some upstart *line*
Give new ones, that are full as fine.
Thou art not *pleasure*; for thy *Rose*
Upon a *thorn* doth still repose;
Which if not cropt, will quickly shed;
But soon as cropt, grows dull and dead.
 Thou art the *sand*, which fills one *glass*,
And then doth to another pass;   50
And could I put thee to a stay,
Thou art but *dust*! then go thy way,
And leave me *clean* and bright, though *poor*;
Who stops thee, doth but *dawb* his floor,

30 skin.] skin: *G*: skin; *C* 32 Or *Convenience*] Or for *Convenience LC*

And *Swallow*-like, when he hath done,
To *unknown dwellings* must be gone!
   Welcom pure thoughts and peaceful hours
Inrich'd with *Sunshine* and with *show'rs*;
Welcom fair hopes and holy Cares,
The not to be repented *shares*   60
Of time and business: the sure *rode*
Unto my last and lov'd *Abode*!
                          O supreme *Bliss*!
The Circle, Center and Abyss
Of blessings, never let me miss
Nor leave that *Path*, which leads to thee:
Who art alone all things to me!
I hear, I see all the long day
The noise and pomp of the *broad way*;
I note their Course and proud approaches: 70
Their silks, perfumes and glittering Coaches.
But in the *narrow way* to thee
I observe only poverty,
And despis'd things: and all along
The ragged, mean and humble throng
Are still on foot, and as they go,
They sigh and say; *Their Lord went so*!
   Give me my *staff* then, as it stood
When green and growing in the Wood.
(Those *stones*, which for the *Altar* serv'd,   80
Might not be smooth'd, nor finely carv'd:)
With this *poor stick* I'le pass the *Foord*
As *Jacob* did; and thy dear *word*,
As thou hast dress'd it: not as *Witt*
And *deprav'd tastes* have poyson'd it:
Shall in the passage be my meat,
And none else will thy Servant eat.
Thus, thus and in no other sort
Will I set forth, though laugh'd at for't;
And leaving the wise *World* their way,   90
Go through; though Judg'd to go astray.

73 poverty,] poverty. *1678*   83 *word,*] *word. 1678*

The Bee.

From fruitful *beds* and flowry *borders*
Parcell'd to wastful Ranks and Orders,
Where *state* grasps more than plain *Truth* needs
And wholesome *Herbs* are starv'd by *Weeds* :
To the wild Woods I will be gone,
And the course Meals of great *Saint John.*
  When truth and piety are mist
Both in the Rulers and the Priest ;
When pity is not cold, but dead,
And the rich eat the Poor like bread ;   10
While factious heads with open Coile
And force first make, then share the spoile :
To *Horeb* then *Elias* goes,
And in the *Desart* grows the *Rose.*
    Hail Christal Fountains and fresh shades,
           Where no proud look invades.
No busie worldling hunts away
The sad Retirer all the day :
Haile happy harmless solitude,
Our Sanctuary from the rude   20
And scornful world : the calm recess
Of faith, and hope and holiness !
Here something still like *Eden* looks,
Hony in Woods, *Julips* in Brooks :
And *Flow'rs*, whose rich, unrifled *Sweets*
With a chast kiss the cool dew greets.
When the toyls of the Day are done
And the tir'd world sets with the Sun,
Here *flying* winds and *flowing* Wells
Are the wise, watchful Hermits *Bells* ;   30
Their buisie *murmurs* all the night
To *praise* or *prayer* do invite,
And with an awful sound arrest
And piously employ his breast.
  When in the *East* the Dawn doth blush,
Here cool, fresh *Spirits* the air brush ;

2 Orders,] Orders. *1678*   16 invades.] invades, *LGC*

Herbs (strait) get up, *Flow'rs* peep and spread :
Trees whisper praise, and bow the head.
Birds from the shades of night releast
Look round about, then quit the neast,   40
And with united gladness sing
The glory of the morning's King.
The *Hermit* hears, and with meek voice
Offers his own up, and their Joys :
Then prays, that all the world may be
Blest with as sweet an unity.
    If sudden storms the day invade,
They flock about him to the shade :
Where wisely they expect the end,
Giving the tempest time to spend ;   50
And hard by shelters on some bough
Hilarion's servant, the sage *Crow*.
    O purer years of light, and grace !
The *diff'rence* is great, as the *space*
'Twixt you and us : who blindly run
After *false-fires*, and leave the *Sun*.
Is not fair *Nature* of her self
Much richer than dull *paint*, or *pelf*?
And are not *streams* at the *Spring-head*
More sweet than in carv'd *Stone*, or *Lead*?   60
But *fancy* and some *Artist's* tools
Frame a Religion for fools.
    The *truth*, which once was plainly taught,
With *thorns* and *briars* now is fraught.
Some part is with bold *Fables* spotted,
Some by strange *Comments* wildly blotted :
And *discord* (old Corruption's Crest,)
With *blood* and *blame* hath stain'd the rest.
So *Snow*, which in its first descents
A whiteness, like pure heav'n presents,   70
When touch'd by *Man* is quickly soil'd
And after trodden down, and spoil'd.
    O lead me, where I may be free
In *truth* and *Spirit* to serve thee !
Where undisturb'd I may converse
With thy great self, and there rehearse
Thy gifts with thanks, and from thy store
Who art all blessings, beg much more ! .

Give me the Wisdom of the *Bee*,
And her unwearied Industry :   80
That from the *wild Gourds* of these days
I may extract Health and thy praise ;
Who can'st turn darkness into light,
And in my weakness shew thy might !
   Suffer me not in any want
To seek refreshment from a *Plant,*
Thou did'st not *set* ! since all must be
Pluck'd up, whose *growth* is not from thee.
'Tis not the *garden* and the *Bowrs,*
Nor *fense* and *forms* that give to flow'rs   90
Their *wholsomness* : but thy *good will,*
Which *truth* and *pureness* purchase still.
   Then since corrupt man hath driv'n hence
Thy kind and saving *Influence,*
And *Balm* is no more to be had
In all the Coasts of *Gilead* :
Go with me to the *shade* and *cell,*
Where thy best *Servants* once did dwell.
There let me know thy *Will,* and see
Exil'd *Religion* own'd by thee.   100
For thou can'st turn dark *Grots* to *Halls,*
And make *Hills* blossome like the *vales* :
Decking their untill'd *heads* with flow'rs
And fresh delights for all sad hours :
Till from them, like a laden *Bee,*
I may fly home, and *hive* with thee.

To Christian Religion.

Farewel thou true and tried Refection
Of the still poor and meek *Election* !
Farewel Souls *Joy,* the quickning *health*
Of Spirits, and their secret *wealth* !
Farewel my *Morning-star,* the bright
And dawning *looks* of the true Light !
O blessed *shiner* ! tell me whither
Thou wilt be gone, when night comes hither ?
A *Seer,* that observ'd thee in
Thy Course, and watch'd the growth of Sin,   10

86 *Plant,*] *Plant.* *1678* : *plant LGC*   8 wilt] will *1678*

Hath giv'n his Judgment and foretold,
That *West-ward* hence thy *Course* will hold:
And when the day with us is done,
There fix, and shine a glorious Sun.
O hated *shades* and *darkness*! when
You have got here the Sway agen,
And like unwholsome *fogs* withstood
The light, and blasted all that's good:
Who shall the happy *shepherds* be
To watch the next *Nativity*   20
Of Truth and brightness, and make way
For the returning, rising day?
O! what year will bring back our bliss,
Or who shall live, when God doth this?
   Thou *Rock* of Ages, and the *Rest*
Of all, that for thee are opprest!
Send down the *Spirit* of thy truth,
That Spirit, which the tender *Youth*
And first *growths* of thy *Spouse* did spread
Through all the world, from one small *head*!   30
Then, if *to blood we must resist*
Let thy mild *Dove*, and our high *Priest*
Help us, when man proves false, or frowns,
To bear the *Cross*, and save our *Crowns*:
O! honour those, that honour thee!
Make *Babes* to still the Enemy:
And teach an *Infant* of few days
To perfect by his death, thy praise!
Let none defile what thou did'st *wed*,
Nor tear the *garland* from her head: 40
But chast and chearful let her dye,
And pretious in the *Bridegrooms* Eye!
So to thy glory, and her praise
These last shall be her brightest dayes.

      Revel. Chap. last, vers. 17.
     The Spirit and the Bride say, Come.

DAPHNIS.

An Elegiac *Eclogue.*

The Interlocutors, *Damon, Menalcas.*

Da. What clouds, *Menalcas*, do oppress thy brow?
Flow'rs in a Sunshine never look so low.
Is *Nisa* still cold Flint? or have thy Lambs
Met with the Fox by straying from their Dams?

Men. Ah! *Damon*, no; my Lambs are safe, & she
Is kind, and much more white than they can be.
But what doth life, when most serene, afford
Without a worm, which gnaws her fairest gourd?
Our days of gladness are but short reliefs,
Giv'n to reserve us for enduring griefs.   10
So smiling Calms close Tempests breed, wch break
Like spoilers out, and kill our flocks, when weak.
I heard last *May* (and *May* is still high Spring,)
The pleasant *Philomel* her Vespers sing.
The green wood glitter'd with the golden Sun
And all the West like Silver shin'd; not one
Black cloud, no rags, nor spots did stain
The Welkins beauty: nothing frown'd like rain;
But e're night came, that Scene of fine sights turn'd
To fierce dark showrs; the Air with lightnings burn'd;   20
The woods sweet Syren rudely thus opprest,
Gave to the Storm her weak and weary Breast.
I saw her next day on her last cold bed;
And *Daphnis* so, just so is *Daphnis* dead!

Da. So Violets, so doth the Primrose fall,
At once the Springs pride and its funeral.
Such easy sweets get off still in their prime,
And stay not here, to wear the soil of Time.
While courser Flow'rs (which none would miss, if past;)
To scorching Summers, and cold Autumns last.   30

Men. Souls need not time, the early forward things
Are always fledg'd, and gladly use their Wings,

17 cloud] cloud appeared *LG*   27 easy] early *LG*   29 past;)] past; *1678*

Or else great parts, when injur'd quit the Crowd,
To shine above still, not behind the Cloud.
And is't not just to leave those to the night,
That madly hate, and persecute the light?
Who doubly dark, all *Negroes* do exceed,
And inwardly are true black Moores indeed.

  Da. The punishment still manifests the Sin,
As outward signs shew the disease within.   40
While worth opprest mounts to a nobler height,
And Palm-like bravely overtops the weight.

  So where swift *Isca* from our lofty hills
With lowd farewels descends, and foming fills
A wider Channel, like some great port-vein,
With large rich streams to feed the humble plain:
I saw an Oak, whose stately height and shade
Projected far, a goodly shelter made,
And from the top with thick diffused Boughs
In distant rounds grew, like a Wood-nymphs house.   50
Here many Garlands won at Roundel-lays
Old shepheards hung up in those happy days,
With knots and girdles, the dear spoils and dress
Of such bright maids, as did true lovers bless.
And many times had old *Amphion* made
His beauteous Flock acquainted with this shade;
A Flock, whose fleeces were as smooth and white
As those, the wellkin shews in Moonshine night.
Here, when the careless world did sleep, have I
In dark records and numbers noblie high   60
The visions of our black, but brightest Bard
From old *Amphion's* mouth full often heard;
With all those plagues poor shepheards since have known,
And Ridles more, which future times must own.
While on his pipe young *Hylas* plaid, and made
Musick as solemn as the song and shade.
But the curs'd owner from the trembling top
To the firm brink, did all those branches lop,
And in one hour what many years had bred,
The pride and beauty of the plain lay dead.   70
The undone Swains in sad songs mourn'd their loss,
While storms & cold winds did improve the Cross.

           39 *Da.*] *Da, 1678*

But Natuie, which (like vertue) scorns to yield
Brought new recruits and succours to the Field;
For by next Spring the check'd Sap wak'd from sleep
And upwards still to feel the Sun did creep,
Till at those wounds, the hated Hewer made,
There sprang a thicker and a fresher shade.

    Men. So thrives afflicted Truth! and so the light,
When put out, gains a value from the Night.   80
How glad are we, when but one twinkling Star
Peeps betwixt clouds, more black than is our Tar?
And Providence was kind, that order'd this
To the brave Suff'rer should be solid bliss;
Nor is it so till this short life be done,
But goes hence with him, and is still his Sun.

    Da. Come Shepherds then, and with your greenest Bays
Refresh his dust, who lov'd your learned Lays.
Bring here the florid glories of the Spring,
And as you strew them pious *Anthems* sing,   90
Which to your children and the years to come
May speak of *Daphnis*, and be never dumb.
While prostrate I drop on his quiet Urn
My Tears, not gifts; and like the poor, that mourn
With green, but humble Turfs; write o're his Hearse
For false, foul Prose-men this fair Truth in Verse.

"Here *Daphnis* sleeps! & while the great watch goes
"Of loud and restless Time, takes his repose.
"Fame is but noise, all Learning but a thought:
"Which one admires, another sets at nought.   100
"Nature mocks both, and Wit still keeps adoe;
"But Death brings knowledge and assurance too.

    Men. Cast in your Garlands, strew on all the flow'rs
Which *May* with smiles, or *April* feeds with show'rs.
Let this days Rites as stedfast as the Sun
Keep pace with Time, and through all Ages run,
The publick character and famous Test
Of our long sorrows and his lasting rest;
And when we make procession on the plains,
Or yearly keep the Holyday of Swains,   110
Let *Daphnis* still be the recorded name
And solemn honour of our feasts and fame.

          106 run,] run. *1678*

For though the *Isis* and the prouder *Thames*
Can shew his reliques lodg'd hard by their streams,
And must for ever to the honour'd name
Of Noble *Murrey* chiefly owe that fame :
Yet, here his Stars first saw him, and when fate
Beckon'd him hence, it knew no other date.
Nor will these vocal Woods and Valleys fail,
Nor *Isca*'s lowder Streams this to bewail, 120
But while Swains hope and Seasons change, will glide
With moving murmurs, because *Daphnis* di'd.

   Da. A fatal sadness, such as still foregoes,
Then runs along with publick plagues and woes,
Lies heavy on us, and the very light
Turn'd Mourner too, hath the dull looks of Night.
Our vales like those of Death, a darkness shew
More sad than Cypress, or the gloomy Yew,
And on our hills, where health with height complied,
Thick drowsie Mists hang round and there reside. 130
Not one short parcel of the tedious year
In its old dress and beauty doth appear ;
Flowr's hate the Spring, and with a sullen bend
Thrust down their Heads, which to the Root still tend,
And though the Sun like a cold Lover, peeps
A little at them, still the Days-eye sleeps.
But when the Crab and Lion with acute
And active Fires their sluggish heat recruit,
Our grass straight russets, and each scorching day
Drinks up our Brooks as fast as dew in May. 140
Till the sad Heardsman with his Cattel faints,
And empty Channels ring with loud Complaints.

   Men. Heaven's just displeasure & our unjust ways
Change Natures course, bring plagues dearth and decays.
This turns our lands to Dust, the skies to Brass,
Makes old kind blessings into curses pass.
And when we learn unknown and forraign Crimes,
Brings in the vengeance due unto those Climes.
The dregs and puddle of all ages now
Like Rivers near their fall, on us do flow. 150
Ah happy *Daphnis* ! who, while yet the streams
Ran clear & warm (though but with setting beams,)

Got through : and saw by that declining light
His toil's and journey's end before the Night.
   Da. A night, where darkness lays her chains and Bars,
And feral fires appear instead of Stars.
But he along with the last looks of day
Went hence, and setting (Sun-like) past away.
What future storms our present sins do hatch
Some in the dark discern, and others watch ;   160
Though foresight makes no Hurricane prove mild ;
Fury that's long fermenting, is most wild.
   But see, while thus our sorrows we discourse,
Phœbus hath finish't his diurnal course.
The shades prevail, each Bush seems bigger grown :
Darkness (like State,) makes small things swell and frown.
The Hills and Woods with Pipes and Sonnets round
And bleating sheep our Swains drive home, resound.

   Men. What voice from yonder Lawn tends hither ? heark
'Tis *Thyrsis* calls, I hear *Lycanthe* bark.   170
His Flocks left out so late, and weary grown
Are to the Thickets gone, and there laid down.

   Da. Menalcas, haste to look them out, poor sheep
When day is done, go willingly to sleep.
And could bad Man his time spend, as they do,
He might go sleep, or die, as willing too.

   Men. Farewel kind *Damon* ! now the Shepheards Star
With beauteous looks smiles on us, though from far.
All creatures that were favourites of day
Are with the Sun retir'd and gone away.   180
While feral Birds send forth unpleasant notes,
And night (the Nurse of thoughts,) sad thoughts promotes.
But Joy will yet come with the morning-light,
Though sadly now we bid good night ! *Da.* good night !

From Dr. Thomas Powell's *Humane Industry : Or, A History Of most Manual Arts, Deducing the Original, Progress, and Improvement of them. Furnished with variety of Instances and Examples, shewing forth the excellency of Humane Wit* ... (1661.)

CAP. I. 'ΩΡΟΛΟΓΙΚΗ': Or The Invention of *Dyals, Clocks, Watches,* and other *Time-tellers.* Page 11.

Of a portable Clock or Watch, take this ensuing Epigram of our Countryman *Thomas Campian, de Horologio Portabili.*

> *Temporis interpres parvum congestus in orbem.*
> *Qui memores repetis nocte dieq̢ sonos.*
> *Ut semel instructus jucundè sex quater horas*
> *Mobilibus rotulis irrequietus agis.*
> *Nec mecum (quocunq̢ feror) comes ire gravaris*
> *Annumerans vitæ damna, levansq̢ meæ :*

Translated H. V.

> Times-Teller wrought into a little round,
> Which count'st the days and nights with watchful sound ;
> How (when once fixt) with busie Wheels dost thou
> The twice twelve useful hours drive on and show.
> And where I go, go'st with me without strife,
> The Monitor and Ease of fleeting life.

CAP. II. ΣΦΑΙΡΟ-ΠΟΙΗΤΙΚΗ': or, Some curious Spheares and Representations of the World. Page 20.

Of this Microcosme or Representation of the World which we now mentioned, the excellent *Grotius* hath framed this Epigram following.

> *In organum motus perpetui quod est penes*
> *Maximum Britanniacum Regem Jacobum.*

> *Perpetui motus indelassata potestas*
> *Absq̢ quiete quies, absq̢ labore labor,*
> *Contigerant cœlo, tunc cùm Natura caducis,*
> *Et solidis unum noluit esse locum.*
> *Et geminas partes Lunæ dispescuit orbe,*
> *In varias damnans inferiora vices.*
> *Sed quod nunc Natura suis è legibus exit*
> *Dans terris semper quod moveatur opus ?*

Mira quidem res est sed non nova (maxime Regum)
Hoc fieri docuit mens tua posse prius.
Mens tua quæ semper tranquilla & torpida nunquam,
Tramite constanti per sua regna meat.
Ut tua mens ergò motûs cælestis Imago :
Machina sic hæc est mentis Imago tuæ.

Translated thus.

The untired strength of never-ceasing motion,
A restless rest a toyl-less operation,
Heaven then had given it, when wise Nature did   H. V.
To frail & solid things one place forbid ;
And parting both, made the Moons Orb their bound,
Damning to various change this lower ground.
But now what Nature hath those Laws transgrest,
Giving to earth a work that ne're will rest?
Though 'tis most strange, yet (great King) 'tis not new ;
This Work was seen and found before in You.   10
In You, whose minde (though still calm) never sleeps,
But through your Realms one constant motion keeps :
As your minde (then) was Heavens type first, so this
But the taught *Anti-type* of your mind is.

De *AQUATICIS MACHINIS*, *Of WATER MOTIONS.*

(Sub-division of CAP. III. ΑΥΤΟΜΑΤΟ–ΠΟΙΗΤΙΚῊ, *Of sundry Machins, and Artificial Motions.*)   p. 39.

There were Amphitheaters both at *Rome* and *Verona*, and elsewhere, which were *prodigious piles*, both for magnificence of cost, and inventions of Art ; whole groves of great Trees (with green branches) were brought and planted upon the sandy Theater, and therein a thousand Estridges, a thousand wilde Boars, and a thousand Stags put in for the people to hunt. This Forrest being removed, they would on a sudden overflow all with a deep Sea, fraught with Sea monsters, and strange Fishes ; then might you see a Fleet of tall Ships ready rigged and appointed, to represent a Sea-fight : then all the water was let out again, and Gladiators or Fencers fight, where the Gallies stood but

5 bound,] bound. *1661*   9 King)] King *1661*

even now; which things are expressed in verse by *Juvenal* in his third *Satyr* thus:

> ———— *Quoties nos descendentis Arenæ*
> *Vidimus in partes, ruptâ‚ voragine terræ*
> *Emersisse feras & iisdem sæpe latebris*
> *Aurea cum Croceo creverunt Arbuta libro?*
> *Nec solum nobis Sylvestria cernere monstra*
> *Contigit, Æquoreos ego cum certantibus Ursis*
> *Spectavi vitulos & equorum nomine dignum*
> *Sed deforme pecus————*

Translated by *H. V.*

How oft have we beheld wilde Beasts appear
From broken gulfs of earth, upon some part
Of sand that did not sink? How often there
And thence did golden boughs ore saffron'd start?
Nor only saw we monsters of the wood,
But I have seen Sea-Calves whom Bears withstood;
And such a kinde of Beast as might be named
A horse, but in most foul proportion framed.

CAP. XI. ʽΗΜΕΡΩΤΙΚΗʹ: Or, *The Art of Cicuration and Taming wilde Beasts.* p. 174.

Many of these examples that I have produced to make good the Title of this Chapter, and the Apostles saying above-mentioned, are briefly sum'd up by *Martial* in his Book of Shows, the 105th *Epigr.* which I have here annexed, with the Translation of M. *Hen. Vaughan Silurist,* whose excellent Poems are publique.

> *Picto quod juga delicata collo*
> *Pardus sustinet, improbæ‚ Tygres*
> *Indulgent patientiam flagello,*
> *Mordent aurea quod lupata Cervi;*
> *Quod Frænis Lybici domantur Ursi,*
> *Et quantum* Caledon *tulisse fertur*
> *Paret purpureis Aper Capistris.*
> *Turpes* [a] *esseda quod trahunt Bisontes* [b],
> *Et molles dare jussa quod choreas:*
> *Nigro* [c] *Bellua* [d] *nil negat Magistro,*
> *Quis spectacula non putet Deorum?*
> *Hæc transit tamen ut minora, quisquis*
> *Venatus humiles videt Leonum,* &c.

[a] Brittish Chariots.
[b] Wild Oxen in the *Hercynian* Forrest called Buffles.
[c] The Negro or Black-Moor, that rides him.
[d] The Elephant.

That the fierce Pard doth at a beck
Yield to the Yoke his spotted neck,
And the untoward Tyger bear
The whip with a submissive fear ;
That Stags do foam with golden bits
And the rough Lybic bear submits
Unto the Ring ; that a wild Boar
Like that which *Caledon* of Yore
Brought forth, doth mildly put his head
In purple Muzzles to be lead :   10
That the vast strong-limb'd Buffles draw
The *Brittish* Chariots with taught awe.
And the Elephant with Courtship falls
To any dance the *Negro* calls :
Would not you think such sports as those
Were shews which the Gods did expose ;
But these are nothing, when we see
That Hares by Lions hunted be, &c.

APPENDIX 1.

POEMS OF UNCERTAIN AUTHORSHIP.

(1) The following lines with the signature H. Vaughan Ies. Col. were published in a thin volume of occasional verses, *Eucharistica Oxoniensia. In Exoptatissimum & Auspicatissimum Caroli . . . E Scotia Reditum Gratulatoria. Oxoniæ . . . 1641.* Mr. Chambers points out in his edition (vol. ii, p. xxviii) that the signature might equally well be that of Henry Vaughan, M.A., Fellow of Jesus College at the time, or of Herbert Vaughan who was a Gentleman-Commoner in 1641. Neither of these, however, seems to be known otherwise as an English poet: 'Hen. Vaugh. Ies. Soc.' has Latin verses in *Eucharistica Oxoniensia,* and both he and Herbert Vaughan contributed Latin verses to ΠΡΟΤΕΛΕΙΑ *Anglo-Batava . . Oxoniæ, . . .* (1641). For the Silurist's connexion with Jesus College see note to p. 667, l. 9.

> *As* Kings *doe rule like th'* Heavens, *who dispense*
> *To parts* remote *and neare their* influence,
> *So doth our* CHARLES *Move also ; while he posts*
> *From* South *to* North, *and back to* Southerne *coasts.*
> *Like to the* Starry Orbe, *which in it's round*
> *Move's to those very* Poynts ; *But while 'tis bound*
> *For* North, *there is (some guesse) a* Trembling fitt
> *And shivering in the* part *that's* opposite.
> *What were our* feares *and* Pantings, *what dire* fame
> *Hear'd we of* Irish Tumults, *sword, and flame !*   10
> *Which now we thinke but* Blessings, *as being sent*
> *Only as Matter, whereupon 'twas mean't*
> *The* Brittish *thus* united *might expresse,*
> *The strength of* joyned Powers *to suppresse,*
> *Or* conquer Foes ; *This is great* Brittaines *blisse;*
> *The* Island *in it selfe a just World is.*
> *Here no commotion shall we find or feare,*
> *But of the* Courts removeall, *no sad teare*
> *Or clowdy* Brow, *but when You leave Vs, then*
> Discord *is loyalty professed, when*   20

Nations *doe strive, which shall the happier bee*
T'enjoy your bounteous ray's *of* Majestie.
Which yet you throw in undivided *Dart,*
For Things divine *allow no* share *or* part.
The same Kind vertue doth at once disclose,
The Beauty of their Thistle, *and our* Rose.
Thus You doe mingle Soules *and firmely knitt*
What were but joyn'd before ; You Scots-men *fitt*
Closely with Vs, *and Reuniter prove,*
You fetch'd the Crowne *before, and now their* Love.   30

      H. VAUGHAN. Ies. Col.

 (2) These lines are printed on page 39 of Dr. Thomas Powell's
Cerbyd Jechydwriaeth (1657). They have sometimes been
ascribed to Henry Vaughan because of the friendship which existed
between him and the author of the book, and because the signature may be interpreted to mean 'Olor Vaughan'. But it seems
probable that if Vaughan had wished to sign himself in such a way
he would not have abbreviated the distinctive word; rather, he
would have given the complete title 'Olor Iscanus'. The lines are
printed, from an Eighteenth-Century (?) Welsh MS., in *Y Cymm-
rodor*, vol. xi, p. 223, with a few variant readings. They are not
ascribed to Vaughan in the manuscript.

   Y Pader, pan trier, Duw-tri a'i dododd
     O'i dadol ddaioni,
   Yn faen-gwaddan i bob gweddi,
    Ac athrawiaeth a wnaeth i ni.

         Ol. Vaughan.

APPENDIX II.

VAUGHAN'S LETTERS TO JOHN AUBREY AND ANTHONY WOOD.

(From the Aubrey and Wood MSS. in the Bodleian Library.)

I. MS. *Wood F* 39, fol. 216. To Aubrey.

Honoured Cousin

Yours of the 10th of June I received att Breckon, where I am still attendinge our Bishops Lady in a tertian feaver, & cannot as yet have the leasure to step home.   butt lest my delayinge of tyme heere should bringe the account (you expect,) too late into your hands : I shall now in part give you the best I can, & be more exact in my next.

My brother and I were borne att *Newton in the parish of St Brigets in the yeare 1621.   I stayed not att Oxford to take any degree, butt was sent to London, beinge then designed by my father for 10 the study of the Law, wch the sudden eruption of our late civil warres wholie frustrated.   my brother continued there for ten or 12 years, and (I thinke) he could be noe lesse than M^r of Arts.   he died (vpon an imployment for his majesty,) within 5 or 6 miles of Oxford, in the yeare that the last great plague visited London. He was buried by Sr Robert Murrey (his great friend,) & then Secretary of Estate for the kingdome of Scotland : to whome he gave all his bookes & manuscripts.   The several Tractates, which he published in his life-tyme, were these followinge :

    Anthroposophia Theo-magica.   20

    Magia Adamica.

    Lumen dè Lumine : all printed by Mr Humphrey Blunden att the Castle in Corn-hill.

---

* In Brecknockshire (*marginal note by Vaughan*).

Aula Lucis, a short discourse printed for William Leak att the Crowne betwixt the two temple-gates in fleet street.

The Historie of the fraternitie of the Rosie Crosse : with his animadversions & Judgement of them. printed for Giles Calvert att the west end of Paules. These are all that came to my cognisance.

30 What past into the presse from me, this short Catalogue comprehends ;

Silex Scintillans : Sacred poems & private Ejaculations in two bookes :

The Mount of Olives : or solitarie Devotions.

Olor Iscanus : A Collection of some poems & translations : printed for Mr Humphrey Moseley.

Flores Solitudinis : A translation of some choice peeces out of the Latine, With the life of Paulinus Bishop of Nola, collected out of his owne writinges, and other primitive Authours.

40   Nollius his Systema medicinæ Hermeticum, & his discourse dè generatione done into English. To these you may adde (if you thinke it fitt,)

Thalia Rediviva, a peece now ready for the presse, with the Remaines of my brothers Latine Poems (for many of them are lost,) never published before : butt (I believe) wilbe very wellcome, & prove inferiour to none of that kind, that is yet extant.

Dr Powell of Cantre I can give you an exact account of, as soone as I have Conference with his brother, whoe is my nighbour : you shall have it in my next. The other persons mentioned in yor lr̄e,
50 were Northwales gent & vnknowne to any in these parts. If tyme will permitt, I advise you to Consult (by lr̄e,) with Dr. Thomas Ellis sometymes of Jesus College, butt livinge now att Dole y gellie in ye County of Merionith.

He hath bine many yeares busied in makinge vp a supplement to Dr Powells Chronicle, & knowes more of him than any man else doth, and (I believe) of all the rest. He is a person of excellent accomplishments, & very solid learninge. My brothers imploymt was in physic & Chymistrie. he was ordayned minister by bishop Mainwaringe & presented to the Rectorie of St Brigets by his
60 kinsman Sr George Vaughan.

My profession allso is physic, wch I have practised now for many years with good successe (I thank god !) & a repute big enough for a person of greater parts than my selfe.

Deare S^r I am highly obliged to you that you would be pleased to remember, & reflect vpon such low & forgotten thinges, as my brother and my selfe : I shalbe ever ready to acknowledge the honour you have done vs, & if you have any Concerne in these parts that I may be serviceable in : I humblie beg, that you would call upon & Command

Honour'd Cousin   70
Breckon June the 15th   Yo^r most affectionate
        —73   & most faithfull, humble
                                              servant
                                         H: Vaughan

My Cousin Walbeoffe is exceedinge glad to heare of yor health & p^rsents you with her true love & respects. her sonne is long since dead without yssue, & left the estate (after his mother's decease,) amongst his fathers nearest relations.

To his ever honoured & obliginge
Kinsman John Awbrey Esq   80
most humblie these

Leave this letter with Mr Henry Coley in Rose & Crowne Court in Grayes Inne Lane to be de-
-livered as above directed
London

75–78 *Written down the left-hand margin of the letter.*
79–86 *On outer leaf.*

II.　MS. *Wood F* 39, fol. 227.　To Aubrey.

Honoured Cousin

In my last (wch I hope, is come to yor hands,) I gave you an account of my brother & my selfe : & what bookes we had written. I have nothinge to add butt this; that he died in the seaven & fortieth year of his age, upon the 27th of februarie, in the yeare 1666.　& was buried upon the first of March.

Thomas Powell of Cantre was since the kinge came in made D^r of divinity att Oxford, by a mandamus, as I have heard.　He was borne att Cantre within the County of Brechon in the year 1608.
10 he dyed att London vpon the last day of December in the year 1660 in the two and fiftieth yeare of his age & lyes buried in S. Dunstans church in fleetstreet.

His printed bookes are these.

Elementa Opticæ.

Recveil de Nowelles Lettres de Monsieur de Balzac, translated into English.

Stoa Triumphans: two l̄res of ye noble & learned Marquesse Virgilio malvezzi, to the illustrious Signior John Vincent Imperiale : translated out of Italian into English.
20 　　Quadriga Salutis : or the 4 general heads of Christian Religion surveyd & explained.

Humane Industrie : Or a short account of most manual Arts: their original, progress & improvement &c

Manuscripts left in my Custodie, & not yet printed.

The Insubrian historie : Conteyninge an exact account of the various fates, Civil commotions, battells & sieges acted vpon the theater of Lumbardie, & the adiacent parts of Italie from the first Irruptions & Conquests of the Goths to their final expulsion by the Emperour Justinian.　Written originalie in the
30 Latine by the Learned Puteanus & now done into English.

The Christian-politic Favourite : or A vindication of the politic transactions of Count-duke de S. Lucar: that great minister of state & favourite Counsellour to Philip the 4th of Spaine. written originalie by Virgilio Malvezzi & now (not tra=duced (as one hath done) butt faithfully translated into English.

Fragmenta de rebus Brittannicis :

A short account of the lives, manners & religion of the Brittish Druids and the Bards &c.

S^r this is all the account I can give you of any writers of Jesus College. The name of the place, where my brother lyes 40 buried, I doe not know ; butt tis a village upon the Thames side within 5 or 6 miles of Oxford, & without doubt well knowne to the Vniversity. My Cousin Walbeoffe p^{r}sents you with her real affections & respects, & would be very glad to see you in these parts. S^{ir} John with his Son & Lady are come well home from London. I begge yor pardon for all this trouble & remaine with all integritie

Honoured Cousin,

Yo^r most affectionate and
faithfull servant   50

Newton Julie 7th

—73 H Vaughan.

To his ever honoured & deservinge
friende : John Awbrey,
Escȝ :

Humblie these.

Leave this l$\overline{\text{r}}$e with Mr Henrie Coley in Rose & Crowne Court in Gray's Inne Lane to be deluv̇ed according to the   60 Directions above written. London.

III.   MS. *Aubrey* 13, fol. 337.   To Aubrey.

Brechon Decemb: 9th
—75.

Honoured Cousin.

Your l$\overline{\text{r}}$e of the 27th of November I received butt the last week. my occasions in Glamorganshire having detained me there the best part of the month : how wellcom it was to me (after your long silence) I will not goe about to express : butt assure you, that noe papyrs (wch I have the honour somtymes to receive from very worthie persons,) refresh me soe much, nor have soe dear an entertainment as yours.   10

II. 53–62 *On outer leaf.*

That my dear brothers name (& mine) are revived, & shine
in the Historie of the Vniversitie ; is an honour we owe vnto your
Care & kindnes : & realie (dear Cousin !) I am verie sensible of
it, & have gratefull reflections vpon an Act of so much love, and
a descendinge from yor great acquaintance & Converse to pick vs
vp, that lay so much below you.

'Tis a noble & excellent Designe that yor learned friend Dr Plott
hath now in hand, & I returne you my humble & hearty thanks
for Communicatinge it with me.   I shall take Care to assist him
20 with a short account of natures Dispensatorie heer, & in order to
it, I beg you would acquaint me with the method of his writinge :

I am in great haste & beg yor pardon for this short & rude returne
to yor kind letter : butt (dear S^r !) accept of my love & all the
effects it can produce in a gratefull Heart, which nowe hath

More than
Honoured Cousin,
Your most obliged, affectionate
friend & servant

H: Vaughan.

IV.   MS. *Aubrey* 13, fol. 338.   To Aubrey.

Brechon June 28th
—680.

Most honoured Cousin.

Yours of the 17th of May, came not to Brechon, till June was
pretty far in ; & then was I a great way from home.   Last week
calling there in my return, I joyfullie received yours, & shall
endeavour withall possible speed to perform yor desire.   I shall not
omitt the most curious search, that can be made into such distant
& obscure nativities : wch none then tooke care to record, & few
are now alive that have them in memorie.   If in my attendance
vpon (rather than speculations into) Nature, I can meet with any
10 thing that may deserve the notice of that learned & Honourable
Societie : I shall humblie present you with it, & leave it wholie to
your Censure and disposal.

That the most serious of our profession have not only an vnkind-
nes for, butt are persecutors of Astrologie : I haue more than once

admired : butt I find not this ill humour amongst the Antients, so much as the modern physicians : nor amongst them all neither. I suppose they had not travelled so far, & having once enterd upon the practise, they were loath to leave off, and learn to be acquainted with another world. for my owne part (though I could never ascend higher,) I had butt litle affection to the skirts 20 & lower parts of learning ; where every hand is graspinge & so litle to be had. butt neither nature, nor fortune favoured my ambition. I am only happy in yor Condescensions, whoe cease not to oblige me in the highest maner, that the most deserving and eminent persons could expect. I never was of such a magnitude as could invite you to take notice of me, & therfore I must owe all these favours to the generous measures of yor owne free & excellent spirit.

S^r I can make noe Returns proportionable to such matchles affections & merits ; butt this I dare assure you, that if any thing 30 happens wherin I may serve you : then I will (without reserves or exceptions) lett you see, that nothing hath bine heer written, butt what was first sincerely resolved vpon by

Honoured S^r

Your most obliged, most affectionate & most faithfull servant

H: Vaughan.

Expect the best account I can give you, within this fortnight.

To his worthily honoured Cousin,
 John Aubrey Esq₃ att 40
 Mr Hookes lodgings
 in Gresham College
London.

Humblie these

39–44 *On outer leaf.*

V.   MS. *Wood F* 45, fol. 68.   To Wood.

Worthy S^r

I received your leter in the declination of a tedious and severe sickness with a very slow recovery; butt as soon as I can gett abroad, I will contribute all I can to give satisfaction to yor Inquiries; especialy about the learned Dr John David Rhesus: a person of great & curious learning; butt had the vnhappines to sojourn heer in an age that vnderstood him not. for the Stradlings I shall imploy a learned friend I have in Glamorgan-shire, to pick vp what memorials remain of them in those parts.

10 I received a leter in the beginning of my sicknes from my Cousin John Awbrey about these inquiries you make now, & writt by him in yor behalf; butt it was my misfortune to continue so very weak and such a forlorn Clinic, that I could not to this day return him an answer. If you intend a second Edition of the Oxford-historie, I must give you a better account of my brothers books & mine; wch are in the first much mistaken, and many omitted. I shallbe very carefull of what you have recommended to my trust: & shall (in any thing els) with much chearfullnes & fidelity pay you the respects & service due to a person of such 20 public & obliging deserts.   I am sincerely

S^r

Yo^r most affectionate
& very willing servant

Newton-St Brigets, within
three miles of Brechon :
   March 25th 1689.

Hen: Vaughan.

To the reverend, his honoured
friend : Mr Antonie
Wood att his lodgings
in Merton-College
30 in Oxford :
Present this

26–31 On verso of letter.

VI.   MS. *Aubrey* 13, fol. 340.   To Aubrey.

Octob: 9th -94.

Honoured Cousin.

I received yours & should have gladly served you, had it b.ne
in my power.   butt all my search & consultations with those few
that I could suspect to have any knowledge of Antiquitie, came to
nothing ; for the antient Bards (though by the testimonie of their
Enemies, the Romans ;) a very learned societie : yet (like the
Druids) they communicated nothing of their knowledge, butt by
way of tradition : wch I suppose to be the reason that we have no
account left vs : nor any sort of remains, or other monuments of
their learning, or way of living.   10
As to the later Bards, who were no such men, butt had a societie
& some rules & orders among themselves : & several sorts of
measures & a kind of Lyric poetrie : wch are all sett down exactly
In the learned John David Rhees, or Rhesus his welch, or British
grammer : you shall have there (in the later end of his book) a most
curious Account of them.   This vein of poetrie they called Awen,
which in their language signifies as much as Raptus, or a poetic
furor ; & (in truth) as many of them as I have conversed with are
(as I may say) gifted or inspired with it.   I was told by a very sober
& knowing person (now dead) that in his time, there was a young   20
lad father & motherless, & soe very poor that he was forced to beg ;
butt att last was taken vp by a rich man, that kept a great stock
of sheep vpon the mountains not far from the place where I now
dwell.   who cloathed him & sent him into the mountains to keep
his sheep.   There in Summer time following the sheep & looking
to their lambs, he fell into a deep sleep ; In wch he dreamt, that
he saw a beautifull young man with a garland of green leafs vpon
his head, & an hawk vpon his fist : with a quiver full of Arrows att
his back, coming towards him (whistling several measures or tunes
all the way) & att last lett the hawk fly att him, w^{ch} (he dreamt)   30
gott into his mouth & inward parts, & suddenly awaked in a great
fear & consternation : butt possessed with such a vein, or gift of
poetrie, that he left the sheep & went about the Countrey, making
songs vpon all occasions, and came to be the most famous Bard in
all the Countrey in his time.
Dear Cousin I should & would be very ready to serve you in any

thing wherein I may be usefull, or qualified to doe it, & I give
you my heartie thanks for yoᵣ continued affections & kind remem-
brances of

40

Sᵣ
Yoᵣ most obliged & faithfull
Servant,
Hen: Vaughan

To his honoured friend & kinsman
John Awbrey, Esꝗ :
present this.

Leave this letter with the truly
honoured & most nobly accomplished
Dᵣ Thomas Gale in S.
Pauls schoole.

50

London.

44-51 *On outer leaf.*

NOTES.

POEMS, WITH THE TENTH SATYRE OF IUVENAL ENGLISHED.

PAGE 1. (*Title-page*) Tam nil, &c. Persius, *Satires*, i. 122–3.

PAGE 2, l. 8. *ægrotari*. Vaughan probably wrote the correct form 'ægrotare'.

PAGE 3. *To my Ingenuous Friend, R. W.* This is no doubt the 'R. W.' who fell at Rowton Heath. Compare page 49 (title). The most probable conjecture as to his identity seems to be that of Professor Firth, who points out that the name Roger Wood occurs among the list of Catholics who fell in the King's service at Chester. For other conjectures see Chambers's edition, vol. ii, pp. 337–8.

l. 13. *the Maze*. I think it likely that Vaughan wrote 'Mace', as the rhyme suggests, in the sense of a mace-bearer (O.E.D. Mace 2 c. 'a Mace was sent to bring Cromwell into the Court'.), or of the occasion when the Serjeant-at-Arms is sent with the mace as a warrant (O.E.D. 2 b.).

ll. 33–5. The first edition of Randolph's works to contain everything mentioned here was that of 1640 ; *The Jealous Lovers*, however, is often missing. In the following notes I refer to the edition of 1643 : *Poems, With the Muses Looking-Glasse, and Amyntas. . . . Whereunto is added, The Jealous Lovers.*

PAGE 4, ll. 57–8. *So they that did &c.* A reminiscence of Habington, *Castara*, p. 8, 'To Castara'. (Here and elsewhere I refer to '*The third Edition. Corrected and augmented . . . 1640*'.)

> So they whose wisdome did discusse
> Of these as fictions : shall in us
> Finde, they were more then fabulous.

PAGE 5, l. 1. Compare *Castara*, 'To Cupid' (ed. cit. p. 22) :

> Nimble boy in thy warme flight,

PAGE 10. (*Title*) *at the Globe Taverne*. The register of St. Saviour's, Southwark, refers to a 'Globe' in 1637—'George White, vintner, at the Globe'. See Rendle and Norman, *Inns of Old Southwark*, p. 326.

PAGE 11, l. 44. *Tower-wharfe to Cymbelyne, and Lud*. From east to west of the City. Statues of the 'early kings' were placed on Ludgate in 1260. When Ludgate was rebuilt in 1586, the statues were renewed. (See Stow's *Survey of London*, ed. C. H. Kingsford, 1908, vol. i, pp. 38, 39.)

PAGES 12 and 13, ll. 15–28. Dr. Beeching compares Donne's *A Valediction : forbidding mourning* (ed. Grierson, p. 50) :

> Dull sublunary lovers love
> (Whose soule is sense) cannot admit
> Absence, because it doth remove
> Those things which elemented it.
> But we by a love, so much refin'd,
> That our selves know not what it is,
> Inter-assured of the mind,
> Care lesse, eyes, lips, and hands to misse.

Habington's reminiscences of the same passage may have helped Vaughan to remember it :

> Yet are we so by Love refin'd,
> From impure drosse we are all mind.
> Death could not more have conquer'd sence
> > (*To the World.   The Perfection of Love*, p. 61.)
> Tis no dull Sublunary flame
> > Burnes in her heart and mine.
> > > (*The harmony of Love*, p. 133.)

PAGE 14, l. 42.   Compare Traherne, ' The Person' (*Poems of Felicity*, ed. Bell, p. 94) :

> Nor *paint*, nor *cloath*, nor *crown*, nor add a *Ray*,
> But glorify by taking all away.

PAGES 15 and 16, ll. 29-36.   Compare Randolph (ed. cit. p. 76), *On the Death of a Nightingale* (see p. 4, 1 above):

> That soul is fled, and to *Elision* gone ;
> Thou a poor desert left ; go then and run,
> Beg there to stand a grove, and if she please
> To sing again beneath thy shadowy Trees ;
> The souls of happy Lovers crown'd with blisses
> Shall flock about thee, and keep time with kisses.

Compare also *The Jealous Lovers*, Act IV, Sc. viii (ed. cit. p. 71) :

> We will be married in Elysium,
> And arm in arm walk through the blessed groves,
> And change a thousand kisses ;

PAGE 17. (*Title-page*) *Nèc verbum &c.*   Horace, *De Arte Poetica*, 133 (' curabis ').

PAGE 29, l. 452. *And why reprov'd.*   Compare Juvenal, 291 ' Cur tamen,' inquit, ' Corripias ? '

ll. 454-9.   Appropriated from Felltham, *Resolves*, 'Of Natures recompencing wrongs ', p. 123.   (Here and elsewhere I refer to the Fifth Edition, 1634.)

> *Lucretia's* fate warnes us to wish no *face*
> Like hers ;   *Virginia* would beneath her grace [read ' bequeath ']
> To Lute-backt *Rutilæ*, in exchange : for till, [read ' still ']
> The fairest Children doe their Parents fill
> With greatest care ;   so seldome *modesty*
> Is found to dwell with *Beauty*.—

PAGE 30, l. 485. *Is of any race.*   I think ' Is ' the form of ' Yes ' used again by Vaughan below, p. 446, 46 : it contradicts the statement in the preceding sentence.   Compare Juvenal, 318-19 :

> Sed tuus Endymion dilectae fiet adulter
> Matronae ; mox quum dederit Servilia nummos, &c.

l. 489.   *Ring* (*King 1646*).   Compare Juvenal, 320-1 ' exuet omnem Corporis ornatum '.

ll. 514-17.   Compare Juvenal, 340-2 :

> Si scelus admittas, dabitur mora parvula, dum res
> Nota urbi et populo contingit principis aurem.
> Dedecus ille domus sciet ultimus ;

Thomas Farnaby's note on Juvenal, 338 ' Non nisi legitime ', &c. (published in an Amsterdam edition of 1633), is as follows : ' Idque vivo marito Claudio Imp.   *Iamque Ostiam tantum profecto sacrificii causa*, &c.'   Vaughan seems to confound ' Ostia ' and ' hostia '.

OLOR ISCANUS.

PAGE 32, l. 6. *Herbertus.* Matthew Herbert, Rector of Llangat-tock. Compare p. 93 below and Wood's life of Vaughan.

ll. 20–8. *Me nullam in tantâ strage fuisse &c.* This passage has often been interpreted as meaning that Vaughan took no part in the Civil War. But see p. 54, 85–6, and p. 50, 50-60 and note. I think he is here merely disclaiming connexion with the Tysiphonae of l. 14.

PAGE 33. (*Title-page*) *Flumina amo &c.* Virgil, *Georgics* ii. 486 ('amem').

PAGE 34. *O quis &c.* Virgil, *Georgics* ii. 489:

> O qui me gelidis convallibus Haemi
> Sistat, &c.

PAGE 35. (*Heading*) *Lord Kildare Digby.* Only son of Robert, Lord Digby, son of Sir Robert Digby and Lettice, Baroness Offaly (q.v. *D.N.B.*). Lord Digby married Lady Sara, daughter of Richard, Earl of Cork. (See Lodge, *Peerage of Ireland*, vi, p. 283.)

PAGE 36. (*Signature*) *T. Powell Oxoniensis.* See Vaughan's letter to Aubrey, p. 670 below, and compare Wood, *Athenae Oxonienses* (ed. Bliss, iii, col. 507). See also pp. 60, 93, 598, 603, 614, 649, 661, 666 below.

PAGE 37, l. 1. *I call'd.* Here and elsewhere, since the original texts print ' I ' or ' O ' outside the line, the second word acquires an initial capital by position. This I have discarded, save where the capital may have its ordinary emphasizing value, as on p. 626 : ' O Subtile Love '.

l. 12. For '*Beard*' read '*Board*'?

(*Signature*) *I. Rowlandson Oxoniensis.* Probably either John or James Rowlandson, both of Queen's College between 1630 and 1640.

PAGE 38, l. 33. *Eugenius Philalethes Oxoniensis.* See Vaughan's letter to Aubrey, p. 667 below, and compare Wood, *Athenae Oxonienses.*

PAGE 39, ll. 5–8. Compare *Castara*, ' His Muse speakes to him ' (ed. cit. p. 104):

> And though Imperiall *Tiber* boast alone
> Ovids Corinna, and to *Arn* is knowne
> But *Petrarch's Laura* ; while our famous Thames
> Doth murmur *Sydneyes Stella* to her streames.

PAGE 40, ll. 51–6. Mr. Gordon Goodwin compares William Browne, *Britannia's Pastorals*, Book i, Song 2 (1616, p. 28):

> May neuer *Euet*, nor the *Toade*,
> Within thy Bankes make their abode !
> Taking thy iourney from the Sea,
> Maist thou ne'er happen in thy way
> On Niter or on Brimstone Myne,
> To spoyle thy taste !

ll. 65–6. Mr. Chambers compares *A Dialogue betweene Sr Henry Wotton and Mr Donne* (attributed to Donne, but see Grierson's edition, pp. 430 and 432):

> Nor roast in fiery eyes, which alwayes are
>   Canicular.

PAGE 41, l. 2. *a second Fiats care.* Mr. Chambers compares Donne, *The Storme* (ed. Grierson, p. 177, 70–2) :

> Since all formes, uniforme deformity
> Doth cover, so that wee, except God say
> Another *Fiat*, shall have no more day.

ll. 11–13. Compare *Castara*, 'To a Tombe' (ed. cit. p. 100) :

> Tyrant o're tyrants, thou who onely dost
> Clip the lascivious beauty without lust ;
> What horror at thy sight shootes through each sence ;
> How powerfull is thy silent eloquence,

Compare also p. 45, 31 below—'*Vocall silence*'.

l. 21. *Aire-monging band.* Compare Felltham, *Resolves*, 'Of Fame' (ed. cit. p. 49) : '*Checke* thy selfe, thou *Ayremonger* :'

PAGE 44, ll. 41–2. Compare Randolph, *In anguem, qui Lycorin dormientem amplexus est. Englished thus* Παραφραστικῶς (ed. cit. p. 11) :

> Hence he slides
> Up to her locks, and through her tresses glides,
> Her yellow tresses ; dazel'd to behold
> A glistring grove, an intire wood of Gold.

and Edward Herbert, *A Vision. A lady combing her hair*, l. 1 (ed. Churton Collins, p. 37) :

> Within an open curled sea of gold.

PAGE 46, l. 13. *her foule, polluted walls.* The walls of Brecon were pulled down by the inhabitants in order to avoid its occupation during the war. See Grose, *Antiquities*, vol. iv, Brecknockshire.

PAGE 48. *Monsieur Gombauld. Endymion,* a prose romance by Jean Ogier de Gombauld (1570?–1666), appeared in 1624. An English translation was published in 1639 : *Endimion. An Excellent Fancy first composed in French by Mounsieur Gombauld. And now Elegantly Interpreted, by Richard Hurst Gentleman.* The dedication of this volume begins with the same four words as Vaughan's dedication of *Olor Iscanus,* p. 35 above : 'It is a position'.

ll. 17–18. Compare *Castara,* 'To the Honourable my much honoured friend, R. B. Esquire' (ed. cit. p. 11) :

> But should she scorne my suite, I'le tread that path
> Which none but some sad Fairy beaten hath.

PAGE 49. *(Title) on the death of Mr. R. W.* Compare title on p. 3 above, and note.

PAGE 50, ll. 50–60. *O that day &c.* Vaughan may have been in the battle or, as Mr. Chambers suggests, among the garrison in Beeston Castle. Compare note on p. 52, 19–20.

PAGE 51, ll. 93–4. Compare Robert Randolph, Dedicatory poem in Thomas Randolph's *Poems &c.* (ed. cit. sig. A 3)

> And like Sun-dialls to a day that's gone,
> Though poor in use can tell there was a sun.

ll. 99–100. *Nomen & arma &c.* Virgil, *Aeneid* vi. 507–8.

PAGE 52, l. 10. *for,* before. Compare *O.E.D.* art. *for.*

ll. 19–20. *that day, when wee Left craggie Biston.* Mr. Chambers points out that after the surrender of Beeston Castle in November 1645 the garrison was allowed to march across the Dee

681

into Denbigh. Compare J. R. Phillips, *The Civil War in Wales and the Marches*, vol. i, p. 343.

PAGE 52, l. 40. *And Bias us'd before me.* The reference may be to 'want of change' and to the saying attributed to Bias of Priene by Cicero, *Paradoxa*, i. 8 'Omnia mecum porto mea'.

PAGE 53, l. 52. *Speeds old Britans.* See *The History of Great Britaine Under the Conquests of ẙ Romans, Saxons, Danes and Normans. . . . by Iohn Speed . . . London . . .* 1611, illustrations on p. 180.

PAGE 54. *Upon Mr. Fletchers Playes, published, 1647.* Vaughan's poem was not published in the folio editions.

PAGE 55, l. 33. *the Eares.* The appearance of the close-cropped Roundheads seems to be glanced at. Compare Cleveland, *Poems*, 1653, p. 68, 'The Hue and Cry after Sir John Presbyter':

With hair in Characters, and Lugs in text ; (Characters=shorthand).

l. 38. *Field's, or Swansteed's overthrow.* Mr. Chambers identifies Swansteed with Eliard Swanston.

Title. In the volume of Cartwright's *Comedies, Tragi-Comedies, With other Poems* . . . 1651, the heading of Vaughan's poem is 'Upon the Poems and Plaies of the ever Memorable Mr. WILL: CARTVVRIGHT'. It is signed HENRY VAUGHAN. *Silurist.*

PAGE 58. (*Title*) *Mr. R. Hall.* For conjectures as to the identity of Mr. R. Hall see Chambers, vol. ii, p. 339.

PAGE 59, ll. 75–6. *Salve æternum &c.* Virgil, *Aeneid* xi. 97–8.

PAGE 60. *Title of poem.* See Vaughan's letter to Aubrey, p. 670 below, and the note on Powell's translation. For *T. Powell* see note on p. 36 above.

l. 10. *Lye Leiguer here.* Compare note on p. 440, 25 below.

PAGE 61. (*First title*) *Master T. Lewes.* 'In 1635, a Thomas Lewis was Incumbent of Llanfigan, a village near Llansaintfread. He was expelled by the Ecclesiastical Commissioners at the same time that Thomas Vaughan was expelled from the latter place ;' [Miss Southall, *Songs of Siluria*, p. 126].

ll. 1–4, 15 sqq. Based on Horace, *Odes* i. 9. 1 'Vides ut alta stet nive candidum', &c., and (13, 14)—

> quid sit futurum cras, fuge quaerere et
> quem Fors . . .

(*Second title*) *Mrs. K. Philips.* Neither these verses nor those on pp. 621–2 below are found in the editions of Orinda's poems published in 1664 and after. See note to p. 597 below.

PAGE 62, ll. 15–16. Compare I. T. A. M., dedicatory poem in Randolph's *Poems, &c.* (ed. cit. sig. A 4ᵛ) :

> Blest Spirit, when I first did see
> The Genius of thy Poetrie,

and Randolph, *An Elegie on the death of . . . Sir Rowland Cotton . . .* (ed. cit. p. 72) :

> That by his vertues might created be
> A new strange miracle, wealth in Poetrie.

PAGE 63, l. 23. *gently spend.* Compare note on p. 509, 11 below.

PAGE 64, ll. 27–30. *This made thy fire &c.* Compare Randolph, *The Jealous Lovers*, Act II, Sc. ii (ed. cit. p. 19) :

> And must her lust break into open flames,
> To lend the world a light to view her shames?

ll. 27–34. *This made thy fire . . . Restraint.* For a discussion of this passage see additional note at p. 707 below.

PAGE **66.** (*Heading*) *De Ponto, Lib.* 3°. *Ex Ponto* iii. 7.

PAGE **68,** l. 47. *with many fancyed Springs And Groves.* A characteristic interpolation; Ovid, *Ex Pont.* iii. 7. 35 'Est tamen utilius, studium cessasse meorum'.

PAGE **74,** ll. 89–92. Mr. Chambers compares Donne, *Elegie,* iv. 3–4 (ed. Grierson, p. 84):

> And as a thiefe at barre, is question'd there
> By all the men, that have been rob'd that yeare,

PAGE **76,** ll. 135–8. *Where ever since . . . Eyes!* Vaughan's (?) addition.

PAGE **84.** *Metra* 6 and 7 should be *Metra* 7 and 8.

Metrum 6, ll. 1–6. Appropriated from Felltham, *Resolves,* 'Of Fame' (ed. cit. p. 50):

> He that thirsts for Glories prize ;
>   Thinking that, the top of all :
> Let him view th' expansed skies,
>   And the Earth's contracted Ball.
> Hee'l be ashamed then, that the name he wanne,
> Fils not the short walke, of one healthfull man.

PAGES **84** and **85.** *Metrum* 7, ll. 1–15. Appropriated from Felltham, *Resolves,* 'Of Charity' (ed. cit. p. 269):

> That the *World* in constant force,
> Varies his concordant course :
> That seeds jarring, *hot* and *cold,*
> Doe the *Breed* perpetuall hold :
> That the Sunne in's golden *Car,*
> Does the *Rosie Day* still rere.
> That the *Moone* swayes all those lights,
> *Hesper* ushers to *darke nights.*
> That alternate Tydes be found,
> *Seas* high-prided *waves* to bound,
> Lest his *fluid waters* Mace,
> Creeke broad *Earths* invallyed face.
> All the *Frame* of things that be,
> *Love* (which rules *Heaven, Land,* and *Sea*)
> Chaines, keepes, orders, as you see.

PAGE **85,** l. 16. *This.* Possibly for 'Thus' (q.v. O.E.D.); but compare ll. 22 and 26.

(*Title*) *Casimirus.* Another translation of Casimir had appeared in 1646 : *The Odes of Casimire Translated by G. H.* [Hils].

PAGE **86.** *Ode* 8. Ode 7 in the edition of Casimir's *Odes* of 1647.

PAGE **89.** (*The Praise of a Religious life*), ll. 1–4. Practically Vaughan's addition.

PAGE **93.** (*First title*) *Mathæo Herbert.* Compare p. 32, 6 and note.

(*Second title*) *Thomæ Poëllo.* See note on p. 36 above. *de Elementis opticæ libellum.* Vaughan refers to *Elementa Opticæ Novâ, facili, et Compendiosa Methodo explicata.* . . . *Londini. 1651* [Dedication signed T. P.].

PAGE **95.** (*Title-page*) *translated in to Latin by I.* Reynolds. Vaughan refers to *D. Iohannis Rainoldi Olim Græcæ Linguæ Prælectoris in Collegio Corporis Christi apud Oxonienses, Orationes 5. cum aliis quibusdam opusculis. Omnia nunc primum edita. Oxoniæ . . .*

Ann. Dom. 1613. (Separate title-pages for the translations from Plutarch and Maximus Tyrius on I 6 and L 7.)

PAGE 95. (*Title-page*) *Dolus, an virtus &c.* Virgil, *Aeneid* ii. 390. *fas est &c.* Ovid, *Metamorphoses* iv. 428.

PAGE 103. (*Note*) *huc venient &c.* Juvenal, *Satires* ix. 131 :

> undique ad illos
> Convenient et carpentis et navibus omnes,
> Qui digito scalpunt uno caput.

PAGE 109. (*Title-page*) *Omnia perversæ &c.* Ovid, *Tristia* ii. 301 'Omnia perversas possunt corrumpere mentes' (*varia lectio* 'poterunt').

PAGE 123. (*Title-page*) *The Praise and Happinesse &c.* A Latin version of the original was published in 1633 with *Oblectatio Vitæ Rusticæ Egidii vander Myle.* At p. 321 begins *Vitæ Rusticæ Encomium Dn. Antonii de Guevara.*

(*Title-page*) *O fortunatos &c.* Virgil, *Georgics* ii. 458.

PAGE 131, l. 1. *that are blown up with the spirit.* Compare Guevara (ed. cit. p. 342) : 'quos supina sapientia inflat'.

ll. 16–18. *and every pious Soule . . . Lord.* Vaughan's addition.

ll. 34–5. *But let us return . . . Country.* Vaughan's addition.

PAGE 133, ll. 15–18. Compare Guevara : ' Non alienos talis heredes, non fiscum, aut bonorum translationes formidat ' ; and *The Mount of Olives,* p. 167, 1–3.

PAGE 135, ll. 26–7. *that claps his Revenues upon his back.* Compare Marlowe, *Edward II,* I. iv. 408 (ed. Brooke, p. 332) : ' He weares a lords reuenewe on his back ' ; and *2 Henry VI,* I. iii. 83. Guevara ad loc.: ' cum divitiarum damno '.

THE MOUNT OF OLIVES.

PAGE 138. (*Heading*) S^r. *Charles Egerton.* Dr. Grosart (vol. ii, p. xxxiii) quotes a monument in Hanbury Church, Staffordshire, ' Caroli Egertoni Equitis Aurati ', who died 1662.

ll. 11–12. *Cœlo dignus &c.* Marcus Aurelius Nemesianus, *Eclogues* i. 50 (' concilio ').

PAGE 141, ll. 13–15. *Choose the better part &c.* Compare Jerome, *Vita S. Pauli Primi Eremitae* (ed. Migne, vol. ii, p. 27) : ' multo magis eligeret ', &c. ; and p. 183, 36–9 below.

PAGE 143, ll. 1–4. Compare Chrysostom, *Homiliae in Epist. ad Hebr.* xiv and xxvii (ed. Migne, vol. xii, pp. 335-6 and 407–8) ; *in Isaiam* (vol. vi, pp. 62–3).

PAGE 147, ll. 23–8. George Herbert, *The Temple,* 'The Church-Porch'.

PAGE 156, ll. 14–15. Compare *De Imitatione Christi,* Lib. IV, cap. xi ' O quam mundae debent esse manus illae ', &c. [Miss Guiney.]

PAGE 163. (*Note*) *Cyprian de cœnâ &c.* The work is *attributed* to Cyprian. See *Opera Omnia* (Oxford, 1682), sig. Ffffff, p. 41.

PAGE 169. (*First note*) *A Proverb in Italy.* Miss Guiney refers to *Select Italian Proverbs; The most significant, very usefull for Travellers, and such as desire that Language. . . . By Gio. Torriano* . . . 1649 (p. 67).

l. 15. *Cremationem habet.* Gregory, *Moralia,* Lib. IX, cap. xlvi (ed. Migne, col. 912).

ll. 29–31. *like holy Macarius &c.* See Macarius, *Apophthegmata* (ed. Migne, col. 258) : ' Iter agens aliquando per eremum, inveni calvariam mortui,' &c.

PAGE 171. (*First note*) *a little book called Speculum Visionis.* The author of *Speculum naturalis cœlestis & propheticæ visionis* was Josephus Grünbeck.

ll. 14–15. *That to all dominions &c.* Grosart compares Ralegh, *The History of the World* (Preface): ' *Others, That the divine providence* (*which* Cratippus *objected to* Pompey) *hath set downe the date and period of every Estate, before their first foundation and erection*'.

Second note. Potest fatum morum &c. Compare Marcellus, *De Doctorum Indagine* (ed. Lindsay, p. 846, 30).

Third note, ll. 1–4. *Non est, falleris &c. Anthol. Lat.* (ed. Buecheler and Riese), I. i. p. 333, No. 444.

ll. 5–8. *Qui vultus &c.* Seneca, *Agamemnon*, 607–10.

PAGE 172, ll. 5–9. *Anacreon &c.* Compare Stobaeus, *Florilegium*, iii (ed. Meineke, p. 185).

l. 22–page 173, l. 4. *But if you will visit . . . desolation.* Roughly translated from Petrarch, *De Otio Religiosorum*, Lib. ii (Opera Omnia, Basileae, 1554, p. 355) ' sed subsiste, obsecro . . . in nihilum abiere'.

(*Note*) *Ingeniosa gula est &c.* Petronius, *Saturae*, ed. Buecheler, 119, 33–8.

PAGE 173. (*First note*) *mors sola fatetur &c.* Juvenal, *Satires* x. 172–3. Quoted by Petrarch in *De Contemptu Mundi*, Dial. ii (ed. cit. p. 384).

ll. 7–22. *and* (*O blessed Jesus!*) *&c.* Partly a reminiscence of Petrarch, *De Otio Religiosorum*, Lib. ii (ed. cit. pp. 355–6) '& ô bonæ *IESV* . . . dabit iocos'.

(*Second note*) *in vitâ Hilar.* See Jerome, *Vita Hilarionis* (ed. Migne, vol. ii, col. 52).

PAGE 174, ll. 4–11. *Natural histories &c.* Miss Guiney notes that this is probably a reminiscence (it is not a direct translation) of Drexelius, *Æternitatis Prodromus* (Opera Omnia, 1647, vol. i, p. 34) ' Sed & volucris' &c.

l. 14. *have their rootes &c.* Compare George Herbert, *The Temple*, ' Vertue':

> Thy root is ever in its grave,
> And thou must die.

l. 23. *Nam mihi &c.* Compare Vaughan's translation on p. 383, 33–8 below, where the lines are attributed to Paulinus. Petrarch (*De Otio Religiosorum*, ed. cit. p. 354) quotes these four lines, attributing them to Prosper. Vaughan's remark on l. 22 is applicable to Prosper, but not to Paulinus.

PAGE 175, ll. 1–3. *Mis mawrddh &c.* These lines (attributed to Aneurin) are printed in *The Myvyrian Archaiology* (second ed., 1870, p. 21), where they form ll. 1, 7, and 8 of the third stanza of the *Englyns of the months*, as follows:

> Mis MAWRTH, mawr ryfyg adar
>
> . . . . .
>
> Pob peth a ddaw trwy'r ddaer
> Ond y Marw, mawr ei Garchar!

PAGE 176, ll. 16–24. *A great Philosopher &c.* Miss Guiney compares Henricus Cornelius Agrippa, *De Occulta Philosophia*, Lib. I, cap. lviii. Three books (of the four) were translated in 1651 by J. F. In the translation the passage referred to is on p. 129: 'And I have often seen a Dor-mouse dissected, and continue immovable, as if she were dead, untill she was boyled, and then presently in boyling the water the dissected members did shew life'.

(*Note*) *Omne quod est &c.* Marcellus Palingenius, *Zodiacus Vitæ*, ix. 180-1, xi. 658-60, viii. 249-51.

PAGE 177, l. 4. *Sic nostros &c.* Manilius, *Astronomicon* ii. 261.

PAGE 178, ll. 4-6. *Sunt qui &c.* Compare Juvenal, *Satires* xiii. 86 :

> Sunt in fortunae qui casibus omnia ponant
> Et nullo credant, &c.

l. 16. *Ex hoc momento &c.* A favourite phrase of Drexelius, e.g. *Æternitatis Prodromus* (1628, page facing first emblem) 'pendet ab hoc momento ÆTERNITAS'.

ll. 19-33. *I remember &c.* Miss Guiney compares Drexelius, *De Damnatorum Rogo* (Opera Omnia, vol. i, p. 146), 'Memini legere, nec sine admiratione,' &c.

ll. 34-41. Compare Drexelius, *De Æternitate Considerationes* (ed. cit. vol. i, p. 11), 'Sit mons,' &c.

PAGE 181. (*First note*) *Est pœna præsens &c.* Seneca, *Phaedra*, 162-4.

ll. 22-37. *Vidi ego, etc.* The passage consists of several extracts from *Prologus sancti Hieronymi ... in libros Vitaspatrum* (wrongly attributed to Jerome).

PAGE 183. (*First note*) *Sinnes are not felt &c.* Compare Stobaeus, *Florilegium* iv. 7 :

> Οὐδεὶς ξύνοιδεν ἐξαμαρτάνων πόσον
> ἁμαρτάνει τὸ μέγεθος, ὕστερον δ' ὁρᾷ.

Quoted by Thomas Gataker in *Cinnus, sive Adversaria Miscellanea*, 1651, Lib. ii (*Opera Critica* 1698, col. 278), with a Latin version :

> Nemo satis, dum peccat, quid faciat, videt :
> Scelere at peracto, atrocitatem intelligit.

(Analysis at head of chapter *A culpa peracta rectus animadvertitur*.)

ll. 19-31, 33-9. *Let me now ... punishments.* Compare Jerome, *Vita S. Pauli Primi Eremitae* (ed. Migne, vol. ii, col. 28) ; and p. 141, 13-15 above.

(*First note*) *Cœlo tegitur &c.* Lucan, *Pharsalia* vii. 819.

(*Second note*) *Jam ruet &c.* Quoted by Petrarch, *De Contemptu Mundi*, Dial. iii (ed. cit. p. 413), from his own *Africa*, ii. 431 and 464 ('Mox ruet' in Petrarch, and 'libris' for 'tumulis').

(*Fourth note*) *O quantum &c.* Compare Seneca, *Thyestes*, 449-51 :

> O quantum bonum est
> Obstare nulli, capere securas dapes
> Humi iacentem ! scelera non intrant casas.

PAGE 184, l. 2. *Hilarion's Crow.* Jerome's story seems to be told of his S. Paul. See *Vita S. Pauli Primi Eremitae* (ed. Migne, vol. ii, col. 25). Compare p. 653, 52 below.

l. 41. *the life of Antonius.* About Antonius in the *life* of Hilarion (ed. Migne, vol. ii, col. 45).

PAGE 185, l. 18 and note. *Arcanas hyemes &c.* Baudouin Cabilliau of Ypres (1568-1652), *Epigrammata Selecta* (Antv. 1620), No. 29, p. 7.

(*Second note*) *Qui jacet &c.* Alanus de Insulis, *Liber Parabolarum*, cap. ii (ed. Migne, col. 584).

PAGE 185, ll. 38–9. *a deaths-head crownd with roses.* Compare p. 491, 6 below.

PAGE 186. (*First note*) *Omnem crede diem &c.* Horace, *Epist.* i. 4. 13. Quoted by Petrarch, *De Contemptu Mundi*, Dial. iii (ed. cit. p. 409).

ll. 7–8. *Soles occidere &c.* Catullus, *Odes* v. 4.

ll. 21–38. Herbert, *The Temple*, 'Life'. It is noticeable that Vaughan singles out three poems which seem to have had no influence on his own work.

PAGE 187, ll. 1–41. *As often &c.* Translated (sometimes roughly) from Petrarch, *De Contemptu Mundi*, Dial. iii (ed. cit. pp. 414–15) 'Quotiens igitur ... nepotibus umbra'.

(*Note*) *Immortalia ne speres &c.* Horace, *Odes* iv. 7. 12 sqq. Not in Petrarch.

ll. 20–1. Virgil, *Aeneid* iii. 515.

PAGE 188, ll. 26–9. *We can go die &c.* Herbert, *The Temple*, 'Death'.

PAGE 192, l. 21. *De Similitud.* Both this and the following are works *attributed* to Anselm.

ll. 22–3. *first made publick at Paris* 1639. *S. Anselmi Cantuariensis Archiepiscopi De Felicitate Sanctorum Dissertatio. Exscriptore Eadinero* [read '*Eadmero*'] *Anglo Canonico Regulari. . . . Parisiis, . . . M. DC. XXXIX.*

PAGE 193, l. 5. *that little hand.* See 1 Kings xviii. 44–5 : 'Behold, there ariseth a little cloud out of the sea, like a man's hand' &c.

FLORES SOLITUDINIS.

PAGE 211. (*Title-page*) *Tantus Amor &c.* Virgil, *Georgics* iv. 2–5.

PAGE 213. (*Heading*) *Sir Charles Egerton.* See note on p. 138 above.

ll. 22–3. *Puella tota &c.* Bisselius, *Icaria* (Ingolstadii, 1637, pp. 215–16).

l. 33. *the Canker-Rose in the mouth of the fox.* Compare Léopold Hervieux, *Les Fabulistes latins*, Tome ii, p. 315, No. xlv 'Vulpes dedit Lupo rosorium involutum sanguine, et cum glutiret et optimum diceret, diceret (read 'dixit') ei Vulpis : In exitu sencies, cum te scindet'.

PAGE 214, l. 22. *Amœna, Petre &c.* Augurellus, *Geronticon*, Lib. i. *Ad Petrum Lipomanum in obitu Claræ sororis* (Antv. 1582, p. 92).

PAGE 216, ll. 30–7. *Whose gentle measure &c.* Herbert, *The Temple*, 'Content'. l. 34, *Cloyster.* Herbert has 'cloisters'.

PAGE 217, ll. 3–5. *Mounsier Mathieu &c.* Pierre Matthieu, *Unhappy Prosperity. Expressed in the History of Ælius Seianus And Philippa the Catanian ... Translated by S^r. T. H.* (second ed. 1639, p. 313) : 'they would have married him to the Princesse of Majorica, he left Roses to make a conserve of Thornes'.

l. 33. *where destruction passeth for propagation.* Vaughan refers to the Act for the Propagation of the Gospel in Wales (1649) under which his brother Thomas and his friend Thomas Powell were ejected from their livings. See John Walker, *Sufferings of the Clergy* (1714) ; compare p. 346, 8 below, and p. 166, 13–15 above.

PAGE 218. *O doe not goe &c.* This poem with the title 'Begging' was also included in the second part of *Silex Scintillans*. The alterations are indicated by the foot-notes to p. 500 below.

PAGE 220. (*Heading*) *Of Temperance and Patience.* Editions of the work from which Vaughan translated (*Ioannis Eusebii Nierembergii Ex Societate Iesu, De Arte Voluntatis, Libri Sex*) were published in 1631, 1639, and 1649. I have used the edition of 1639. Beginning on p. 105 (Lib. Sec. Appendix I, 'Tolerantia, & temperantia rerum') Vaughan translates from 'Breuis est' to p. 161 (end of Appendix III), corresponding to p. 267, 2 below. He then goes back to p. 93 (Epistasis to Lib. I).

PAGE 225, l. 12. *that troublesome Tympany.* Vaughan's addition.

PAGE 226, l. 11. *as the heart with Dittany.* Compare Nieremberg (ed. cit. p. 113): 'quo velut dictamo expellimus aciem'. 'heart'= 'hart' (see O.E.D. art. *Dittany*).

PAGE 227, l. 30. *his relatives.* Nieremberg (ed. cit. p. 115): 'quod nostra refert'. Compare p. 390, 37 below: 'the *sacred Relatives* of *God*'; also p. 295, 4.

PAGE 233. (*Note*) *Volater.* Compare Raphael Volaterranus, *Commentarii* (Basileae, 1559, p. 357). The last sentence of the note is Vaughan's. Most of the material for the preceding note (p. 231) is also in Volaterranus (p. 140).

PAGE 243, ll. 7–8. *for God . . . Divell.* Vaughan's addition.

PAGE 253, l. 41–254, l. 2. *The brest that conceives &c.* Compare Nieremberg (ed. cit. p. 145): 'inque ipso peccaturi pectore dum concipitur malignitas, iam grauida est, imò puerpera suæ pœnæ'; 'he is delivered' apparently refers to the 'peccaturus'.

PAGE 254, ll. 4–12. *Conscience &c.* Compare Nieremberg (ed. cit. p. 145): 'Quin ipsius culpæ ipsa est maxima, & prima pœna: nullum non capitale scelus cuique apud se est, etiam post indulgentiam omnium'.

PAGE 255, ll. 32–4. *or if she doth . . . hurt him.* Vaughan's addition.

l. 42–page 256, l. 18. *In the affaires &c.* Compare Nieremberg (ed. cit. p. 147): 'namque tristitia, quam fors ardua immisit, potest in se eleuari; quam verò dimisit culpa, non dimissa, non debet, etiamsi possit'.

PAGE 256, ll. 37–40. *he that dryes . . . precaution.* Vaughan's addition, replacing five lines of original (ed. cit. p. 147). From this point Vaughan omits longer passages of his original.

PAGE 259, ll. 10–11. *Indiscretion . . . importance.* Vaughan's addition.

PAGE 263, ll. 23–9. *Care thou &c.* Compare Nieremberg (ed. cit. p. 157): 'Cura, quæ tibi transire modò putas, actiones, vt rectæ sint: hæc manebunt'.

ll. 40–1. *though they may disturb . . . immortality.* Compare Nieremberg (loc. cit.): 'liberum immortalitati post mortem ius relinquit'.

PAGE 264, ll. 4–5. *Gold . . . unrighteousnesse.* Vaughan's addition.

ll. 15–17. *strain, and point . . . corruption.* Vaughan's addition.

ll. 36–7. *Knowledge . . . dead.* Vaughan's addition.

PAGE 265, ll. 25–32. *Christians . . . Humility.* Vaughan's addition.

PAGE 266, ll. 3–4. *He was . . . hastie.* Vaughan's addition.

ll. 12–14. *Rivers would fall . . . sterility.* Vaughan's addition.

l. 37–page 267, l. 6. *Nothing hath commerce . . . Calamities.* Vaughan's addition.

PAGE 269, l. 2. *No man can take up a Child.* Compare Nieremberg (ed. cit. p. 96): 'Nullus iacentem suscitabit'.

PAGE 270, ll. 2–3. *yea . . . men.* Vaughan's addition.

ll. 31–2. *which . . . private.* Vaughan's addition.

PAGE 271, ll. 22–6. *All the glory &c.* Compare Nieremberg (ed. cit. p. 98): 'Currunt & simulatæ: compar his fiet, qui saltem se dissimulat'.

ll. 29–30. *nor that Christian peace . . . hope.* Vaughan's addition.

PAGE 272, ll. 22–4. *He saw . . . Veyle.* Vaughan's addition.

PAGE 272, l. 41–page 273, l. 3. *They are still &c.* Compare Nieremberg (ed. cit. p. 100): 'Quò? rogabis. Meta, nihilum est: euanent, non sinunt, vt fumus è camino'.

PAGE 273, ll. 15–20. *but the Soul . . . the Soul.* Vaughan's addition.

ll. 24–37. *He applied &c.* A very free paraphrase. Compare Nieremberg (ed. cit. p. 101).

PAGE 274, l. 8. *these . . . peace.* Vaughan's addition.

l. 10. *What . . . them.* Vaughan's addition.

(*Note*) *Vixere fortes &c.* Horace, *Odes* IV. ix. 2. 25–8.

l. 39–page 275, l. 2. *which tears the Crowne . . . planted.* Compare Nieremberg (ed. cit. p. 103): 'quominùs fortunam ibi radicatam, non videremus reuulsam'.

PAGE 275, ll. 16–17. *Seeing the World . . . earnest.* Vaughan's addition.

ll. 21–8. *Why should I . . . Cap.* Compare Nieremberg (ed. cit. p. 103): 'Quia nemo alienis rebus afficitur, qui vixerit alienam vitam sine affectu, id est, suus erit : omnia, vt histrio, fabulam putabit'.

PAGE 276, l. 10—end. *In all the tumults &c.* Vaughan's addition.

l. 14. *Gloria tibi mitissime Jesu!* With these words Herbert closes *The Temple.*

PAGE 277. Here Vaughan begins to translate *De Arte Voluntatis,* Lib. VI, Diorismus v. *Ex comparatione vitæ, & mortis.*

(*Note*). Compare Volaterranus, Lib. xiv (ed. cit. p. 325).

ll. 23–6. *hee would not . . . despised her.* Vaughan's addition.

PAGE 278, ll. 3–5. *Whose . . . blockish.* Vaughan's addition.

ll. 18–26. *some old . . . Conscience.* Vaughan's addition.

PAGE 281, ll. 16–17. *and glorifies . . . cause.* Vaughan's addition.

ll. 19–22. *It was &c.* Compare Nieremberg (ed. cit. p. 477): 'omnium malorum remedium est, quo desinunt omnia'.

PAGE 283, l. 15. *like a great and violent fall.* Vaughan's addition.

l. 23. *The Rod blasteth all their innocent joyes.* Compare Nieremberg (ed. cit. p. 478): 'Terret pueros flagellum'.

PAGE 284, ll. 2–9. *And indeed . . . blood.* Almost entirely Vaughan's addition, replacing seven lines of original (p. 479).

l. 40. *It is . . . troubles.* Vaughan's addition.

PAGE 285, ll. 2–5. *that having reach'd . . . before them.* Compare Nieremberg (ed. cit. p. 481): 'quò procedant iam placidius per decliuia & plana'.

l. 21. *in the shade.* l. 22. *the shadow of death.* l. 33. *in its shadow and projection.* Vaughan's additions.

PAGE 286, ll. 15–16. *and make . . . fairest faces.* Vaughan's addition.

ll. 29–32. *Thou mayst lye watching . . . sleepes.* Vaughan's addition.

l. 41–page 287, l. 1. *the Nurse . . . to it.* Vaughan's addition.

PAGE 287, ll. 19–22. *by which . . . world.* Vaughan's addition.

ll. 35–6. *impieties, tyranny &c.* Compare Nieremberg (ed. cit. p. 483): 'malitia'.

PAGE 288, ll. 18–21. *They plot . . . prevail.* Vaughan's addition.

ll. 35–6. *by turning . . . lease was out.* Vaughan's addition.

ll. 38–9. *Before . . . veile.* Vaughan's addition.

l. 41–page 289, l. 10. *It was . . . Christ.* Compare Nieremberg (ed. cit. p. 484): 'fauor fuit non properare illò, vbi nec meritum, nec præmium futurum erat. Nunc, quia Cælum nos expectat, mora mortis non promittitur, potiùs commendatur intempestiua

& violenta, beatitudinis exaggerata titulo, quia illuc conuehat morientes pro Christo'.

PAGE 289, ll. 30-1. *which cannot . . . sorrowes.* Vaughan's addition.

PAGE 291, ll. 36-7. *Rom. Chap. . . . Sinne.* Vaughan adds the quotation.

PAGE 292, ll. 4-8. *Life . . . intimations.* Compare Nieremberg (ed. cit. p. 487) : 'feriata mens sensibus idoneè diuina excipit'.

PAGE 294, ll. 15-16. *That humble . . . mouth.* Compare Nieremberg (ed. cit. p. 490): 'nemini non honorificus defunctus est'.

ll. 18-19. *He saw . . . downe.* Vaughan's addition.

PAGE 295, ll. 1-2. *and discerning . . . humanity.* Vaughan's addition.

ll. 11-12. *and the Depositum . . . Restauratour.* Vaughan's addition.

ll. 32-3. *whose Musick . . . any.* Vaughan's addition.

PAGE 296, ll. 6-7. *in that great . . . day.* Compare Nieremberg (ed. cit. p. 491): 'post mortem'.

ll. 31-9. *God gave it not . . . the body.* Vaughan's addition.

PAGE 297, ll. 37-40. *He quarrelled . . . Almighty.* Vaughan's addition.

PAGE 298, ll. 13-17. *The ignorance . . . so well.* Vaughan's addition.

PAGE 299, ll. 10-12. *though . . . believers.* Compare Nieremberg (ed. cit. p. 494): ' omnibus mutatis '.

ll. 23-4. *Life . . . out.* Vaughan's addition.

ll. 30-3. *therefore it delaies . . . protractions.* Compare Nieremberg (ed. cit. p. 495): 'protractius protelat. Mors optima est, ideò sine lege moræ.'

PAGE 300, ll. 26-8. *it is a flower . . . weather.* Compare Nieremberg (ed. cit. p. 496): ' Caduca possessio vita est,' &c.

PAGE 301, ll. 5-6. *Good . . . bolts.* Vaughan's addition.

ll. 32-5. *and by a compendious . . . feet.* Compare Nieremberg (ed. cit. p. 497): 'infantiam per compendium maturat, ianuam Cæli gratis aperiens, viâ rectâ, & sine obice dirigens '.

ll. 37-9. *Death . . . divinity.* Compare Nieremberg (ed. cit. p. 497) : ' fuisse argumentum Diuinitatis '.

l. 40-page 302, l. 6. *The Divell . . . daies.* Compare Nieremberg (ed. cit. p. 497): '-Æmulus Diabolus cultum falsum beneficio mortis fulciit, petentibus magnum domum, exiguam vitam concedens '.

⊦ PAGE 302, ll. 15-24. *What greater good &c.* Compare Nieremberg (ed. cit. p. 497) : ' Quid felicius Pompeio accidisset, quàm antè, aut in sua felicitate perire, cùm sui desiderium relinqueret, si non expecteret fastidium fortunæ'.

PAGE 303, ll. 9-13. *For those . . . morning.* Vaughan's addition, replacing five lines of original (p. 498).

ll. 14-19. *but he expired . . . dissolution.* Compare Nieremberg (ed. cit. p. 498): 'sed casum putares, intempestiuam mortem, non consilium Dei, non donum '.

PAGE 304, ll. 27-32. *Life is a Terrace-walke . . . dust.* Vaughan's addition.

ll. 32-42. *Sleepe . . . cares.* Compare Nieremberg (ed. cit. p. 500) : ' Somnus quædam effigies mortis, & prælibatio est : somnum appetimus, somno recreamur, somnus requies laborum est, reparatio hominis, depositio curarum '.

PAGE 305, ll. 19-25. *Paracelsus writes . . . flesh.* Vaughan's addition. Compare Paracelsus, *De Meteoricis Expressionibus* (*Philosophiæ et Medicinæ . . . Compendium,* 1568, p. 34) : ' Non est spiritui tamen sabathi requies imposita, sed corpori solùm hominis, vt aliorum animalium auxiliantium illi. Spiritus verò semper & in assiduo labore positus est, vt neᴄᴣ nox, neᴄᴣ sabathum ad requiem eum compescat, in omnibus etiam creaturis.'

l. 32. *like the Phœnix.* Vaughan's addition.

ll. 39–41. (*more) then for . . . joyes.* Vaughan's addition.

PAGE 306, ll. 34–5. *imitation . . . World.* Vaughan's addition.

PAGE 307, ll. 31–2. *and not sneak . . . fellow.* Vaughan's addition.

ll. 35–9. *That death . . . head.* Compare Nieremberg (ed. cit. p. 503) : ' quæ suffragio pereuntis expectatur, quâ crescit illæsus etiam minutus capite '.

l. 41—page 308, l. 1. *Whose sufferer . . . joy.* Vaughan's addition.

PAGE 308, ll. 16–17. *the Elixir &c.* Vaughan supplies the alchemical metaphor.

l. 27. *politick, irreligious Tyrants.* Compare Nieremberg (ed. cit. p. 504) : ' instantem tyrannum '.

PAGE 309, l. 1. *they dare not . . . of it.* Vaughan's addition.

ll. 5–7. *Death . . . hands.* Vaughan's addition.

ll. 13–14. *Sickness and death &c.* Vaughan's addition.

PAGE 312, l. 1. *published this peece at Antwerp* 1621. Vaughan refers to *D. Eucherii Episcopi Lugdunensis De Contemptu Mundi Epistola parænetica ad Valerianum cognatum. Accedit Vita D. Paulini Nolani Veri Mundi Contemptoris. Antverpiæ, . . . M. DC. XXI.*

l. 2. *Gennadius cap.* 63. ed. Migne, *Patrologiæ Cursus,* vol. lviii, col. 1096.

l. 3. *and Erasmus &c. Epistola Parænetica . . . Cum Scholijs D. Erasmi Roterodami . . . M. D. XXXI.*

l. 9. *placed by Helvicus.* See *Theatrum Historicum* (Editio Quinta Oxoniæ M. DC. LI. p. 100).

ll. 15–19. *Some will have him to be &c.* The conjectures are taken from a note on p. 185 of Vaughan's original.

PAGE 318. (*Note) An excellent Dilemma.* The note is in Vaughan's original.

l. 42. *this rope of sands.* Vaughan's addition.

PAGE 320, ll. 2–4. *and in the custody . . . goods.* Compare Eucherius (ed. cit. p. 13) : ' proscriptionesq; ipsas quodammodò ostentant & inuitant ? '

PAGE 324. (*Third note) St. Augustine.* The reference to Augustine is made in Vaughan's original.

PAGE 325, ll. 25–6. *What Covert . . . things.* Vaughan's addition.

ll. 37–40. Vaughan adds the last two verses.

PAGE 329, ll. 8–9. *from the farthest North . . . Christ.* Compare Eucherius (ed. cit. pp. 28–9) : ' ab Aquilone & mari Christum resonat '.

(*Note).* This is in Vaughan's original.

PAGE 330, ll. 28–31. *Hence . . . heaven.* Compare Eucherius (ed. cit. p. 31) : ' Hinc sæpè illa cæli cernuntur signa '.

PAGE 333, ll. 12–14. *the disputers . . . wisedome.* Vaughan's addition.

PAGE 336, l. 34. *Gloria tibi &c.* Vaughan's addition. See note on p. 276, 14 above.

PAGE 337. (*Title-page) Collected out of his own Works . . . by Henry Vaughan.* The title of the work following Eucherius' *Epistola* in the 1621 edition is as follows : *Vita Diui Paulini Episc. Nolani ex scriptis eius, & veterum de eo Elogiis concinnata.* The Preface by

Heribertvs Rosweydvs begins: 'Vti Româ hanc Vitam ab amico Socio concinnatam accepi, ita tecum communico'. In 1622 Rosweydus and Ducæus brought out an edition (with notes and a reprint of the *Vita*) of the Works of Paulinus. Vaughan uses the works and the notes, and since he translated the *Epistola* presumably had both publications (i. e. those of 1621 and 1622).

PAGE 338, ll. 15-20. *Desine tandem &c.* From *Ioh: Baptistæ Ferrarii Senensis, S. I. Flora, seu De Florum Cultura Lib. IV.* (Ed. nova, 1646, Lib. I, cap. i, p. 3.)

PAGE 339, ll. 8-21. Ecclesiasticus l, vv. 6-11.

PAGE 340, ll. 4-5. *Which silently &c.* Miss Guiney compares Horace, *Odes* i. 12. 45-6:

> Crescit occulto velut arbor aevo
> Fama Marcelli.

ll. 7-15. *And this &c.* Here Vaughan begins his series of paraphrases and translations from the *Vita*. See note on page 337 above. His dependence is illustrated in the following notes.

ll. 25-30. *In a Golden Age &c.* Compare *Vita*, p. 51 'Sæculo aureo . . . multiplicandæ suæ'.

ll. 30-41. *It was the fashion &c.* Compare *Vita*, p. 49 'Quippe ea tempestate . . . gloriantur'.

PAGE 341, ll. 2-16. *His Patrimonies &c.* Compare *Vita*, pp. 50-1 '*Patrimonium . . . fleamus*'.

ll. 19-30. *Ergo nihil &c.* Compare *Vita*, p. 47 '*Ergo nihil . . . negligamus*'.

ll. 31-6. *He had conferred &c.* Compare *Vita*, pp. 46-7 'Humanae vitae ornamenta . . . suauissimis'.

l. 36—page 342, l. 2. *To bring &c.* Compare *Vita*, pp. 51-2 'Ita factum est . . . formaritque'.

ll. 39-40. *who at that time &c.* Compare *Vita*, p. 60 'Burdigalæ . . . rexit'.

PAGE 342, ll. 3-26. For the origin of this passage, including the note, see *Vita*, pp. 51, 52, 55, 56, 57, 60.

l. 41—page 343, l. 5. *In these travells &c.* Compare *Vita*, p. 60 'Quos inter errores . . . norint'.

PAGE 343, ll. 12-14. *associating &c.* Compare *Vita*, p. 63.

ll. 15-25, 31-4. Compare *Vita*, pp. 65-6.

l. 40. *calling her Tanaquil &c.* Compare *Vita*, p. 63 'Tanaquilem . . . imperitaretque viro'.

PAGE 344, l. 2. *Thus Ausonius barks at him.* Compare *Vita*, p. 63 'Sic enim latrat'.

ll. 3-14. *Undè istam &c.* Ausonius, *Epist.* xxviii. 5-9, 17, 14 (ed. Peiper, p. 285) and xxviii. (p. 284) 30-1. This couplet is also in *Vita*, p. 63.

ll. 17-33. *Continuata &c.* Paulinus, *Epist. ad Aus.* xi. 1-5 and x. 189-92 (*Corpus Script. Eccl. Lat.*, pp. 39 and 32).

PAGE 345, ll. 3-23. *Hoc pignus &c.* Paulinus, *Carm.* xxxi. (ed. cit. p. 328) 581-2, 585-90, 601-2, 607-8, 615-16, 624, 626. ll. 20-1 are practically Vaughan's addition.

ll. 39-41 (*with note*) *The first step . . . men.* Compare *Vita*, p. 78.

PAGE 346, l. 2. *Superstitie.* Apparently a coinage.

ll. 11-22 and 23-5. *Utinam . . . Christ.* Compare *Vita*, p. 80.

l. 34—page 347, l. 34. *Four yeares . . . called.* Compare *Vita*, p. 86 'Porrò . . . expaui'; p. 87 'Data . . . vocauit'.

PAGE 348, l. 41-page 350, l. 6. *Revocandum &c.* Paulinus, *Carm.* x. 110-13, 131-3, 137, 283-331.

PAGE 350, ll. 19-28. *And here . . . himself.* Compare *Vita*, pp. 89-90 'Hîc (vt loquitur Vranius) . . . restituens'.

l. 30-page 351, l. 1. *Paulinum &c.* Compare *Vita*, pp. 72-3 'Paulinus . . . charitatis diuitiis'.

PAGE 351, ll. 2-5, 20-38, 38-page 352, l. 15. *Saint Augustine &c.* Compare *Vita*, pp. 124-31.

PAGE 352, ll. 35-9. *for he onely is a stranger &c.* Compare p. 440, 9 sqq. below, and the note on that poem.

PAGE 353, ll. 23-6. *His Estate . . . Sea.* Compare *Vita*, p. 90 'Rebus in Gallia . . . accessit'.

l. 40-page 354, l. 9. *From Millaine . . . edicts.* Compare *Vita*, pp. 90-1.

PAGE 354, ll. 23-4. *In a pleasant field . . . Felix.* Compare *Vita*, p. 92 'Amoeno in agro', &c.

l. 31-page 355, l. 11. *Eusebius &c.* Part of a note to the edition of Paulinus's works published in 1622 (p. 847 'Constantinus in templo . . . *requiescere terrâ*'). See note on p. 337 above.

PAGE 355. (*Note*). Compare Paulinus, *Carm.* xii. 9 'sine sanguine martyr'.

ll. 25-30. *This Felix &c.* Compare Paulinus, *Carm.* xv. 72-80.

l. 32-page 356, l. 4. *Saint Augustine . . . them.* Compare *Vita*, p. 97 'S. Augustinus . . . propalatum'.

PAGE 356, ll. 5-6. *Paulinus . . . sicknesse.* Compare *Vita*, p. 98 'Verùm non multis', &c.

(*Note*). Compare Paulinus, *Epist.* xl (ed. cit.—*Corpus Script. Eccl.*—pp. 346-7).

l. 38-page 357, l. 9. *viderant pueri . . . comfort me.* Compare *Vita*, pp. 98-9.

PAGE 357, ll. 13-16, 22-page 360, l. 23. *As touching the letters &c.* Compare *Vita*, pp. 99-103.

PAGE 360, l. 40-page 361, l. 22. *Librum tuum . . . Martyrs.* Compare *Vita*, pp. 105-6, 172, 171.

PAGE 361, l. 23-page 362, l. 22. *Much about this time . . . Burdeaux.* Compare *Vita*, pp. 106-15.

PAGE 362, l. 32-page 363, l. 1. *Potiore . . . ashamed of me.* See Paulinus, *Epist.* xi (ed. cit., p. 61, 22–p. 62, 4).

PAGE 363, ll. 2-7. *If I shall have need &c.* Compare *Vita*, p. 116 'Præterea peto . . . debitores'.

ll. 13-17. *The Ape &c.* Compare *Locmani Sapientis Fabulæ* (Leidæ, 1615, p. 15), Lepus & Leaena. See note on 29-35 below.

l. 21. *Cabanes.* See *Unhappy Prosperity* (ed. cit. note to p. 217 above), p. 326 sqq.

l. 22. *some Son of a Butcher.* Cardinal Wolsey? See Miss Guiney's edition, p. 124.

ll. 29-35. *the Apologues &c.* Compare Locmannus, *Fabulæ* (ed. cit. p. 38), Faber & Canis.

PAGE 364, ll. 1-33 (*including note*). *And on the other side &c.* Compare *Vita*, pp. 116-19 'At laudes . . . *quod non sum*'.

l. 38-page 365, l. 10. *Abluitis &c.* Compare Paulinus, *Epist.* xxxii (ed. cit. p. 277, 19-24).

PAGE 365, ll. 12-25. *Hic reparandarum &c.* Compare Paulinus, ed. cit. p. 279, 9-20.

ll. 26-43, *all his Garments &c.* Compare *Vita*, p. 123.

PAGE 365, l. 31. *Righteousnesse . . . poor.* Vaughan's addition.

PAGE 366. (*Note*). See Paulinus, *Epist.* xl (ed. cit. p. 349, 18–p.350, 3).

l. 31. Τὸ πτωχὸν ἦθος &c. Georgius Pisida, Εἰς τὸν μάταιον βίον, l. 237 (ed. Migne, col. 1598).

l. 35–page 367, l. 25. *In the four hundred . . . poore man.* Compare *Vita*, p. 127 ' Namq; sub annum ', &c.

PAGE 367, ll. 26–9. *In his owne Workes . . . glory.* Compare *Vita*, pp. 144–5 ' Quæ extant ', &c.

l. 38–page 368, l. 33. *Cum autem . . . falshood.* Compare *Vita*, pp. 148–50 ' Cùm autem ', &c.

PAGE 368, ll. 34–40. *Nola was at this time . . . honour him.* Compare *Vita*, p. 151 ' per id tempus ', &c.

l. 42–page 369, l. 9. *Prosper . . . them.* Compare *Vita*, p. 152 ' vt inde ostendat ', &c.

PAGE 369, l. 16. *one of his Epistles.* See Paulinus, *Epist.* iii (ed. cit. p. 17, 4–5).

ll. 29–39. *Victor the Monk . . . hands.* Compare *Vita*, pp. 121–2 ' Immensis ', &c.

PAGE 370, l. 8–page 371, l. 30. *In the year . . . long for.* Compare *Vita*, p. 152 ' docet epistola ', &c.

PAGE 372, l. 5–page 374, l. 5 (except note on p. 373). *Whose charity . . . the fire.* Compare *Vita*, pp. 154–8 ' Sed misericordia ', &c.

ll. 6–7. *This iron age . . . mercy.* Vaughan's addition.

PAGE 374, l. 40–page 375, l. 2. *He repaired . . . Christ.* Compare Paulinus, *Epist.* xxxii (ed. cit. p. 286, 1–3).

PAGE 375, ll. 9–13. *Cælestes intrate &c.* Compare Paulinus, *Epist.* xxxii (ed. cit. p. 288).

ll. 24–8. *Ardua floriferæ &c.* Compare Paulinus, loc. cit. (p. 289).

l. 41. *in his twelfth Epistle.* *Epist.* xxxii (ed. cit. pp. 291–2).

PAGE 376, ll. 1–16, *his ninth Natalis &c.* Paulinus, *Carm.* xxvii. 387–92.

ll. 17–45. *Having finished . . . light.* Compare Paulinus, *Epist.* xxxii (ed. cit. pp. 291–2).

PAGE 377, ll. 3–4. *they were good works &c.* Compare *The Temple* ('The Printers to the Reader ') : ' With the remembrance whereof, as of an especiall good work, when a friend went about to comfort him on his deathbed, he made answer, *It is a good work, if it be sprinkled with the bloud of Christ:* otherwise then in this[,] respect he could finde nothing to glorie or comfort himself with, neither in this, nor in any other thing '.

ll. 6–14. *Nisi dominus &c.* Compare Paulinus, *Epist.* xxxii (ed. cit. p. 297, 6 and 12–15).

ll. 16–17. *Cum suis &c.* Compare Paulinus, *Epist.* xxxii (ed. cit. p. 295) ' ut tunc ibi locupletemur '.

l. 39–page 378, l. 28. *hos per longa morantes &c.* Paulinus, *Carm.* xxvii. 3–11, 107–16, 119–23, 127–34.

PAGE 379, ll. 32–3. *These two they have utterly taken away.* Compare p. 443, 17–18 below.

ll. 40–2. *the forerunners . . . with years.* Compare George Herbert, *The Temple*, ' The Forerunners ' :

The harbingers are come. See, see their mark ;
White is their colour, and behold my head.

PAGE 380, l. 7–page 381, l. 29. *Three daies . . . Master.* Compare *Vita*, pp. 161–4 ' Ante triduum ', &c.

PAGE 381, ll. 32–3. *Gregory the great &c.* Compare *Vita*, loc. cit.

l. 35–page 382, l. 4. *Three daies &c.* Compare *Vita*, pp. 166–7 'Ante diem', &c.

PAGE 382, ll. 8–10, 12–13. *Blessed Paulinus ... Tombe.* Compare *Vita*, pp. 167–8 'Decessit', &c.

PAGES 382–5. *Poem.* Attributed to Paulinus and given in the edition of 1622, p. 643. Compare note on p. 174, 23 above. See Appendix to *Carmina*, ed. cit. pp. 344–8.

SILEX SCINTILLANS.

PAGE 387 (*Title-page*). *Silex Scintillans.* Compare Nieremberg, *De Arte Voluntatis*, ed. cit. p. 139 'Subsiliunt è plagis quædam animo diuinæ luces, velut scintillæ è silice afflicto,' translated p. 249, 10–11 above, 'Certaine Divine Raies,' &c. ; and p. 462, 58–60.

PAGE 388, l. 8. (*with a Predecessor of theirs*) *term Parricides.* Grosart compares Greene, *Groats-Worth of witte* (1592, &c.): 'Ah Gentlemen, that liue to read my broken and confused lines, looke not I should (as I was wont) delight you with vaine fantasies ; and as yee would deale with so many parricides, cast them into the fire'.

ll. 26–30. *Os dignum &c.* Prudentius, *Contra Symmachum*, i. 636–40 ('tentet').

PAGE 390, ll. 3–13. *That he would read &c.* From Felltham, *Resolves*, Second Century I. 'Of Idle Bookes,' ed. cit. pp. 323–4. The differences suggest that Vaughan was quoting from memory.

l. 37. *Relatives.* See note on p. 227, 30 above.

PAGE 391, l. 26. *a most flourishing and admired wit of his time.* The reference is probably to Andrew Melville or Melvin. Compare Walton, *Life of Mr. George Herbert*, ed. Bullen, p. 274. Mr. Chambers suggested Donne, though noting the difficulty of Herbert's age.

l. 27. *Sed non passibus æquis.* Virgil, *Aeneid* ii. 724 'sequitur-que patrem non passibus aequis'.

PAGE 392, l. 8. *Hierotheus.* See *Vita S. Dionysii Areopagiticae* (P. Halloix), ed. Migne, p. 839 &c.: '*Haec etiam praeclarus ille noster sacrorum moderator* (Hierotheus) *in hymnis amatoriis divine exposuit*'.

PAGE 397, ll. 1–16. *A Ward &c.* Compare Thomas Vaughan, *Lumen de Lumine: Or A new Magicall Light discovered, and Communicated to the World By Eugenius Philalethes. . . .* London, . . . 1651, p. 1–2: 'It was about the *Dawning* or Day-breake, when tyr'd with a tedious *solitude*, and those *pensive Thoughts* which *attend it*, after much *Losse* and more *Labour*, I suddainly fell *a sleep.* Here then the *Day* was no sooner *borne*, but *strangled*; I was reduc'd to a *night* of a more deep *tincture* than that which I had *formerly spent.* My *fansie* placed me in a *Region* of inexpressible *Obscuritie*, and as I thought more than *Naturall*; but without any *Terrors.* . . . I moved every way for *Discoveries*, but was still intertained with *Darknesse* and *silence*, and I thought my self translated to the *Land* of *Desolation*.'

ll. 3–4. *and all the way &c.* Compare *Lumen de Lumine*, p. 6: 'Her *walk* was *green*, . . . and purl'd all the Way with *Daysies* and *Primrose*'.

PAGE 398, ll. 33–48. *Here, I repos'd &c.* Compare *Lumen de Lumine*, p. 2: 'Being thus troubled to no purpose, and wearied with long Indeavours, I resolved to rest my self, and seeing I could find nothing, I expected if any thing could find me. I had not long continued in this humor, but I could heare the *whispers* of a *soft wind*, that *tra-vail'd* towards me, and suddainly it was in the *Leaves* of the *Trees*, so that I concluded my self to be in some *Wood*, or *Wildernesse*. With this gentle *Breath* came a most *heavenly*, *odorous Ayre*, much like that of *sweet Briars*, but not so *rank*, and *full*.'

l. 44. *Checqur'd with snowie fleeces.* Compare *Lumen de Lumine*, p. 4: 'The *Ground* both neer and far of, presented a *pleasing* kind of *Checquer*'.

PAGE 399, ll. 65-80. *It was a banke &c.* Compare *Lumen de Lumine*, p. 15: 'Now verily was I much troubled, and somewhat disordered, but composing my self as well as I could, I came to a *Cop* of *Myrtles*, where resting my self on a *Flowrie Bank*, I began to consider those Things which I had seen'.

l. 70. *A rushing wind.* Compare note on p. 398 above.

l. 75. *if any leafe.* Compare note on p. 398 above.

PAGE 401, ll. 9-14. *Untill at last &c.* Compare Felltham, *Resolves*, 'Of Death' (ed. cit. p. 149) : 'That grosse object which is left to the spectators eyes, is now onely a composure but of the two *baser Elements*, *Water*, and *Earth* : that now it is these two onely, that seeme to make the *body*, while the two purer, *Fire* and *Ayre*, are wing'd away, as being more fit for the compact of an *elementall* and *ascentive Soule*'.

l. 25. *For no thing &c.* Compare Donne, *The broken heart* (ed. Grierson, p. 49, l. 25), 'Yet nothing can to nothing fall'.

ll. 31-4. *For a preserving spirit &c.* Compare Sir Thomas Browne, *Religio Medici* (ed. Herford, p. 36) : 'Now, besides these particular and divided Spirits, there may be (for ought I know) an universal and common Spirit to the whole World. It was the opinion of Plato, and it is yet of the Hermetical Philosophers.'

PAGE 402, l. 59. *To reade some Starre.* Compare Vaughan's letter to Aubrey, p. 672, 13 sqq. below.

PAGE 404, ll. 5-8. *Under a Juniper &c.* Compare George Herbert, *The Temple*, 'Decay' :

> One might have sought and found thee presently
> At some fair oak, or bush, or cave, or well.

PAGE 412. *The Showre.* Compare note on p. 445, 31-7 below.

PAGE 414. *The Pursuite.* Compare *The Temple*, 'The Pulley'.

(*Mount of Olives*) l. 9. *Cotswold, and Coopers.* See *Annalia Dubrensia. Vpon the yeerely celebration of M*ʳ· *Robert Dovers Olimpick Games vpon Cotswold-Hills ... London, ... 1636.* But Vaughan was perhaps thinking only of one poem in that volume, Randolph (ed. cit. p. 103) *An Eglogue on the noble Assemblies revived on Cotswold Hills by M*. Robert Dover. *Coopers Hill* was published in 1642.

PAGE 416, (*second poem*) l. 1. *Thou that know'st for whom I mourne.* Compare p. 420, 28 (With him I weep); p. 426, 28 ; p. 479, 61 ; p. 512, 12, &c.; and Thomas Vaughan, *Anthroposophia Theomagica* (1650), p. 65 : 'this *Piece* was compos'd in *Haste*, and in my *Dayes* of *Mourning*, on the sad *Occurence* of a *Brother's Death*'.

PAGE 418, ll. 51-2. *And sweeter aires &c.* Compare *The Temple*, 'Sion' :

> All Solomons sea of brasse and world of stone
> Is not so deare to thee as one good grone.

and *Gratefulnesse*, st. vi.

PAGE 419. *The Retreate.* Vaughan may have read John Earle's Character of a Child (*Micro-cosmographie*, 1628) : ' *A Child* is a Man in a small Letter, yet the best Copie of *Adam* before hee tasted of *Eue*, or the Apple ; and hee is happy whose small practice in the World can only write his Character. Hee is natures fresh picture newly drawne in Oyle, which time and much handling dimmes and defaces. . . . His father hath writ him as his owne little story, wherein he reades those dayes of his life that he cannot remember; and sighes to see what innocence he ha's out-liu'd. The elder he growes, he is a stayre lower from God ; and like his first father, much worse in his breeches. He is the Christians example, and the old man's relapse: The one imitates his purenesse, and the other falls into his simplicitie . . . '

PAGE 419, l. 20. *Bright shootes of everlastingnesse.* Compare Felltham, *Resolves*, ' Of the Soule ' (ed. cit. p. 197): ' The *Conscience*, the *Caracter* of a *God* stampt in it, and the apprehension of *Eternity*, doe all prove it a *shoot of everlastingnesse* '.

PAGE 424, ll. 21-4. *So shall that storme &c.* Compare *The Temple*, ' The Storm ' :

> Poets have wrong'd poore storms : such dayes are best ;
> They purge the aire without, within the breast.

(*The Morning-watch*) l. 1. *O Joyes! Infinite sweetnes!* Compare *The Temple*, ' The Holy Scriptures,' I :

> Oh Book ! infinite sweetnesse !

ll. 18, 19. *Prayer is The world in tune.* Compare *The Temple*, ' Prayer ' :

> A kind of tune, which all things heare and fear ;

PAGE 429, l. 1. *Sure, there's a tye of Bodyes!* Compare Felltham, *Resolves*, ' That Sufferance causeth Love ' (ed. cit. p. 253): ' Nothing surer tyes a friend . . . Sure, there is a *Sympathy of soules* '.

l. 9. *Absents within the Line &c.* Compare p. 497, 9 and p. 483, 20. Vaughan apparently means ' Those who are absent from one another, and yet not dead, feel sympathy '.

PAGE 431, ll. 15-18. *Most blessed Vine &c.* Compare *The Temple*, ' The Agonie ' :

> Love is that liquor sweet and most divine,
> Which my God feels as bloud ; but I, as wine.

PAGE 432, ll. 11-16. Compare *The Temple*, ' Employment ' (second poem with that title) :

> Oh that I were an Orenge-tree,
>> That busie plant !
> Then should I ever laden be,
>> And never want
> Some fruit for him that dressed me.

PAGE 433, ll. 9-12. Compare *The Temple*, ' Discipline ' :

> Throw away thy rod,
> Throw away thy wrath
>> O my God,
> Take the gentle path.

PAGE 434, l. 1. Compare *The Temple*, ' The Reprisall ' :

> I have consider'd it, and finde
> There is no dealing with thy mighty passion:

ll. 11-28. These lines were printed in the 1650 edition of *Recreation for Ingenious Head-peeces. Or, A Pleasant Grove for their Wits to walke in* [Wit's Recreations] and in the subsequent editions of 1654, 1663, and 1667. They form a conclusion to the volume : ' Having now fed thy youthfull frencies, with these Juvenilian Fancies ; let me invite thee (with my selfe) to sing *Altiora peto.* And then to meet with this thy noble resolution; I would commend to thy sharpest view and serious consideration ; The Sweet Cælestiall sacred Poems by Mr. *Henry Vaughan,* intituled *Silex Scintillans.*

> There plumes from Angels wings, he'l lend thee,
> Which every day to heaven will send thee.
> (*Heare him thus invite thee home.*)'

PAGE 434, ll. 23-4. *All strewed with flowres &c.* Compare *The Temple,* ' Affliction ' (first poem with that title) :

> My dayes were straw'd with flow'rs and happinesse ;
> There was no moneth but May.

and p. 505, 18 below.

(*The Match*) l. 1. *Dear friend!* Presumably Vaughan refers to George Herbert.

PAGE 435, ll. 7-12. *Two Lifes &c.* Compare *The Temple,* ' Love unknown ' :

> A Lord I had,
> And have, of whom some grounds which may improve,
> I hold for two lives, and both lives in me.

PAGE 436. *Rules and Lessons.* Compare (for the form) *The Temple,* ' The Church-porch '.

ll. 13-16. *Walk with thy fellow-creatures &c.* Compare Thomas Vaughan, *Anima Magica Abscondita* (1650), p. 52 : ' In the *Summer* translate thy self to the Fields, where all are green with the Breath of God, and fresh with the Powers of Heaven. Learn to refer all Naturals to their Spirituals, *per viam Secretioris Analogiæ* ; for this is the way the *Magicians* went, and found out Miracles.'

PAGE 437, l. 45. *a Judas Jew.* Compare *The Temple,* ' Self-con-demnation ' :

> For he hath sold for money his deare Lord,
> And is a Judas-Jew.

PAGE 439, l. 118. *Ther's one Sun more &c.* Compare *The Temple,* ' Sunday ' :

> The Sundaies of mans life
> Thredded together on times string. &c.

l. 134. *In that dead age.* Compare Felltham, *Resolves,* ' Of Death ' (ed. cit. p. 149) : ' when thou shalt see the *body* put on *Deaths* sad and ashy countenance, in the dead age of *night* '.

PAGE 440. *Corruption.* Compare p. 352, 35-9 above, *The Temple,* ' Miserie ' ad fin., and Thomas Vaughan, *Magia Adamica : Or The Antiquitie of Magic, And the Descent thereof from Adam downwards, proved* (1650, p. 17) : ' He was excluded from a *glorious Paradyse,* and confin'd to a *base world,* whose *sickly infected Elements* conspiring with his *own Nature,* did assist and hasten that *Death,* which already began to reign in his *Body.* Heaven did mourn over him, The Earth, and all her Generations about him. He look'd upon himself as a *Felon,* and a *Murtherer,* being *guilty* of that *Curse* and *Corruption,* which succeeded in the *world* because of his *fall,* . . .'

l. 9. Compare op. cit. p. 18 : ' He was a meer stranger in this World '.

PAGE **440**, l. 19. Compare op. cit. p. 18 : ' He heard indeed sometimes of a *Tree* of *Life* in *Eden*'.

l. 25. *Angels lay Leiger here.*   Compare *The Temple*, ' The H. Scriptures', I : ' thou art heav'ns Lidger here,' and p. 60, 10 above.

PAGE **441**, (*H. Scriptures*) ll. 3–4. *The Doves spotless neast &c.* Compare *The Temple*, ' Whitsunday' :

> Listen sweet Dove unto my song,
> And spread thy golden wings in me ;
> Hatching my tender heart so long,
> Till it get wing, and flie away with thee.

and p. 446, 47 below.

PAGE **442**, l. 7. Compare *The Temple*, ' Man's Medley ' :

> Heark how the birds do sing,
> And woods do ring.

ll. 11–12. *Man is their high-priest &c.*   Compare *The Temple*, ' Providence' :

> Man is the worlds high Priest : he doth present
> The sacrifice for all ;

PAGE **443**, ll. 17–18. *Thy birth now here &c.*   See p. 379, 32–3 above.

PAGE **445**, ll. 31–7. *Some sleeping Exhalation &c.*   Compare *The Temple*, ' The Answer ' :

> As a young exhalation, newly waking,
> Scorns his first bed of dirt, and means the sky ;
> But cooling by the way, grows pursie and slow,
> And settling to a cloud, doth live and die
> In that dark state of tears :

and *The Showre*, p. 412 above.

PAGE **446**, l. 46. *O, is!*   See O.E.D. art. *is* and *yes*, and note on p. 30, 484 above.

PAGE **447**, (*Idle Verse*) l. 16. *Sick with a scarf, or glove.*   Compare *The Temple*, ' Love ' (first poem with that title) :

> Who sings thy praise ? onely a skarf or glove
> Doth warm our hands, and make them write of love.

(*Son-dayes*) l. 1–end. Compare *The Temple*, ' Prayer' (for the form and some of the images), and (for other images) *The Temple*, ' Sunday'.

PAGE **449**, l. 41. *All that have signature.*   Compare p. 583, 11–13 below.

ll. 75–6. *Profanenes on my tongue &c.*   Compare *The Temple*, ' Aaron ' :

> Profaneness in my head,
> Defects and darkenesse in my breast,

PAGE **453**, ll. 5–6. *for Marble sweats &c.*   Compare *The Temple*, ' The Church floore ' :

> But all is cleansed when the marble weeps,

l. 17. *Wee are thy Infants, and suck thee.*   Compare *The Temple*, 'Longing ' :

> Mothers are kinde, because thou art,
> And dost dispose
> To them a part :
> Their infants, them ; and they suck thee
> More free.

Page 454. *Praise.* Compare *The Temple*, 'Praise,' for the form.

Page 456. *Easter-day.* Compare *The Temple*, 'The Dawning,' for the form.

Page 460, ll. 29–40. *Vicissitude plaies all the game &c.* Compare Felltham, *Resolves*, 'That all things are restrained' (ed. cit. pp. 131–2): 'Every string has his *use*, and his *tune*, and his *turne*. When the *Assyrians* fell, the *Persians* rose. When the *Persians* fell, the *Grecians* rose. The losse of one *Man*, is the gaine of another. 'Tis *vicissitude* that maintains the *World.* As in infinite *circles* about one *Center*, there is the same *Method*, though not the same *measure*: So, in the smallest *creature* that is, there is an *Epitome* of a *Monarchy.*'

ll. 37–40. *Tuning his brest &c.* Compare *The Temple*, 'The Temper' (first poem with that title):

> Yet take thy way; for sure thy way is best:
> Stretch or contract me thy poore debter:
> This is but tuning of my breast,
> To make the musick better.

Page 461, ll. 25–40. *All things here &c.* Compare *The Temple*, 'Man,' stanzas 5, 6, 7.

ll. 37–9. *but man Though he knows these &c.* Compare *The Temple*, 'Miserie':

> But Man doth know
> The spring, whence all things flow:

> And yet, as though he knew it not,
> His knowledge winks, and lets his humours reigne;

l. 45. *Yet hugs he &c.* Compare *The Temple*, 'Miserie':

> He doth not like this vertue, no;
> Give him his dirt to wallow in all night:

l. 49. *Life's but a blast, he knows it.* Compare *The Temple*, 'Miserie':

> Man is but grasse,
> He knows it, fill the glasse.

ll. 51–2. *grows ne'r a flowr &c.* Compare *The Temple*, 'The Collar':

> Is the yeare onely lost to me?
> Have I no bayes to crown it?
> No flowers, no garlands gay?

Page 462, l. 53. *O foolish man &c.* Compare *The Temple*, 'Miserie':

> Oh foolish man! where are thine eyes?
> How hast thou lost them in a croud of cares?

ll. 58–60. *for flints will give no fire &c.* Compare note on the title of *Silex Scintillans*, p. 387 above.

l. 22. *My love-twist &c.* Compare *The Temple*, 'The Pearl':

> But thy silk-twist let down from heav'n to me,
> Did both conduct and teach me,

Page 464, (*Love, and Discipline*) ll. 17–18. *'twixt joyes, and tears &c.* Compare *The Temple*, 'Hope':

> With that I gave a viall full of tears:
> But he a few green eares:

PAGE **468**, ll. 11–12. *who made poor sand &c.* Compare *The Temple*, ' Providence ' :

> Thou hast made poore sand
> Check the proud sea, ev'n when it swells and gathers.

PAGE **470**, l. 1. *livers.* The emendation, necessary on metrical grounds, is justified by Vaughan's frequent use of the word ' liver '. Compare e. g. p. 642 (*Retirement*), 4.

PAGE **473**, ll. 35–6. *who of that Cel &c.* Compare *The Temple*, ' The Glimpse ' :

> O make me not their sport,
> Who by thy coming may be made a court !

ll. 65–7. " *The Age &c.* Compare *The Temple*, ' Giddinesse ' :

> Now he will fight it out, and to the warres ;
>   Now eat his bread in peace,
> And snudge in quiet :

PAGE **474**, l. 96. *To look him out &c.* Compare *The Temple*, ' The Glasse ' :

> When thou shalt look us out of pain,

PAGE **475**, ll. 13–35. *the Prince of Salem &c.* Compare *The Temple*, ' Peace,' stanza 4 sqq. :

> There was a Prince of old
> At Salem dwelt, &c.

PAGE **477**, l. 5. *Where Bees &c.* Compare *The Temple*, ' The Starre ' :

> To flie home like a laden bee
> Unto that hive of beams.

PAGE **478**, ll. 3–4. *Where I sometimes &c.* Compare *The Temple*, ' Peace ' :

> Then went I to a garden, and did spy
>   A gallant flower, &c.

PAGE **480**, ll. 13–16. *O it is thy only Art &c.* Compare *The Temple*, ' Nature ' :

> O tame my heart ;
> It is thy highest art
> To captivate strong holds to thee.

PAGE **481**, l. 23. ' the ' probably means ' thee '. Compare p. 90, 33 : ' the *Sun* o're night deceast '.

PAGE **483**, l. 20. *Within the line.* Compare note on p. 429, 9.

PAGE **484**, ll. 39–40. *Or else &c.* Compare *The Temple*, ' Grace ' :

> O come ! for thou dost know the way.
> Or if to me thou wilt not move,
> Remove me, where I need not say,
>   *Drop from above.*

PAGE **488**, ll. 45–8. *think on thy dream &c.* Compare *The Temple*, ' The Size ' :

> Call to minde thy dream,
>   An earthly globe,
> On whose meridian was engraven,
> *These seas are tears, and heaven the haven.*

PAGE **489–90**. *The Starre.* Compare Thomas Vaughan, *Magia*

Adamica ('To the Reader') : 'Look up then to *Heaven,* and when thou seest the Cœlestiall fires move in their swift and glorious *Circles,* think also there are here *below* some *cold Natures,* which they *over-look,* and about which they *move* incessantly to *heat,* and *concoct* them'. *Magia Adamica,* p. 68 : 'To speak plainly, *Heaven* it self was *originally extracted* from *Inferiors,* yet not so *intirely,* but some *portion* of the *Heavenly Natures* remained still *below,* and are the *very same* in *Essence* and *Substance* with the *separated starrs* and *skies*'. Compare also *The Favour,* p. 492, 7-10 below, and Thomas Vaughan's master, Cornelius Agrippa, *De Occulta Philosophia,* Lib. I, cap. lxvii '*Quomodo animus humanus potest coniungi cum cœlestium animis & intelligentiis, atq₃ simul illis mirabiles quasdam virtutes rebus inferioribus imprimere*'.

PAGE 489, ll. 3-4. *And winde and curle &c.* Compare *The Temple,* 'The Starre' :

> That so among the rest I may
> Glitter, and curle, and winde as they :

PAGE **490**, l. 1. *Deare friend sit down.* Compare *The Temple,* 'Love unknown' :

> Deare Friend, sit down,

l. 11. *By flowers &c.* Compare *The Temple,* 'Sion' :

> The wood was all embellished
> With flowers and carvings ; mysticall and rare :

PAGE **491**, l. 6. *a Deaths-head crown'd with Roses.* Compare p. 185, 39-40 above.

l. 8. *by a winde or wave.* Compare *The Temple,* 'The Glimpse' :

> Wert thou a winde or wave,

l. 30. *shaking fastens thee.* Compare *The Temple,* 'Affliction' (the fifth poem with that title) :

> We are the trees, whom shaking fastens more,

PAGE **492**, (*The Favour*) ll. 7-10. *Some kinde herbs &c.* See note on *The Starre,* p. 489 above.

PAGES **493**-4. *Trinity-Sunday.* Compare *The Temple,* 'Trinitie-Sunday'.

PAGE **497**, l. 9. *Line.* Compare p. 429, 9, and p. 483, 20.

PAGE **498**, l. 50. *Begetting Virgins.* Compare p. 407, 70 : 'Faire, virgin-flowers', and p. 92, 1 : 'Isca *parens florum*'.

PAGE **500.** *Begging.* This poem first appeared in *Flores Solitudinis* (1654). See p. 218 above.

PAGE **501**, l. 13. *which all at once.* 'which' may be kept if this stanza is regarded as carrying on the construction of the preceding one.

PAGE **502**, ll. 35-6. *I'le get me up &c.* Compare *The Temple,* 'Easter' :

> I got me flowers to straw thy way ;
> I got me boughs off many a tree :

PAGE **505**, l. 18. *no moneth but May.* Compare note on p. 434, 21-4.

PAGE **506**, ll. 46-7. *like Pontick sheep &c.* See Pliny, *Nat. Hist.,* Lib. xxvii, cap. 28 (ed. Janus, p. 137) 'Absinthi genera plura sunt : . . . Ponticum e Ponto, ubi pecora pinguescunt illo et ob id sine felle reperiuntur'. 'their wormwood-diet' means 'a wormwood-diet like theirs'.

PAGE **507**, l. 16. *the sheep-keeping Syrian Maid.* Rebekah ? Compare *Isaac's Marriage,* pp. 408-9.

PAGE **508**, l. 21. *Pistic Nard.* Compare S. John xii. 3 ἡ οὖν Μαριὰμ λαβοῦσα λίτραν μύρου νάρδου πιστικῆς. . . .

PAGE **509**, l. 11. *Rain gently spends &c.* Compare *The Temple,* 'Providence':

> Rain, do not hurt my flowers; but gently spend
> Your hony drops:

and p. 63, 23 above.

PAGE **521**, ll. 14-16. *But flowers &c.* Compare *The Temple,* 'Life':

> Farewell deare flowers, sweetly your time ye spent,
> Fit, while ye liv'd, for smell or ornament,
> And after death for cures.

PAGE **524**. *Righteousness.* Compare Psalm xv and *The Temple,* 'Constancie,' for the form.

PAGE **534**, *(Death)* ll. 21-5. *As harmless violets &c.* Compare note on p. 521, 14-16 above.

PAGE **536**, ll. 61-3. *O thorny crown &c.* Compare *The Temple,* 'The Thanksgiving':

> Shall thy strokes be my stroking? thorns, my flower?
> Thy rod, my posie? crosse, my bower?

PAGE **543**, ll. 63-5. *S. Clemens apud Basil.* Basilius, *Liber de Spiritu Sancto,* cap. xxix (ed. Migne, vol. iv, col. 201).

HERMETICAL PHYSICK.

PAGE **547**. *(Title-page) Hermetical Physick . . . Nollius.* The work which Vaughan translates is not, as stated by Dr. Grosart, *Naturae Sanctuarium : quod est Physica Hermetica,* but *Systema* Medicinae Hermeticæ Generale, In quo

I. Medicinæ veræ fundamentum.
II. Sanitatis conseruatio. } Methodo dilucidissima generaliter explicantur.
III. Morborum cognitio & Curatio.

Ab Henrico Nollio Philo-chymiatro. [Figure] Prostat. *In nobilis Francoforti Paltheniana.* Anno MDCXIII. [12mo.]

I have used the copy in the Library of the Royal Society of Medicine. Vaughan begins to translate at page 60, where (after *Prodromus Medicus,* pp. 7-60) *Systema Medicinæ Hermeticæ generale* begins.

PAGE **548**, l. 10. *Veritatem tempus manu-ducit.* Compare Menander, *Monosticha* 11 ἄγει δὲ πρὸς φῶς τὴν ἀλήθειαν χρόνος (Otto, *Die Sprichwörter der Römer,* p. 343), and Seneca, *De Ira* ii. 22. 3 'Dandum semper est tempus : veritatem dies aperit'.

PAGE **550**, ll. 10-14. *Now all . . . leader.* Vaughan's addition.

PAGE **554**, l. 22. *Saints.* Compare Nollius (p. 67) : 'homines'.

ll. 27-9. *for they . . . deliver them.* Vaughan's addition.

PAGE **558**, ll. 1-2. *The dose &c.* Out of original setting; p. 115 in Nollius.

PAGES **558, 560,** and **561**. The notes, as usual, are Vaughan's additions.

PAGE **567**, ll. 22-9. *I mean . . . Law.* Shorter in original.

ll. 29-page 568, l. 1. *For thus . . . possessest.* Vaughan's addition.

PAGE **568**, ll. 2-9. *The Lord . . . Deuteron.* 28. Shorter in original.

PAGE **569**, l. 8. ἀπνευστί. In Nollius the word is written ἀπνϐϛῇ. The first contraction, apparently, was mistaken for *a.*

PAGE 572, l. 4. *Bergkranckheiten.* The mistake in the original seems to be due to a misreading (which is probably Vaughan's) of the German 'f'; see Nollius, p. 91, and compare the mistake on p. 588, 19 below, where 'ArƷt' is read as '*Arkt*'.

PAGE 576, ll. 25–6. *Eucherius &c.* Compare Nollius, p. 97 'Eucharius Rosenbader ex Weissenburg, Noricorum oppido, ac Ioannes ab Ettenstet chirurgi'.

PAGE 577, l. 7. *seven Sections.* Compare Nollius, p. 97 'sectiones . . . octo', and p. 98 '8. Quid sit vniuersalis medicina; ex qua materia fiat, & quis eius legitimus vsus'.

PAGE 581, l. 12. *And after all the coyl . . . Doctors.* Vaughan's addition.

PAGE 583, ll. 11–13. *That is to say &c.* Vaughan's addition.

PAGE 584, l. 29. *a Pythagorical Metempsuchosis.* Vaughan's addition.

ll. 31–32. *as an old womans Recipe.* Vaughan's addition.

PAGE 585, ll. 5–6. *by those fatal Tormentors &c.* Vaughan's addition.

ll. 17–19. *and the success . . . impostors.* Compare Nollius, p. 108 'aut salus nocentibus adscribatur'.

l. 20. *Medicasters.* Compare Nollius, p. 108 'medicorum'.

l. 25. *who suffer most by them.* Vaughan's addition.

ll. 31–2. *that is to say . . . diseases.* Vaughan's addition.

PAGE 586, l. 22. *but for a bad one &c.* Vaughan's addition.

PAGE 587, ll. 5–6. *in imitation . . . Sonne.* Vaughan's addition.

PAGE 588, ll. 13–14. *not omitting his own observations.* Vaughan's addition.

l. 19. '*Arzt*' written '*Arkt*'. See note on p. 572, 4 above.

PAGE 589, ll. 12–15. *and he was not ashamed . . . heaven.* Compare Nollius, p. 113 'eosq; instruere non erubuerit'.

PAGE 590, l. 39–page 591, l. 3. *Let him &c.* Compare Nollius, p. 113 'Deum sibi reconciliato poenitentia vera, ac deinceps Deum adorato, vt auxilietur'.

PAGE 592, ll. 26–end. Shorter in original. After this Nollius goes on with 'Sectio viii. *Quid sit universalis medicina*' &c. (pp. 118–26) and *Epilogus* (pp. 126–7). Blank page, then (in Royal Society of Medicine copy) *De Generatione Rerum naturalium Liber ex vero naturæ lumine in gratiam sincerioris philosophiæ studiosorum conformatus ab Henrico Nollio. Christus Iesus Dominus noster: . . . Francoforti, . . . Anno M. DC. XV.* [pp. 1[31]–52 including Epistola Nuncupatoria and Præfatio.] See Vaughan's letter to Aubrey below, p. 668, 40–1.

THALIA REDIVIVA.

PAGE 593. (Title-page) *Nec erubuit &c.* Virgil, *Eclogues* vi. 2.

PAGE 594. (*Heading*) *Earl of Worcester.* See *D.N.B.* art. Somerset, Henry. Grosart notes that he was a distant kinsman of Vaughan's. Frances Somerset, granddaughter of Henry, Earl of Worcester, married William Vaughan of Tretower, the poet's great-great-grandfather.

PAGE 595. (*Signature*) *J. W.* Compare the signatures on pages 596 and 602. The most probable conjecture as to J. W.'s identity seems to be that of Professor Firth, who suggests John Williams, son of Sir Henry Williams of Brecon. He matriculated from Brasenose College in 1642. See Chambers, vol. ii, p. 344.

PAGE 597. This poem is included in the editions of Orinda's poems of 1644, 1667, 1678, and 1710. Only the more important variants are given in the foot-notes.

PAGE 598, l. 19. *Tho. Powel, D.D.* See note on p. 36 above.

PAGE 600. (*Signature*) *N. W. Jes. Coll. Oxon.* Professor Firth suggests that N. W. might be either Nathaniel Williams of Swansea, who matriculated in 1672, or Nicholas Wadham of Carmarthen, who matriculated in 1669. See Chambers, vol. ii, p. 344.

PAGE 602. (*Signature*) *I. W. A.M. Oxon.* See note on p. 595 above.

PAGE 605. (*Title of poem*) *The King Disguis'd.* Compare *The Kings Disguise.* [MS. note in B.M. copy 'Jan: 21 1646 London by Jo: Cleveland Poet' (Thomason Tract).]

l. 2. *into his Coffin.* The idea is paralleled in the 1677 edition of Cleveland's *The King's Disguise*:

> And why so coffin'd in this vile Disguise,
> That who but sees blasphemes thee with his eys?

In 1647 and 1653 the passage runs:

> And why a Tenant to this vile disguise,
> Which who but sees . . .

PAGE 608. (*Title*) *To Mr. M. L. &c.* Probably Matthew Locke, as Grosart suggested. *D. N. B.* quotes Roger North (*Memoires of Musick*, p. 95) to the effect that Locke 'set most of the Psalms to musick in parts for the use of some vertuoso ladyes in the city'. But the setting appears not to have been published.

PAGE 609. (*Title*) *C. W. Esquire.* For notes on the life of Charles Walbeoffe see Chambers, vol. ii, pp. 345-7, where the inscription on his tombstone in Llanhamlach Church is given: 'Here lieth the body of Charles Walbeoffe, Esqre., who departed this life the 13th day of September, 1653, and was married to Mary, one of the daughters of Sir Thomas Aubrey of Llantrydid, in the county of Glamorgan, Knt., by whom he had issue two sonnes, of whom only Charles surviveth'. Compare Vaughan's letter to Aubrey, p. 669, 75, below for a reference to another member of the family: 'My Cousin Walbeoffe.'

PAGE 611, l. 86. *and the bright day's Forlorn.* A modernized text obscures rather than elucidates the meaning. For '*Forlorn*' meaning 'vanguard' see O.E.D.

PAGES 614–17. *The importunate Fortune.* With this poem compare Randolph's *On the Inestimable Content he injoyes in the Muses*; *to those of his Friends that dehort him from Poetry* (ed. cit. p. 1).

PAGE 617, l. 105. *My purse as Randolph's was.* See Randolph, *A parley with his empty Purse* (ed. cit. p. 112).

(*Title*) *I. Morgan of White-Hall Esq.* Mr. Chambers (vol. ii, p. 348) notes that a John Morgan of Wenallt (or Whitehill) was a kinsman of Vaughan's, being a grandson of Charles Vaughan of Tretower. See Harl. MS. 2,289, fol. 39.

PAGE 621. (*Title*) *the matchless Orinda.* Compare note on p. 61 above.

PAGE 622. (*Title*) *Judge Trevers.* See *D.N.B.* art. Trevor, Sir Thomas (1586–1656).

PAGE 623. (*Title*) *To Etesia.* Compare p. 81, *Metrum* 3, 7–8:

> Thus, when the warm Etesian wind
> The Earth's seald bosome doth unbind,

Notes. 705

PAGE **626**, (*In Etesiam*) l. 8. *perit*. I think it probable that Vaughan wrote ' periit ', which explains the misprint better than the more metrically correct ' perit '.

PAGE **629**, ll. 35–48. *And humbly &c.* Compare Boethius, Lib. iii, Met. 12:

> Et dulci ueniam prece
> Vmbrarum dominos rogat.
> Captus carmine ianitor.

PAGE **635**, ll. 13–24. *by fruits, not Consuls &c.* Vaughan is indebted to Randolph's translation of the same poem: *De Sene* Veronensi: *Ex Claudiano* (ed. cit. p. 29):

> From fruits, not Consuls, computation brings,
> By Apples Autumnes knows, by flowers the springs.
> Thus he the day by his own orb doth prize;
> In the same field his Sun doth set and rise.
> That knew an oak a twig, and walking thither
> Beholds a wood and he grown up together,
> Neighbouring *Veron* he may for India take,
> And think the Red-sea is *Benacus* lake.
> Yet is his strength untam'd, and firm his knees ;
> Him the third age a lusty Grandsire sees.
> Go seek who s' will the far *Iberian* shore,
> This man hath liv'd, though that hath travel'd more.

PAGES **635–6**, ll. 1–14. *When Jove &c.* Vaughan is indebted to Randolph's translation of the same poem: *In Archimedis Sphæram*, *ex Claudiano* (ed. cit. p. 26):

> *Iove* saw the Heavens fram'd in a little glasse,
> And laughing, to the gods these words did passe:
> Comes then the power of mortall cares so far?
> In brittle Orbes my labours acted are.
> The statutes of the Poles, the faith of things,
> The laws of gods this *Syracusian* brings
> Hither by art : Spirits inclos'd attend
> Their severall sphears, and with set motions bend
> The living work : Each yeer the faigned Sun,
> Each month returns the counterfeited Moon,
> And viewing now her world, bold Industry
> Grows proud, to know the heavens her subjects be.
> Believe *Salmonius* hath false thunders thrown,
> For a poor hand is Natures rivall grown,

PAGE **641**, (*Discipline*) l. 3. *the mule man.* Compare p. 459, 18 above. See foot-note.

PAGE **645**, (*The Nativity*) l. 9. *A Tax? 'tis so still!* Vaughan probably refers to the ' Decimation ' tax levied on the Royalists in 1655.

PAGE **648**. (*Title*) *Servilii Fatum.* Vaughan is probably writing, with intentional obscurity, of a contemporary. But he may also refer to Pliny, *Nat. Hist.* vii. 53 (54), § 182, where among examples of people who ' nullis evidentibus causis obiere' mention is made of 'C. Servilius Pansa, cum staret in foro ad tabernam hora diei secunda in P. fratrem innixus ',—although among 'felicia exempla'.

PAGE **649**. (*First title*) *D. Thomam Poellum Cantrevensem.* See note on p. 36 above.

PAGE **653**, l. 52. *Hilarion's servant, the sage Crow.* See note on p. 184, 2 above.

PAGES **656-60**, *Daphnis.* This poem is on the death of Thomas
Vaughan, some of whose poems follow in 1678. See title-page,
p. 593 above, and note on p. 38, 33 above.

PAGE **656**, ll. 3–4. *or have thy Lambs &c.* This may be a reminiscence of Milton, *Comus*, 497–8. On account of their uncertainty I have
not mentioned other possible reminiscences of Milton's early poems
in Vaughan's works. For possible *references* to Milton, see an article
by Miss L. I. Guiney, *Quarterly Review*, April 1914, 'Milton and
Vaughan'.

PAGE **657**, ll. 36–8. *That madly hate &c.* These lines refer to Dr.
Henry More's criticisms of Thomas Vaughan's works. Henry Vaughan
was not the first to make the pun on l. 38. Compare his brother's
pamphlet—answering *The Second Lash of Alazonomastix—The Second
Wash: Or the Moore Scour'd once more . . .* 1651.

ll. **55** and **62**. *Amphion.* Perhaps Matthew Herbert, as Mr.
Chambers suggests. Compare *Ad Posteros*, p. 32, 6, and the first
poem on p. 93 above. To those who wish to interpret the details of
the allegory it may be of interest that on July 19, 1655, 'Mat. Herbert begs discharge of sequestration of Langattock Rectory, co.
Brecon, . . . sequestered for delinquency of the present Earl [of
Worcester]'. *Calendar of Proceedings, Committee for Compounding,
&c.*, p. 1713. It may have a bearing on ll. 67–78 below.

l. **61**. *The visions of our black, but brightest Bard.* In the
above-mentioned article (*Quarterly Review*, April 1914, p. 356)
Miss Guiney suggests that the 'black Bard' is Myrddin Emrys (Merlin
Ambrosius), and mentions Thomas Heywood's work, *The Life of
Merlin, Sirnamed Ambrosius. His Prophesies, and Predictions Interpreted; and their truth made good by our English Annalls . . . from
Brute to the Reigne of our Royall Soveraigne King Charles* (London,
1641, 4°). Compare (title) *The Mad-merry Merlin, or the Black Alma-
nack* (1653).

PAGE **659**, l. 116. *Noble Murrey.* See Vaughan's letter to Aubrey,
p. 667, 16 below.

PAGE **661**. *Dr. Thomas Powell's Humane Industry.* In this volume
there are many other fragmentary translations besides those given
here; but they are not specially assigned to Vaughan. One is by
Thomas May; the rest may be by Powell himself. For Powell see
note on p. 36 above.

PAGE **664**, l. 18. *Hares by Lions.* This may be a misprint for
'Lions by Hares', though it is possible that Vaughan misunderstood
his text, if he had no more than is given on p. 663.

THE LETTERS.

The proper names in the letters might often have been printed in
italics to correspond with the larger hand in which they are written,
and in accordance with contemporary usage. But as they are not
always marked off in a sufficiently distinct way from the ordinary
context, roman type has been used throughout. 'D^r', 'M^r', 'w^ch',
and similar forms are, in the MSS., usually accompanied by a dot
under or after the raised letters. The lists of works on pages 667, 668,
and 670 are inset in narrow columns.

PAGE **667**, l. 8 sqq. The biographical matter given here was used
as a basis for the lives of Henry and Thomas Vaughan in *Historia*

et Antiquitates Universitatis Oxoniensis (1674) and in *Athenæ Oxonienses.* Henry Vaughan's life was one of those added to *Athenæ Oxonienses* in 1720.

l. 9. *I stayed not att Oxford.* Henry Vaughan's name appears neither in the University Matriculation Register nor in the Jesus College Battel-books for 1638 and 1640 (that for 1639 is missing). But he was regarded by Aubrey and Wood as a member of Jesus College.

PAGE **668**, ll. 40–1. *& his discourse dè generatione.* See note on p. 592 above.

l. 47. *D* Powell of Cantre.* See p. 670 below and note on p. 36 above.

ll. 51–2. *Dr. Thomas Ellis.* See *D.N.B.* art. Ellis, Thomas.

PAGE **669**, ll. 79–86. Aubrey notes ' I p^d 3^d for y^s '.

PAGE **670**, l. 15. *Recveil &c.* I have not found any trace of this book.

l. 24. *& not yet printed.* Apparently never printed.

ll. 34–5. *not traduced (as one hath done).* Presumably the version published in 1647.

PAGE **672**, ll. 17–21. *yor learned friend Dr Plott &c.* Compare Aubrey's letter to Wood of March 19, 1680/1 (Bodleian MS. *Ballard* xiv, fol. 80) : ' When you see Dr. Plott, mind him to send me halfe a dozen printed Queres, wch I would send to my Cosen Hen: Vaughan in Breck[nock ?]shire, whom I have engaged to follow his method. he has great & steady practise there, & may unâ fidelia duas dealbare parietes. He is very fitt for ††.'

PAGE **674**, l. 5. *Dr John David Rhesus.* Compare p. 675 below, and Aubrey's life, Bodleian MS. *Aubrey* 8, fol. 11 : ' he wrote a Compendium of Aristotles Metaphysiques in the British Language, mentioned in his Eple [to S^r . . . Stradling] before his Welsh Gramer. 'Twas in Jesus coll. library Oxd. & my cos. Henry Vaughan [Olor Iscans] had it in his custody. Dr. Rhees ^averres_sayes there, that the British language is as copious in expressing congruous Termes of Art, as the Greeke : or any language whatsoever. I have [sent ?] to H. Vaughan, for it.' Compare also Wood's life (ed. Bliss, vol. ii, p. 62) : ' He hath written other excellent things, but are lost, as I have been assured by OLOR ISCANUS '. See also *D.N.B.* art. Rhys, Ioan Dafydd.

ADDITIONAL NOTE

PAGE **64**, ll. 27–34. *This made thy fire &c.* This passage contains difficulties which I cannot completely solve. It is clear that ' *a forlorn Restraint*' (l. 34) refers to Davenant's imprisonment in 1650 at Cowes, where he brought *Gondibert* to its premature conclusion.

Two explanations of ll. 27–33 have been suggested :

(i) Mr. Chambers's, that the ' aged *Sire* ' with an inferior ' fancy ' was Shakespeare. Compare Spence, *Anecdotes,* 1820, p. 82 : ' That notion of Sir William D'Avenant being more than a poetical child only of Shakspeare was common in town, and Sir William himself seemed fond of having it taken for truth.—[*Mr. Pope.*]' Compare the next anecdote. The story is first explicitly told by Vaughan's cousin Aubrey (*Brief Lives,* ed. Clark, vol. i, p. 204), but see the lines of 1655 quoted in *D.N.B.* art. D'Avenant.

(ii) Mr. Percy Simpson's, that the 'aged *Sire*' who wore 'bayes' was Ben Jonson, succeeded as Poet Laureate by Davenant in 1638. James Howell addresses Jonson as 'Father Ben' (*Familiar Letters*, ed. Jacobs, p. 267, '*To my Father, Mr.* Ben. Jonson'). Thomas Randolph, whom Vaughan quotes at this point, was another 'son'.

With either explanation, two difficulties remain:

(i) l. 30. *his fancy darker than his sight.* thy sight? 'his' might be caught from l. 32, 'his *bayes*'.

(ii) l. 31. *the bars and length of dayes.* bars, perhaps difficulties in the poet's career. 'length of dayes' seems more applicable to Jonson than to Shakespeare.

It should be added that Vaughan's poem seems to repeat thoughts in the congratulatory poems by Cowley and Waller accompanying *Gondibert*. But these appear to throw no light on Vaughan's meaning.

ERRATA

PAGE 101, l. 21 : for *canst* read *canst,* (*canst 1651*)

PAGE 142, foot-note : for Enemies read *Enemie*

PAGE 183, l. 35 and marginal note : *One* asterisk in *1652*

PAGE 185, l. 16 : for upbraids read upraids (cp. foot-note)

PAGE 213, ll. 3–4, foot-note omitted : 3 *into*] *i misplaced 1654*   4 *into*] *nto 1654*

PAGE 453, l. 8 : Set in as l. 16

INDEX OF FIRST LINES.

*The poems marked * are fragments and translations to be found among the prose works. Those marked † are commendatory poems addressed to Vaughan.*

	PAGE
A grove there grows round with the *Sea* confin'd	636
A King and no King! Is he gone from us,	605
A tender Kid (see, where 'tis put,)	113
A Ward, and still in bonds, one day	397
A wit most worthy in tryed Gold to shine,	389
Accept, dread Lord, the poor Oblation,	435
Accipe prærapido Salmonem in gurgite captum,	649
Against the Virtuous man we all make head,	294
Ah! he is fled!	410
Ah! what time wilt thou come? when shall that crie	451
All *sorts* of men, that live on Earth,	634
All worldly things, even while they grow, decay,	273
All-mighty *Spirit*! thou that by	85
Amyntas *goe, thou art undone,*	6
And do they so? have they a Sense	432
And for lifes sake to lose the crown of life?	259
And is the bargain thought too dear,	352
And rising at midnight the Stars espi'd	187
And will not hear the Crie	243
As Egypts *drought by Nilus is redrest,*	268
As Kings doe rule like th' Heavens, who dispense	665
As time one day by me did pass	512
As travellours when the twilight's come,	464
Aske Lover, ere thou dyest; let one poor breath	6
Awake, glad heart! get up, and Sing,	442
Base man! & couldst thou think Cato alone	241
Be dumb course measures, jar no more; to me	491
Be still black Parasites,	486
Blesse me! what damps are here? how stiffe an aire?	41
Blessed, unhappy City? dearly lov'd	502
Blessings as rich and fragrant crown your heads	57
Blest be the God of Harmony, and Love!	426
Blest Infant Bud, whose Blossome-life	450
Boast not proud *Golgotha*: that thou can'st show	613
Bright, and blest beame! whose strong projection	450
Bright books! the *perspectives* to our weak sights:	639
Bright Queen of Heaven! Gods Virgin Spouse!	506
Bright shadows of true Rest! some shoots of blisse,	447
But night and day doth his owne life molest,	254
Can any tell me what it is? can you,	649
Chance taking from me things of highest price	104
Come, come, what doe I here?	420
Come, drop your branches, strow the way	501
Come my heart! come my head	416
Come my true Consort in my Joyes and Care!	382
Come sapless Blossom, creep not stil on Earth	475
Curtain'd with Clouds in a dark night	80

PAGE

Darknes, Stars i' th' mid day ! they invite 10
Dear, beauteous Saint ! more white then day, ... 507
Dear friend ! whose holy, ever-living lines 434
Dear Lord, 'tis finished ! and now he 394
Deare friend sit down, and bear awhile this shade . . . 490
Dearest ! if you those fair Eyes (wondring) stick 70
Death, and darkness get you packing, ... 457
Diminuat ne sera *dies* præsentis *honorem* 32
*Draw neer, fond man, and dresse thee by this glasse, . . . 168
Dust and clay 482

Early, while yet the *dark* was gay, ... 643
Esteem it no point of revenge to kill, ... 554
Eternal God ! maker of all 540
Et sic in cythara, *sic in* dulcedine *vitæ* 648
Excell then if thou canst be not withstood, ... 101

Fair and yong light ! my guide to holy 513
Fair, order'd lights (whose motion without noise . . . 469
Fair prince of life, lights living well ! 641
Fair, shining *Mountains* of my pilgrimage, ... 640
Fair, solitary path ! Whose blessed shades 524
Fair *Vessell* of our daily light, whose proud . . . 644
†Fairly design'd ! to charm our *Civil* Rage 598
False life ! a foil and no more, when 538
Fancy, and I, last Evening walkt, ... 8
Farewel thou true and tried Refection 654
Farewell ! I goe to sleep ; but when 425
Farewell you Everlasting hills ! I'm Cast . . . 411
Father of lights ! what Sunnie seed, ... 488
Feeding on fruits which in the heavens doe grow, . . . 101
Flaccus not so : That worldly *He* 89
Fool that I was ! to believe blood 620
For shame desist, why should'st thou seek my fall ? . . 614
For, with brave rage he flung it on the Sand, . . . 241
Fortune (when with rash hands she quite turmoiles . . 80
Fresh *fields* and *woods* ! the Earth's fair *face,* . . . 642
From fruitful *beds* and flowry *borders* 652
*From the first hour the heav'ns were made 179

Go catch the *Phoenix,* and then bring 624
Go, go, queint folies, sugred sin, ... 446
Go, if you must ! but stay—and know 626

†Had I ador'd the Multitude, and thence 597
Haile sacred shades ! coole, leavie House ! . . . 15
Happy is he, that with fix'd Eyes 628
Happy that first white age ! when wee 83
Happy those early dayes ! when I 419
He that thirsts for glories prize, ... 84
*Here holy *Anselme* lives in ev'ry page, ... 193
Here, take againe thy *Sack-cloth* ! and thank heav'n . 52
*Here the great well-spring of wash'd Soules, with beams . 365
His deepe, dark heart (bent to supplant) . . . 105
Hither thou com'st : the busie wind all night . . . 495
*how could that paper sent, ... 344
How is man parcell'd out ? how ev'ry hour . . . 460
How kind is heav'n to man ! If here 443
*How oft have we beheld wilde Beasts appear . . . 663

PAGE

How rich, O Lord! how fresh thy visits are! 441
How shril are silent tears? when sin got head 453

I am Confirm'd, and so much wing is given 49
I 'ave read thy Souls fair night-peece, and have seen . . 48
†I call'd it once my *sloth*: In such an age 37
I cannot reach it; and my striving eye 520
I did but *see* thee! and how *vain* it is 55
I, do not go! thou know'st, I'le dye! 500
I have consider'd it; and find 434
I have it now: 514
I knew it would be thus! and my Just fears 58
I knew thee not, nor durst *attendance* strive 54
I saw beneath Tarentum's *stately towers* 184
I saw Eternity the other night 466
I see the Temple in thy Pillar rear'd, ... 527
I see the use: and know my bloud 423
I walkt the other day (to spend my hour,) 478
I whose first year flourish'd with youthfull verse . . . 76
I wonder, *James*, through the whole Historie 44
†I write not here, as if thy *last* in store 37
I wrote it down. But one that saw 528
Iesus, my life! how shall I truly love thee? 493
If *Amoret*, that glorious Eye, ... 7
If any have an ear 516
If I were dead, and in my place, ... 8
If old tradition hath not fail'd, ... 633
If sever'd Friends by *Sympathy* can joyn, ... 603
If this worlds friends might see but once 510
If *weeping Eyes* could wash away 89
If with an open, bounteous hand 81
In all the parts of Earth, from farthest West, ... 18
In March birds couple, a new birth 175
In those blest fields of *Everlasting aire* 72
Isca *parens florum, placido qui spumeus ore* 92
It is perform'd! and thy great Name doth run . . . 611
It lives when kill'd, and brancheth when 'tis lopt. . . 248
It would lesse vex *distressed man* 86

Joy of my life! while left me here, ... 422

King of Comforts! King of life! 454
King of Mercy, King of Love, ... 480
Knaves tongues, and calumnies no more doth price . . 105

Learning and *Law* your *Day* is done, ... 622
Leave, *Amoret*, melt not away so fast 13
Let me not weep to see thy ravish'd house 341
Let not thy *youth* and *false delights* 86
Life, Marcellina, leaving thy faire frame, ... 355
Like some faire Oke, *that when her boughes* . . . 248
Long life, opprest with many woes, ... 301
Long since great witts have left the Stage 621
Lord, bind me up, and let me lye 472
Lord Jesus! with what sweetness and delights, . . . 481
Lord, since thou didst in this vile Clay 448
Lord! what a busie, restless thing 414
Lord, when thou didst on *Sinai* pitch 465

PAGE

Lord! when thou didst thy selfe undresse 415
Lord, with what courage, and delight 428
Love, the Worlds Life! what a sad death 627

Man should with Virtue arm'd, and hearten'd be, ... 258
Marke, when the Evenings cooler wings 12
Most happy man! who in his own sweet *fields* 635
My dear, Almighty Lord! why dost thou weep? 503
My God and King! to thee 526
My God, how gracious art thou! I had slipt 433
My God! thou that didst dye for me, ... 394
My God, when I walke in those groves, ... 404
My soul, my pleasant soul and witty, ... 173
My Soul, there is a Countrie 430

Nature even for her selfe doth lay a snare, ... 259
Nimble Sigh on thy warme wings, ... 5
Nothing on *Earth*, nothing at all 88
Now I have seen her; And by *Cupid* 618
Now, that the publick Sorrow doth subside, ... 609

O book! lifes guide! how shall we part, ... 540
O come, and welcom! Come, refine; 642
O come away, ... 534
O day of life, of light, of love! 530
O doe not goe, thou know'st I'le dye, ... 218
O dulcis luctus, risuque potentior omni! 626
O health the chief of gifts divine! 117
O holy, blessed, glorious three, ... 493
O in what haste with Clouds and Night 76
O Joyes! Infinite sweetnes! with what flowres, ... 424
O knit me, that am crumbled dust! the heape 413
O my chief good! 430
O Quæ frondosæ per amœna Cubilia *sylvæ* 93
O Subtile Love! thy Peace is War; 626
O tell me whence that joy doth spring 539
O the new worlds new, quickning Sun! 541
O thou great builder of this starrie frame, ... 78
O thou that lovest a pure, and whitend soul! 492
O thou! the first fruits of the dead, ... 427
O thou! who did'st deny to me 647
O thy bright looks! thy glance of love 492
*O what pure things, most pure, must those hands be 156
O when my God, my glory brings 526
*Obdurate still, and tongue-tyed you accuse 344
Oft have I seen, when that renewing breath 400
one food the best for all 249

Patience digesteth misery 248
Peace? and to all the world? sure, one 645
Peace, peace! I blush to hear thee; when thou art . . . 443
Peace, peace! I know 'twas brave, ... 422
Peace, peace; It is not so. Thou doest miscall . . . 459
*Peter, *when thou this pleasant world dost see,* 214
Praying! and to be married? It was rare, ... 408

Quid celebras auratam undam, Et combusta pyropis . . . 648
Quite spent with thoughts I left my Cell, and lay . . . 418
Quod vixi, Mathæe, dedit Pater, *hæc tamen olim* . . . 93

PAGE

Sacred and secret hand! 505
Sad, purple well! whose bubling eye 523
Saw not, Lysimachus, last day, when wee 612
Say wittie fair one, from what Sphere 61
†See what thou wert! by what Platonick round . . . 600
See you that beauteous *Queen*, which no age tames? . . 625
Sees not my friend, what a deep snow 61
*Shall I beleeve you can make me return, ... 349
Shall I complain, or not? Or shall I mask 68
Sickness and death, you are but sluggish things, . . . 309
Silence, and stealth of dayes! 'tis now 425
Since dying for me, thou didst crave no more . . . 536
Since I in storms us'd most to be 539
Since in a land not barren stil 463
Since last wee met, thou and thy horse (my dear,) . . 46
Sions true, glorious God! on thee 531
So from our cold, rude World, which all things tires . . 617
*So our decays God comforts by 177
So stick up *Ivie* and the *Bays*, ... 646
Still yong and fine! but what is still in view . . . 509
Struggle & grone as if by Panthers *torne* . . . 235
Sure, It was so. Man in those early days 440
Sure Priam *will to mirth incline*, ... 100
Sure, there's a tye of Bodyes! and as they 429
Sure thou didst flourish once! and many Springs, . . 497
Sweet, harmles livers! (on whose holy leisure . . . 470
Sweet Paulinus, *is thy nature turn'd?* 348
Sweete, sacred hill! on whose fair brow 414

Tentâsti, fateor, sine vulnere sœpius, & me . . . 386
Thanks mighty *Silver*! I rejoyce to see 43
That man for misery excell'd 111
*That the fierce Pard doth at a beck 664
That the world in constant *force* 84
The lucky world shewd me one day 507
The naked man too getts the field, ... 220
*The paines of Saints, and Saints rewards are twins, . . 376
*The painfull Crosse with flowers and Palms is crown'd, . 375
*The plenteous Evills of frail life fill the old: . . . 283
*The strongest body, and the best 570
*The trees, we set, grow slowly, and their shade . . 187
*The untired strength of never-ceasing motion, . . . 662
*The whole wench (how compleat soe'r) was but . . 213
*There are that do believe all things succeed . . . 178
*There's need (betwixt his clothes, his bed and bord,) . . 553
They are all gone into the world of light! 483
*They faine would (if they might) 253
This is the day (blith god of *Sack*) which wee . . . 65
*This pledge of your joint love, to Heaven now fled, . . 345
*Those sacred daies by tedious time delai'd 378
Thou that know'st for whom I mourne, ... 416
Thou the Nepenthe *easing griefe* 238
Thou! who didst place me in this busie street . . . 518
Thou, who dost flow and flourish here below . . . 492
Thou, whose sad heart, and weeping head lyes low, . . 456
Though since thy first sad entrance by 533
*Through pleasant green fields enter you the way . . 375
Through that pure *Virgin-shrine*, ... 522
*Times-Teller wrought into a little round 661

PAGE

*'Tis a sad Land, that in one day 399
'Tis dead night round about : Horrour doth creepe . . . 410
'Tis madness sure ; And I am in the *Fitt,* 606
'Tis not *rich furniture* and *gems* 87
'Tis now cleare day : I see a Rose 405
'Tis true, I am undone ; Yet e're I dye, ... 9
* *To live a stranger unto life.* 275
* *To speedy posts, bear hence the Lamp of life.* 271
* *True life in this is shown,* 267
'Twas so, I saw thy birth : That drowsie Lake 412
Tyrant farewell : This heart, the prize 4

Unfold, unfold ! take in his light, ... 643
Up, O my soul, and blesse the Lord.   O God, ... 494
Up to those bright, and gladsome hils 458

Vain, sinful Art ! who first did fit 503
Vain Wits and eyes 396
* *Virtues faire cares some people measure* 257
Vivaces *oculorum* Ignes & lumina dia 93

Waters above ! eternal Springs ! 641
Weary of this same Clay, and straw, I laid 468
Wee thank you, worthy Sir, that now we see 60
Weighing the stedfastness and state 477
Welcome dear book, souls Joy, and food !   The feast . . . 441
Welcome sweet, and sacred feast ; welcome life ! . . . 457
Well, wee are rescued ! and by thy rare Pen 64
Wellcome white day ! a thousand Suns, ... 485
What can the man do that succeeds the King? 519
What clouds, *Menalcas,* do oppress thy brow ? 656
What ever 'tis, whose beauty here below 489
What fix'd *Affections,* and lov'd Laws 631
* *What greater good had deckt great* Pompey's *Crown* . . . 302
What happy, secret fountain, ... 516
* *What is't to me that spacious rivers run* 174
†What *Planet* rul'd your *birth* ? what *wittie star* ? . . . 36
What smiling *Star* in that fair Night, ... 623
* *What though they boast their riches unto us ?* 108
When *Daphne's* Lover here first wore the *Bayes,* . . . 39
* *When ever did (I pray,)* 553
When first I saw true beauty, and thy Joys 476
When first thou didst even from the grave 444
When first thy Eies unveil, give thy Soul leave . . . 436
When *Jove* a heav'n of small glass did behold, ... 635
When the Crabs fierce Constellation 79
When the fair year 499
When the Sun from his Rosie bed 81
When through the North a fire shall rush 402
When to my Eyes 421
When we are dead, and now, no more 3
When with these eyes clos'd now by thee, ... 533
†Where Reverend Bards of old have sate 599
*Where-e'r my fancy calls, there I goe still, ... 551
* *Which silently, and by none seen,* 340
Whither, O whither did'st thou fly 641
Who on yon throne of Azure sits, ... 462
Who wisely would for his retreat 82
Who would unclouded see the Laws 631

PAGE

*_Whome God doth take care for and love,_ 303
Whose calme soule in a settled state 77
*_Whose guilty soul with terrours fraught, doth frame_ 258
*_Whose hissings fright all Natures monstrous Ills,_ 280
*_With restless cares they wast the night and day,_ 553
With what deep murmurs through times silent stealth 537

*_Y Pader, pan trier, Duw-tri a'i dododd_ 666
You have Consum'd my language, and my pen 66
You have oblig'd the _Patriarch._ And tis known 608
* _You minister to others wounds a Cure,_ 101
*You see what splendour through the spatious Isle 376
*You that to wash your flesh and Soules draw near, ... 364
Youth, Beauty, Vertue, Innocence 63

OXFORD : HORACE HART M.A.
PRINTER TO THE UNIVERSITY